SAGGISTICA 7

A Toni
Carbone,

with affection
and admiration-

Luigi Fontanella

Luigi Fontanella

Migrating Words
Italian Writers in the United States

Translated from the Italian by
Joan Taber
with the collaboration of the author

Library of Congress Control Number: 2011945040

Revised and expanded edition of
La parola transfuga: scrittori italiani in America. Florence, Italy: Cadmo, 2003

*The author and publisher thank Guernica Editions
for their kind permission to cite from Giose Rimanelli's English novels*

Printed in the United States.

Published by
BORDIGHERA PRESS
John D. Calandra Italian American Institute
25 West 43rd Street, 17th Floor
New York, NY 10036

SAGGISTICA 7
ISBN 978-1-59954-041-2

In memory of Pascal D'Angelo

TABLE OF CONTENTS

CHAPTER ONE

Italian Emigration and Literature in Early Twentieth-Century America:
Arturo Giovannitti, Emanuel Carnevali and Others.
Theoretical Questions and Methods

And hunger is the patrimony of the emigrant;
Hunger, desolate and squalid—
For the fatherland,
For bread and for women, both dear
America, you gather the hungry people
And give them new hungers for the old ones.
—Emanuel Carnevali

PRELIMINARY OBSERVATIONS

This first chapter, originally titled in Italian "*Poeti emigrati e emigranti poeti negli Stati Uniti*" (*Migrant poets and poet emigrants in the United States*), first appeared in one of my essays readily available in a volume of Proceedings edited by Sebastiano Martelli (*Il sogno italo-americano* 1999, 299-319). Here the essay has been significantly revised and expanded both to serve as an introduction and to stimulate some initial thoughts based not only on the personal experiences of the writer (an Italian intellectual who has resided in the United States for many years) but also on the title's more subtle implications and meanings. The original title might imply a broader inquiry than our focus here, which as I have already mentioned in the Preface, is limited to particular examples drawn chronologically from the personal experiences of selected Italian expatriate writers in America from approximately the beginning of the twentieth century to the 1950s.

My preference, however, is to focus on certain preliminary theoretical and methodological questions.

1

The original title also suggested (or suggests) two distinct categories of authors that co-exist on historical/temporal and stylistic/thematic levels.

The first "group" consists of established Italian writers who emigrated to the United States about a century ago and very quickly inserted themselves into the mainstream American literary scene, some with greater, others with less success. (Arturo Giovannitti, for example, the first important Italian emigrant author in America, who arrived in 1901, would fall into this category.) For all intents and purposes, therefore, this group became American writers of their own volition and by (it goes without saying) the expressive use of the adopted language.

We can also add to this group of expatriates those poets and thinkers who were born in America and are defined today as "Italian-American writers," even though their surname may be all that they retain of their Italian heritage. Only a few of these writers at times convey indirectly in their creative work a degree of hidden or veiled Italian cultural references and "reflections." This category includes such writers as Pietro Di Donato, John Fante, John Ciardi, Michele Rago, and Felix Stefanile. I am aware that the term "reflections" is an approximation; later, I will explain in more depth what I mean by the "reflections" conveyed occasionally in their work.

Finally, we can also add to these two groups a third category of Italian migrant writers / emigrant writers who became more relevant beginning with the Post-World War II period. These are writers who have (1) successfully assimilated the new language, (2) consciously opted for one language or the other, (3) write easily in both Italian and English (Niccolò Tucci, Joseph Tusiani, and Giose Rimanelli are three fine examples), or (4) have experimented in an interesting multilingual mix (for example, some recent compositions by Giose Rimanelli, whom I consider to be the most versatile Italian expatriate writer in the United States today).

I would also like to clarify the double meaning of the terms "migrant/emigrant" in the original subtitle of this chapter. The term "migrant writer" refers to a person who was *already* a writer prior to leaving Italy. The migrant writer may be someone who has, among other accomplishments, already produced a profound body of work in his or her native language (as with Giovannitti), or a writer who maintains his or her profession after emigrating permanently—or to use an old expression of Prezzolini that still has currency—after being "transplanted" into another culture. Such a writer has made a determined effort to assimilate the manners, themes, forms, and, above all, the new expressive language. There are, in other words, Italian writers, who at a certain point in their lives chose to relocate and establish residence in the United States, maintaining their profession as writers but *desiring* to now consider themselves American writers.

Take Emanuel Carnevali, for example. Carnevali was born in Florence in 1897 and emigrated to America in 1914, where he became a poet and polemicist, establishing close relationships with some of the most important American writers: Carl Sandburg, Sherwood Anderson, Ernest Walsh, and William Carlos Williams, among others. In a letter to Harriet Moore (Poetry 11.6 [1918]: 343) Carnevali forthrightly declares, "I want to become an American poet." Such an admission is not simply a declaration of the finality of his physical emigration; it also serves as an ideological literary statement signifying his intention not only to write in the English language, but also a desire that his work belong to the literature of English.

But is it enough for a writer to adopt a new language and, for that alone, to be considered adept in that role? How much of the culture that has been left behind remains in the creative expression in a *new* language? Doesn't this represent a challenge that is perhaps the challenge of all authentic, innovative literature?

It may be impossible to answer these questions because that would require penetrating into the deepest recesses of a writer to discover and ascertain, for example, to what degree and precisely how the writer has maintained elements of his own spiritual, cultural, and emotional background, and, at the same time, to pinpoint to what degree and precisely how he has absorbed the adopted culture. Besides, to what degree are such declarations proper and valid or just abstract? I believe we can only succeed in identifying and evaluating the *causes* of this desire that in most cases can be condensed into the following aspirations: to be read, valued, and *accepted* no longer by the public that you have left behind but by the one in which you have decided to live and work for the rest of your life.

To this aspiration, which I consider to be basic, other considerations can be added: the opportunity to express oneself as writers in the most pervasive, hegemonic language (as mentioned previously, this was the youthful dream of Mario Soldati); the advantages (and fertile contradictions) of being multilingual; the sense of working with great "freedom" and in the broadest of geographical and literary spaces, with the secret ambition perhaps to fill a unique void. Carnevali, whose mastery of English had been already proven by 1932, wrote in his letter to Peter Neagoe, editor of *Americans Abroad* (The Hague: The Service Press, 1932, cited by D. Biagi, 1991, 423), "I believe that I occupy a unique space in American literature." This last point seems central to all Italian writers transplanted abroad who are never completely accepted by the American literary establishment, who are often regarded with a certain suspicion, or who are generically classified as "ethnic writers." Although this conviction may seem naïve, even vain, it also conceals a truth—a relatively profound awareness of not belonging to the literary culture in which this expatriate poet, who has lost his own cultural/ethnical center of gravity, lives.

This last point seems to me to be central to all Italian writers transplanted abroad, *but never completely accepted by the American literary establishment,* or regarded often with a certain suspicion, or generically classified as "ethnic writers." Apart from the diverse (or rather nominally diverse) cultural anthropology, the primary problem obviously resides in language: an acquired (applied) tool that places one in an antagonistic or altered position with respect to one's native language, which one loses little by little, although never entirely. Again, it seems to me that the case of Carnevali—to which one could also add Giovannitti—is exemplary.

A "second" applied language cannot entirely sweep away the original, "primary" language. This crucial point about Carnevali's language was dramatically illustrated years ago by an attentive scholar speaking of the "linguistic disguise" and of the "inevitable process of conscious internal translation, discernible in every poem and in the prose itself" (Fink, 1973, 85-88). If not taken to an extreme, this assessment is one that I can, at least in part, share. In fact, the problem seems to me to be much more complex: the language of a Carnevali cannot be interpreted as a simple process of "conscious internal translation," because at a certain point a writer who has lived for years in America (with a linguistic reality significantly different from his original one) succeeds in naturally absorbing the "new" language and expressing himself directly in/with it, without intermediate operations of disguising or superimposing. My point is that the problem—more than being one of internal translation—*is of a translinguistical nature.* In many instances, it's a matter of a true and proper marriage, not a temporary arrangement. Once again, Carnevali's uncertainties of syntax and root words can be used as a demonstration of this concept. As early as 1919 (after just five years of living on Ameri-can soil), Carnevali admitted in a letter to Papini, "I am no longer completely Italian." It's significant that when he returned to Italy in 1922, sick, traveling from one clinic to another, his contacts and literary exchanges were primarily with American writers, some of whom even came to visit him. This is confirmed by his correspondence with a few—really only a few—Italian intellectuals (Linati, Papini, Cro-ce, and a few others) filled with anglicisims and English sentences inserted directly, in a completely spontaneous way, in the text of his letters, used especially when his *Italian does not immediately flow.*

It is astonishing to see the degree to which this interlinguistic problem is still noticeable today, surfacing in all of the best Italian writers transplanted to the United States. Recently, I had the opportunity to review a new novel of Giose Rimanelli, a writer from Molise fairly well known in Italy in the 1950s, who had been living in the United States for several decades. Reference to Rimanelli will serve to better elucidate this aspect of Carnevali.

In Rimanelli's novel, *Detroit Blues* (1977), a professor of anthropology and son of Italian immigrants investigates the brutal, racially motivated assassination of his cousin Larry, a talented musician, deeply committed to the cause of equality for African-Americans.

Dark skinned himself, Larry was the son of a well-known jazz guitarist, Nebraska Dope, an Indian from Omaha, whom everyone thought was black. The background: Detroit, a volcano erupting with racial tensions following the bloody riots that overturned the city in a hot July in 1967, a year before the assassinations of Robert Kennedy and Martin Luther King.

The letters of Emanuel Carnevali—albeit from a different period—inevitably made me think, from a translinguistic perspective, of the Rimanelli novel—a dense, multilingual mixture where English is spontaneously inserted into the narrative as the natural sequel to Italian discourse. This union is intended not as a simple linguistic mixture but rather as a natural fluid interference of one language with another, which binds them inextricably to each other. We should not forget that Rimanelli is also the author of novels written directly in English, such as *Benedetta in Guysterland* (1993), *Accademia* (1997), and *The Three-legged One* (2009), the first two published by Guernica in Canada, the third by Bordighera Press in the United States. These novels seem to repeat and parallel the writing experiences of Carnevali, over half a century earlier. Many examples can be cited from each writer; here are a few, juxtaposed, to demonstrate this point:

CARNEVALI
- (...) E siccome he knows all about Italy, la sua parola valse.
- (...) Lei sarà sport abbastanza da aiutarmi e loving enough da non buttarmi fuori dalla sua stima.

RIMANELLI
- Well my friends, stavo propio addeso passado per questa lovely city of yours perché la mia missione has a universal worth.
- Quel camioncino è una ghiacciaia . . . His best food, *Black Magyk*, is solid frozen.

As you can see, the writing represents an interlingual cohabitation that no longer demands a conscious internal translation, but is a direct expression in a natural continuum of phrases. I'd like to underscore again that we are speaking here of two very different writers from quite distant periods. For Carnevali, this difference entails an actual forgetting of Italian, which tends to detract from its use, as opposed to the *voluntarily acquired* English. On the other hand, Rimanelli's use of multiple languages is a conscious and sophisticated creation of his own expressive idiom, which is also, however, a sign of a definitive interference of another language with the native language.

Naturally, while in the case of Rimanelli (who came to America for the first time more than a half century ago, in 1953, the year of Mondadori's publication of *Tiro al piccione*), this "interference" of English is the fruit of a conscious, exquisitely experimental wish not to put aside Italian but to enrich it until it forms an interesting idiosyncratic multilingual mixture whose creation is the result of a radical choice to willfully and violently oppose the language of his parents. This passage from the emigration historian Emilio Franzina seems to me to clarify this central point:

> The English language, which should break down humanity's walls of ethnic separation, and whose prompt adoption has sometimes been considered as a kind of primal glue binding the myths produced by the first Italian communities of emigrants who had difficulty asserting themselves. ("Couldn't one of the reasons for the force of the American myth—which was then transferred into the English language—be the emigrants' lack of loyalty to their native language?" asks Sollers [Werner Sollors, Alchimie d'America. Identità etnica e cultura nazionale, Editori Riuniti, 1990, 179].) This represents one of the reasons for their essential weakness, along with the proliferation of criminal and Mafia behavior in some of these communities—the *Little Italies* of North America. Or it might be the other way around. The very broad loyalty of children and grandchildren to the adopted language—as documented in Italian-American fiction from Forgione to Carnevali and from Fante to Puzo—across great distances of time and constrained very rigidly within the family environment is transformed into a rapid and irreversible loss of linguistic identity. This theme has brought together not only scholars and observers from Giocosa on, but also writers and other image-makers in the bitter and reoccurring realization that the first emigrants didn't learn and almost never spoke

English, while their children and their descendants do not speak and almost never understand Italian. (Franzina 1996, 198-199)

Obviously the migrant writer is handicapped within the new literary establishment, for he must operate with only his own cultural strength. Indeed, he no longer has the support of familiar places and people, and the new context is difficult to absorb. However, if one cannot resolve the problem of which language or voice to give one's own text, one should not assume that this problem will automatically disappear in American-born authors of Italian descent who should be considered simply as American writers.

But this poses another question. Can these writers really be considered entirely American? Is it fair—as is often now done—to label such writers as Di Donato, Puzo, Talese, Stefanile, Mangione, and Gambino "Italian-American writers"? What does it mean to be a "purely American writer"? And what does it mean to be an "Italian-American writer?" And again: that attribute ("Italian") placed beside "American" but often preceded by a hyphen—at once divisive and unifying, about which some scholars have had long and polarizing discussions in recent years (Tamburri, Alfonsi, Gardaphè, etc.) proposing more "modern" solutions, such as "Italian/American" or (if said in Italian) "italiano americano." So, in what way and to what degree should that attribute "Italian" assume that a so-called "Italianness" is present in their work? Moreover, doesn't the term "Italianness" still evoke something ambiguous and ideologically dangerous? And in this regard, we haven't even mentioned the cinema, including Martin Scorsese's documentary film, *ITALIANAMERICANS*, which should be remembered in the context of this discussion. For this work, I would refer the reader to the excellent essay by Ben Lawton, "What is 'Italian-American' Cinema?" (Lawton 1995).

I can now better explain the term "reflections" that I introduced at the outset, confirming that almost all of these writers have only an abstract image of their so-called "Italian-ness." In most instances, this refers to a sentiment that could be called "bookish," echoed in the home by parents or grandparents—in short, a derived or superimposed culture that doesn't require a direct knowledge of the Italian language or literature, other than the classics read in translation

(Dante, Petrarch, Boccaccio, Machiavelli, Manzoni, Pirandello are the favored authors), or of the arts (in general, only Renaissance art reproduced in art history books).

This is the prevailing situation. I personally know American intellectuals, excellent scholars of English literature or Italian-American culture, who come up with translations from Italian to English without knowing Italian (some indeed who have never been to Italy) and boast that they can be translators without even knowing the language they are translating!

Yes, this is the prevailing situation, but not entirely, because there are a few scholars who are "exceptions"—American intellectuals and writers of Italian descent who are not constrained by this "derived culture." They have felt compelled to repossess the linguistic tools that after a generation or two had gradually fallen into neglect. The old workshop has been set up again: the fathers' or grandfathers' tools have been cleaned up, polished, and put back in use. Or they have been replaced with others that are stronger and more up-to-date. Not only do they want to master the language, they also want to master its expressive functions. They have embraced Italian literature in its original language; they have seen the masterpieces of Italian Renaissance art (and other periods) in person; they have finally rediscovered (and encountered) Italian life and society through frequent trips to the motherland. I am thinking of writers like John Fante, Lawrence Ferlinghetti (who is actually more French than Italian), John Ciardi, Felix Stefanile, Jerre Mangione, Fred Gardaphè, Anthony Tamburri, and Robert Viscusi, who are (and have been) true bicultural ambassadors as well as authentic translators of a language that has been lost, studied, and finally recaptured.

AMERICAN-ITALIANS, ITALIAN-AMERICANS, ITALIAN-ITALIANS

Let's return for a moment to the witty, though impetuous and uneven, John Ciardi (1916-1986), who, in my opinion, represents a significant and symbolic benchmark. Ciardi is the author of numerous books, including *Homeward to America* (1940), winner of the 1939 Hopewell Award. His work explicitly and dramatically demonstrates "the dichotomy of the old and new worlds, where America is now home" (Tamburri 1997, 34). At a certain point, Ciardi, a quintessential American writer (and proud of it), feels the irresistible desire to re-appropriate the Italian language. The effort is enormous: the comprehensive, palpable result is his translation of the *Divine Comedy* (1954), among the best existing translations of Dante's poem, despite its poetic liberties.

Along with Ciardi, we should also consider Felix Stefanile, who published his early poetry in the *Saturday Review,* the important journal where Ciardi served as Editor. Born in 1920, Felix (Felice) Stefanile was an accomplished Anglicist, professor emeritus at Purdue University, and one of the most significant American poets. Like Ciardi, he gradually returned to his father's native language, with a touching accent that truly and "felicitously" evokes a genuine sense of nostalgia. This sense of nostalgia is not meant to serve as a lament as is the case with the majority of Italian-American poets and would-be poets of which Ferdinando Alfonsi provides an obvious if generic example (Alfonsi 1985, 1989). Stefanile's historic and cultural nostalgia is accompanied by a literary and linguistic precision that enabled him to translate with a great finesse much Italian poetry—from Cecco Angiolieri to the futurists to Umberto Saba. In contrast to the more well-known work of Ciardi or Ferlinghetti, I would like to provide at least one example of this writer's poetry, citing his poem, "How I Changed My Name" (*A Fig Tree in America,* 1970).

> In Italy a man's name, here a woman's,
> transliterated so I went to school
> for seven years, and no one told me different.
> The teachers hardly cared, and in the class
> Italian boys who knew me said Felice.
> although outside they called me fee-LEE-tcahay.
>
> I might have lived, my noun so neutralized,
> another seven years, except one day
> I broke a window like nobody's girl,
> and the old lady called a cop, whose sass
> was wonderful when all the neighbors smiled

and said that there was no boy named Felice.
And then it was it came on me, my shame,
And I stepped up, and told him, and he grinned.

My father paid a quarter for my sin,
called me inside to look up in a book
that Felix was American for me.
A Roman name, I read. And what he said
was that no Roman broke a widow's glass
and fanned my little Neapolitan ass.

"How I Changed My Name" can be considered a manifesto of Italian-American poetry. Stefanile speaks of *transliteration*, and many of the lines in the poem point to a translinguistic problem, which is perhaps the primary problem that all American writers of Italian descent must confront. (In this case, Felix is the son of Antonio Stefanile, who was born in Nola in 1873 and emigrated at a very young age to America; his son Felice—alias Felix—was born in New York in Queens, one of the most populated areas of the city.) The problem is of a surname that remained Italian, a linguistic spy, "damaging" and, in some cases, resulting in discrimination on the part of official American literary establishment.

This problem of nomenclature—though somewhat superfluous or irrelevant in itself—is perhaps important and relevant in relation to the actual American cultural-linguistic values to which these writers naturally subscribe. They are very proud to represent, even ethnically, such values, which have been central to their education. As I have already stated, this last point is a disparaging attribute that "official" American writers and intellectuals have at times used to marginalize a literary phenomenology that also should, by all rights, belong to the composite *external form* of American literature.

A sensational episode in the literary life of Ciardi serves as a perfect example. In their Introduction to *From the Margin* (1991, second edition revised and expanded in 2000), editors Anthony Julian Tamburri, Paolo Giordano, and Fred Gardaphè recall an incident that happened to Ciardi at the height of his poetic career. The *Atlantic Monthly* had published one of Ciardi's poems with a reference to Fascist Italy under Mussolini. Robert Lowell was a contemporary of Ciardi and a fellow American citizen (both were born in Boston; the former in 1917, the latter in 1916). According to Ciardi, Lowell, a poet who was also at his peak (but with a Yankee surname), judged his poem as:

> ... The best Italian-American poem he had ever seen. And I thought, "Does this son of a bitch think he is more American than I am?" Where does he think I was brought up? Because my name is Ciardi, he decided to hyphenate the poem. Had it been a Yankee name, he would have thought, "Ah, a scholar who knows about Italy." Sure he made an assumption, but I can't grant for a minute that Lowell is any more American than I am.

Not entirely self-explanatory, this incident bears further analysis. On the one hand, it underscores how a poet like Lowell could distance himself from one of his most talented American colleagues, whose only "sin" was an Italian surname. This detail was more significant because it was more evident in a poet like Ciardi, a well-known and well-regarded American writer at the time of this poem's publication in the *Atlantic Monthly*. On the other hand, the incident also underscores the socio-cultural distance from the Italian Motherland that had already occurred in the first generation of Italian-Americans.

Ciardi never doubted that he belonged to the category assigned to him, or imposed upon him, by the literary milieu in which he had been shaped—that is, an American writer among American writers. This brings us to another—and at this point unavoidable—preliminary theoretical consideration: To maintain a certain ethnic credibility with respect to the dichotomy implied by the *hyphenation* of the term Italian-American, is it not time to call writers such as Ciardi, Mangione, Fante, and Sefanaile simply and more accurately *American-Italian* writers? As I have noted elsewhere, I realize that this nomenclature, which suggests something extremely tenuous or questionable on a semantic level, now deserves a more comprehensive and concrete definition.

I define as "American-Italian" writers (and naturally I am very cognizant of the socio-grammatical inversion of the typical expres-

sion) all those American intellectuals of Italian descent from the first
and second generation whose fathers (first generation) and grandfathers (second generation) were born in Italy and emigrated permanently to America. "American-Italians" can therefore be considered
all those Americans of Italian origin who were *born in America*, are
above all American, and live and operate perfectly integrated in the
American social system. They do not necessarily have direct knowledge of the Italian language or, in some cases, of Italian culture, that
is, apart from a chance exposure to it in the homes of their fathers
and grandfathers, or by having chosen to study it in American schools
and, subsequently, having traveled more or less frequently to their
parents' and grandparents' country of origin. The term and the meaning of "American-Italian" should be applied only to first- and second-
generation Americans of Italian descent, when the Italian culture has
been experienced within the domestic walls and still possesses an
original yeast and an *active* reverberation. After two generations, it is
absolutely incongruous to refer to any American of Italian descent
as Italian-American or American-Italian, especially when that individual has retained nothing of Italian culture other than his great
grandfather's surname, now unrecognizable or irreparably deformed.

Without necessarily arriving at my proposed terminology, whose
value is in orienting readers, this question, among others, has been
debated in recent years by the American poet and intellectual Dana
Gioia in his essay titled "What is Italian-American Poetry?" (1993).
Gioia argues, fairly but also questionably, that if a category of "Italian-American poets" exists, it should be considered historically transitory within American literature, and to study it with the tools and
criteria of ethnicity, as, for example, is done with African-American
literature, would be a methodological error, in as much as the identity of Italian-American writers is *profoundly linked to a historical
problem rather than one of race* ("The Italian-American writer's
identity is rooted in history not race" [1993, 61]). And history, unlike race, progresses and evolves; and so the history of Italians in
America has evolved for generations and generations, and, slowly but
surely, the ties with Italy have been broken. Slowly but surely, the
families of the various "Little Italies" have fragmented and dispersed

all over America. Slowly but surely the cultural values have been transformed by mixed marriages, which, rather than an exception, have become a rule. But—and this partially corrects the finality of Dana Gioia's statements—it's always just a question of *history.* Consequently, the scholar who wishes to examine the American literary evolution will not be able to set aside the fact that literary history itself is composed of diverse sources of inspiration, including those of American writers of Italian descent theoretically tied to the culture of origin.

From this perspective, I find equally debatable, though admittedly troubling, the position of a scholar like Richard Alba who speaks of the "twilight" of ethnicity at the core of the Italian-American experience. Alba essentially adopts a sociological point of view, but considering, as he does in his book, *Italian Americans: into the Twilight of Ethnicity,* the ethnic impact in American society to be tantamount to a weakening of its historical force. From a different historical vantage point, this is comparable to claiming that the influence on the future of Italy as a result of current immigration, as well as the subsequent pockets of heterogeneous cultures within Italian society today, is anthropologically similar to that of North America in the period of massive immigration of a century ago that continued until World War II, then drastically diminished, until it created the opposite phenomenon of the "return."

It will be convenient, therefore, for the scholar of Italian emigrant literature in America to perform, at least preliminarily, a work of literary reconstruction or a true and proper "archeology"—going back to the historical origins of the phenomenon in question—rather than focusing on current authors by now American(ized). If one really wanted to study such writers as Ciardi, Fante, and Stefanile under the rubric of "Italian-American" literature, then one would need to do a lengthy and painstaking direct study of their texts (and not of the preceding context, the *"ur-context,"* that risks becoming only a para-ethnic ornamentation), examining, as I mentioned earlier, how the "where-how-when" of authentic (not "derived") native "Italian-ness" has filtered into their creative work.

Obviously, when encountered first hand, this literary art is even more present (and serves as a dialectical agent) in those generations that arrived in the new world from the 1960s on when there were fewer emigrants than there had been in preceding generations. No longer were emigrants forced to leave their homeland due to brutal economic necessities; indeed, these new emigrants were often professionals, entrepreneurs, scientific researchers, or simply people who had an anthropological curiosity. This category includes the most recent authors (such as Franco Ferrucci, Paolo Valesio, Luigi Ballerini, etc.) who, if we wish to continue the "naming game," could paradoxically be called "Italo-Italian" writers or, to be more precise, "ubiquitous" writers who have made biculturalism a natural component of their literary cosmopolitanism.

I am not, therefore, very inclined to accept the evocative term "literary *tribe*" that Paolo Valesio has assigned to this last category of "Italo-Italian" writers in his excellent essay ("I fuochi della tribù"), which he subsequently revised (Valesio, 1993, 2000). Beyond its original meaning, the term "tribe" also carries a fatal association with forms of primitive society, with certain populations of "inferior" closed societies that have been isolated, and are without external contact. This concept is very far removed from the mobile, cosmopolitan, ambassador-like image that distinctively characterizes today's Italian writers who are (inter)active in North America and Europe—a category of writers (including Valesio himself) that will not be examined in this book, as I already stated in the Preface.

The "Offended" and "Forgotten"

The time is long overdue, therefore, for a literary recovery—which is by now inevitable and I would say ethically required—of writers who are overlooked even today, such as Arturo Giovannitti, Pascal D'Angelo, and Emanuel Carnevali—even though, an important general book on Carnevali appeared over thirty years ago in Italy: *Il primo Dio* (1978). In addition, however, many other very worthy writers need to be "recovered" and offered to the American public, which has "forgotten" them after having 'offended" them, and to the Italian public, which is completely or almost entirely unaware of them (into this black hole, writers such as Francesco Durante, Emilio Franzina, Martino Marazzi, and Sebastiano Martelli have been relegated in part).

And here is just a quick list of a few names: Bernardino Ciambelli, author of various pamphlets (on the long wave of Eugene Sue) such as *I misteri di Mulberry Street* (1893), *I misteri di Bleeker Street* (1899), *La trovatella di Mulberry Street: ovvero la stella ei cinque punti* (1919). Silvio Villa: *The Unbidden Guest* (1923). Louis Forgione (to whom D'Angelo's *Son of Italy* is dedicated), author in the 1920s of three works of fiction: *Reamer Lou* (1924), *The Men of Silence* (1928), and *The River Between* (1928). As an aside, it should be said that Ciambelli, Forgione, and Villa are remembered by Prezzolini who refers to them in his essay, "Scrittori americani d'origine italiana," in his book, *America in pantofole* (1956).

And other authors should also be mentioned: Constantine Panunzio, whose important biography, *The Soul of an Immigrant* (1924), came out in the same year as the autobiography of Pascal D'Angelo and is the perfect accompaniment to D'Angelo's poignant work. Prosper Buranelli: *You Gotta Be Rough* (1930). Charles Calitri: *Rickey* (1952). Giuseppe Cautela: *Moon Harvest* (1925). Guido D'Agostino, author of three volumes: *Olives on the Apple Tree* (1940), *Hills Beyond Manhattan* (1942), and *My Enemy My World* (1947). Michael De Capite, also the author of three novels: *Maria* (1943), *No Bright Banner* (1944), and *The Bennett Place* (1948).

Mario Garibaldi Lapolla, with three very interesting works of fiction self-published in the 1930s: *The Fire in the Flesh* (1931), *Miss Rollins in Love* (1932), *The Grand Gennaro* (1935). As cited in the Bibliography, Roberto Viscusi has written intelligently on Lapolla.

Pietro Di Donato, quite well known in the 1940s for the publication of *Christ in Concrete,* published in 1939 and also turned into a film. This novel, which was translated into several languages, including Italian, was followed twenty years later by *This Woman* (1959), *Three Circles of Light* (1960), and his last collection of stories, *Naked Author* (1970).

John Fante (no bibliographical information is needed since this writer is well known in Italy today even by the general public, but until about twelve years ago he had been known only by the "specialists").

Jerre Mangione, an outstanding writer and intellectual (a professor of English literature at the University of Pennsylvania for several years), known especially between the 1940s and 1960s: *Mount Allegro* (1942), published also in Italian translation in 1954 and republished in 1985, *Reunion in Sicily* (1950), published in Italian in 1992.

Jo Pagano, well known in the 1940s, author of, among other works, three successive novels: *The Paesanos* (1940), *The Golden Wedding* (1943), and *The Condemned* (1947). Rocco Fumento: *Devil by the Tail* (1954) and, in the same year, *Tree of Dark Reflection*. George Panetta, who is remembered at least for the novels: *We Ride a White Donkey* (1944) and *Jimmy Potts Gets a Haircut* (1947). Arturo Vivante, well respected and widely read in the 1950s: *The French Girls of Killini* (1958), *A Goodly Babe* (1959), and *Doctor Giovanni* (1959)

We are considering, therefore, a broad spectrum of authors who were well known at one time in North America, but who have now fallen into neglect or complete oblivion. Their work, I'd like to underscore, had been published by major publishers (many now consolidated) such as McGraw-Hill, Doubleday, Knopf, Harcourt, Houghton Mifflin, Little Brown, and Random House.

We should remember that, except for a few sporadic exceptions, such as Ciambelli, all of the writers mentioned wrote in English, and should by necessity be studied by scholars of American literature (quite significantly, Prezzolini refers to them as "American writers of Italian origin"). By way of introduction, I'd like to clarify again that in this book, we will focus primarily on *Italian expatriate writers*, that is, writers born in Italy who have become expatriates in America, who write in Italian, even though they have adopted the English language or become perfectly bilingual, if not indeed multilingual.

I've already spoken of Carnevali. It should be repeated that his expressive language remains exclusively English with all of the implications that fact implies: collaboration with poetry journals in the

United States; his career as an editor with *Poetry* magazine (for several months, Carnevali was the journal's Associate Editor, notably in 1918, and his work continued to be well represented in the magazine; his last collaboration was in August 1931) along with his love/hate relationship with his friend Harriet Monroe, "the savior of all poets," as he affectionately refers to her in his autobiography; the frequent controversies and exchanges of correspondence with American writers; a posthumously published autobiography edited by Kay Boyle (*The Autobiography of Emanuel Carnevali*); his fairly regular inclusion in histories of American poetry from 1910 on (and not from 1911 as it has been mistakenly written). In fact, we find that Carnevali makes his first appearance in an anthology in *A History of Poetry*, an edition edited by James D. Hart in 1941 (second edition in 1948). But even other anthologies, in this respect, should be remembered in which Carnevali or Giovannitti regularly appear (Kunitz 1942; Benèt 1948; Hine-Parisi 1978; refer to the Bibliography in this book).

It should be remembered that Carnevali and Giovannitti regularly appear in other anthologies (Kunitz 1942; Benèt 1948; Hine-Parisi 1978; refer to the Bibliography in this book). It should also be noted that after Carnevali returned to Italy in 1922, he continued to write primarily in English (although, due to his illness, his writing became increasingly sporadic) and maintained contact with his American writer friends.

℘

The example of Arturo Giovannitti (Ripabottoni, Campobasso 1884-New York 1959) is more complex and pronounced. Up until now, very little has been written about his literary work by Italian critics (among others, Portelli 1977; Tusiani 1976, 1988; Lalli 1981; Tedeschini Lalli 1986; Candeloro, Gardaphé, Giordano 1990).

The case of this poet, who, amid the thick forest of many nostalgic, lamenting, ardent, or rebellious poets as well minor poets from the first wave of migration, is perhaps destined to remain among the strongest Italian-American writers, is very different from that of Carnevali. But in America today Giovannitti is hardly remembered at all as a poet and even less so as a dramatist. His memory is tied almost exclusively to the dramatic union struggles from 1910 to 1929, particularly to an episode in 1912, reconstructed by the historian Franzina. A union strike broke out in Lawrence, Massachusetts, with serious disorder "during which an Italian-American woman, Anna Lo Pezzo, was killed by a bomb of a provocateur, perhaps paid for by the police. The strikers, who belonged to about twenty different nationalities and were fighting against a forced wage reduction, enjoyed the support of the immigrant community and of progressive New York intellectuals. From prison, Giovannitti composed one of his most successful poems ("The Walker") and succeeded in defending himself in court during the trial for his alleged homicide, speaking in perfect English and displaying an eloquence that Prezzolini compared to the legal rhetoric of attorneys in Southern Italy" (Franzina 1996, 153). This self-defense troubled and astonished the judge and the jury, enabling the socialist-anarchist to avoid what would have been a certain condemnation to death (in contrast to what happened a few years later to Sacco and Vanzetti). From the distance of four decades, Prezzolini returns to this incident in a somewhat elitist, half serious/half ironic minor article titled "Elogio di un trapiantato molisano bardo della libertà." Commenting on Giovannitti's English, which, according to him, was sufficiently sophisticated for conversation, "the Italian that he wrote maintained all of the cadences and defects of the literary language of D'Annuzio" (*Il Tempo*, May 10, 1964).

Giovannitti achieved an extraordinary mastery of English, and it is in English that his major works of poetry can be found (*Collected Poems*, 1962, reprinted in 1975; his first self-published monograph, *Arrows in the Gale*, is from 1914). Unlike Carnevali, Giovannitti never forgot Italian, the language in which he continued to write until the last years of his life (as in the tender and memorable *Nenia sannita*); he also translated or rewrote poetry that he had originally written in English, demonstrating a perfect facility with both languages, which Carnevali lacked.

From the diverse scope of Giovannitti's work, which has assumed an almost mythical aura as transformed by today's critics, one must underscore its original thematic and stylistic merits, setting aside the degree to which there is already a nineteenth-century legacy—especially from Carducci, and the late nineteenth-century verists—in his secular verse, which is both messianic and oracular. More significant is the heated rhetoric that Giovannitti utilized in the passionate political battles that he successively conducted in the United States. I am thinking, among others, of the biweekly literary/artistic/political periodical, *Il Fuoco,* which he founded and edited in New York along with Onorio Ruotolo (first issue: September 20, 1914; last issue: December 1, 1915; in addition to poetry, Giovannitti published in this journal several plays and spirited pamphlets). After the sad episode in Lawrence, Massachusetts, this was an ideal continuation of *Il proletario,* which he had edited in 1911. I am also thinking of his introduction to the socialist Pouget's *Sabotage* (Emile Pouget 1913, 11-36) and of the contemporaneous work of the "rebellious romantics" gravitating around *The Masses,* the American revolutionary socialist journal of the 1910s that seemed to be a countermelody to the more cautious and respectable *Poetry* magazine of Harriet Monroe. These aspects influenced the work of the militant political poet Giovanniti, filling his verse with a fervent exaltation as we find in certain volcanic little poems like "New York and I", or the celebrated "The Walker," written feverishly in the jail in Lawrence, a poem that I mentioned earlier and that is today considered to be his political masterpiece, translated in all major languages and included in 1919 (already at its height of popularity) in the *Modern American Poetry* anthology edited by Louis Utermeyer. I will cite two excerpts with my translation into Italian (in the Appendix) from "The Walker" and "New York and I," poems respectively from the collections *Arrows in the Gale* and *Wind Before Dawn,* that best express the impetuous, if uneven, vehemence of this writer:

"The Walker"

I hear footsteps over my head all night.
They come and go. Again they come and they go all night.
They come one eternity in four paces and they go one eternity
    in four paces, and between the coming and the going

there is Silence and the Night and the Infinite.

For infinite are the nine feet of a prison cell, and endless is
    the march of he who walks between the yellow brick
    wall and the red iron gate, thinking things that cannot
    be chained and cannot be locked, but that wander far
    away in the sunlight, each in a wild pilgrimage after a
                                        destined goal.

Throughout the restless night I hear the footsteps over
                                        my head.
Who walks? I know not. It is the phantom of the jail,
    the sleepless brain, a man, the man, the Walker.
One-two-three-four: four paces and the wall.
One-two-three-four: four paces and the iron gate.
He has measured his space, he has measured it
                                        accurately,
        scrupulously, minutely, as the hangman measures the
                                        rope
        and the gravedigger the coffin—so many feet, so
                                        many inches,
        so many fractions of inch for each of the four paces.
One-two-three-four. Each step sounds heavy and
                hollow over my head,
        and the echo of each step sounds hollow within my
                                        head
        as I count them in suspense and in dread that once,
                                        perhaps,
        in the endless walk, there may be five steps instead
                                        of four
        between the yellow brick wall and the red iron gate.
But he has measured the space so accurately, so scrupulously,
        so minutely that nothing beaks the grave rhythm
        of the slow, fantastic march.

(. . .)

My brother, do not walk any more.
It is wrong to walk on a grave. It is a sacrilege to walk
four steps from the headstone to the foot and four steps

from the foot to the headstone.

If you stop walking, my brother, no longer will this be a grave,
    for you will give me back my mind that is chained
      to your feet and the right to think my own thoughts.
I implore you, my brother, for I am weary of the long vigil,
    weary of counting your steps, heavy with sleep.
Stop. Rest, sleep, my brother, for the dawn is well nigh
    and it is not the key alone that can throw open the gate.

"New York and I"

City without history and without legends,
City without scaffolds and without monuments,
Ruinless, shrineless, gateless, open to all wayfarers,
To all the carriers of dreams, to all the burden bearers,
To all the seekers for bread and power and forbidden ken;
City of the Common Men
Who work and eat and breed, without any other ambitions,
O Incorruptible Force, O Reality without visions,
What is between you and me?

You have narrowed my vast horizons
To the coil of your cold embrace,
You have shortened my star-girt heights
To the height of your bludgeoning mace;
You have pinioned my falcon flights
With the shears of your thieving measure,
You have seared my eyes with the sights
Of the stew where you rot and gloat;
You have parched my war-shouts in my throat
With the smudge of your hot bitumes,
You have choked my white prayers with the fumes
Of your toils and the dust of your streets.

(. . .)

You have sealed in my lungs the cough
Of your sick and voracious breath;
You have poured the squalid death

Of your pleasures into my veins;
And all the things that are red,
And all the things that are vain.

(. . .)

I shall sing of your slums where you bleed,
Your machines, iron claws of your greed,
And your jails, viscid coils of your mind,
The light of your eyes that dazzles the sun
And turns your midnights into noons,
The Street where you buy and resell
Each day the whole world and mankind,
Your foundations that reach down to hell
And your towers that rend the typhoons,
And your voice drunk with bloody libations,
And your harbor that swallows the nations,
And the glory of your nameless dead,
And the bitterness of your bread,
And the sword that shall hallow your hand,
And the dawn that shall garland your head!

ARTURO GIOVANNITTI EDITOR OF *IL FUOCO* AND *VITA*

The eclectic and passionate Giovannitti must certainly be re-membered for his editorial work both as contributor to various pe-riodicals and as founder of a number of journals between 1914 and 1915. I am referring to his many contributions, in Italian and in Eng-lish, to publications such as *Solidarity, The Liberator, The New Masses,* and *The Hammer* [*Il Martello*]. Furthermore, he must be remembered for his fiery antifascist activities during the twenties and thirties, which culminated in his editorship of *The New World* (1928-1930), as well as his translation from Italian into English, *Mussolini: The Story of a Corpse* by former socialist deputy Vincenzo Vacirca (1934).

At this point, I would like to spend a short time considering the periodical *Il Fuoco*, which Giovannitti and his friend Onorio Ruo-tolo published from September 1914 until December of the follow-ing year—first issue: September 20, 1914, last issue: September 30, 1915. This period, which is both emblematic of and central to Giovannitti's American experience, is virtually unknown to the Italian culture. At the same time, it exemplifies the ideals and ambitious artistic projects that burned in the spirit of Giovannitti.

During these years, the thirty-year-old author from Molise envisioned the actions of Italian Futurists, especially those in Florence, as the ideal interlocutor. (This is just before the publication of *Lacerba*.) This becomes crystal clear when we consider the publication's title, its subtitle, "A Biweekly of Art and Battle," as well as its motto, which ran, in capital letters, from the top to bottom of the first edition's cover—"CIÒ CHE NON VIVE NON ARDE, CIÒ CHE NON ARDE NON VIVE" ["What does not live, does not burn; what does not burn does not live."]

Imbued with the principles and typical avant-garde vehemence of anti-conventionalism, the first editorial published in *Il Fuoco* boldly proclaimed its somewhat anarchistic spirit. Let us read a few passages that clearly reflect some key writings of F.T. Marinetti and Giovanni Papini just a few years, or even months, earlier:

> La vita reale di oggi, quella dei forti, degli atleti, dei creatori, è come una fiammata rapidissima di sarmenti secchi: brucia, crepita, divampa e si disfa in cenere senza tizzi e senza bracia.

> I maestosi ceppi umani che ardevano per settimane sui grandi alari ferrei della storia sono roba del passato come i mostri antidiluviani e i giganti arborei delle foreste vergini. Le individualità solitarie che torreggiavano come cime inaccessibili sugli orizzonti piatti e livellati sono scomparsi ritirandosi sempre più nel folto delle ombre dei trapassati remoti. (...) Le nicchie della storia sono tutte piene di mummie in decomposizione ed i tripodi offertorii son passati alle vetrine dei musei con tutte le altre muffe.

> (...) Il genio non è più nei secoli, è nell'ora. La gloria è nell'istante, come la felicità, come l'amore, come il piacere. (...) Noi siamo dell'OGGI e del QUI; oltre questo giro di sole non ci importa la vita ma solo ci ammalia la visione della morte bella. (...) Noi vogliamo essere intesi soltanto da coloro a cui parliamo e che ci ascoltano. Vogliamo ardere e risplendere nel fuoco del presente per la gioia degli occhi di coloro che ci vedono e per le anime di coloro che si scaldano alla nostra fiammata.

(...) Ecco perché il nostro Alcorano è un giornale e il nostro nume è IL FUOCO: arde di noi soltanto e quando il nostro combustibile sarà finito si spegnerà con noi. Per riaccenderlo vi bisogneranno altre fascine umane, sarà d'uopo che altri vivano di nuovo per rilucere e conflagrare. Non i morti, non le idee sepolte, non le sapienze sotterrate, non i fossili immobili né le ceneri sacre bagnate di lagrime devote, daran luce e fiamma e calore. Le cose inerti non si accendono, le cose eterne non divampano perché non sono distruggibili. La vita soltanto è nell'incendio e la fiamma soltanto è nella vita.

[Real life today—that of the strong, of the athlete, of the creator, is like a rapidly blazing pile of dry kindling: it burns, crackles, blazes, flares up, and consumes itself in ashes, without embers and without coal.

The majestic human logs that burned for weeks on the great andirons of history are as much a part of the past as antediluvian monsters and the giant trees of virgin forests. The solitary individuals who towered like inaccessible peaks over flat and level horizons have disappeared, retreating ever deeper into dense shadows of the remote past. (...) The niches of history are completely filled with rotting mummies.

(...) Genius is no longer a thing of centuries past; it is now. Glory is the in the moment, like happiness, like love, like pleasure. (...) We are of TODAY and we are HERE; beyond this revolution of the sun, life is not important to us, and we are bewitched only by the vision of the beautiful death. (...) We want to be understood only by those to whom we speak and by those who listen to us. We want to burn and glow in the fire of the present for the joy in the eyes of those who see us and for the souls of those who warm themselves in our flame.

(...) This is why our Koran is a newspaper and our god is *Il fuoco*: it burns only because of us, and when the light goes out, it is we who will turn it off. To turn it back on, there will have to be other human kindling; it will be incumbent upon others to bring it back to life, to relight its flame, and let it explode. Not the dead, not buried ideas or buried wisdom, not buildings or the ashes of sacred fossils wet with devout tears—none of these will give light or heat or flame. Inert things do not light, and eternal things do not consume themselves, because they are not destructible. Only life is in the fire, and only the flame is in life.]

In the above passage, it is impossible not to notice the bombastic tone and even some dangerous terms, or slogans, that would become part of Italy's ultra-nationalistic apparatus and eventually be picked up by the fascist regime (for example, "beautiful death," etc.).

Giovannitti ambiguously and generally exposed *Il fuoco's* parafuturistic and anticlerical "agenda" on page two of an article palinodially titled "Instead of a Program." Here, he calls the newspaper's editors "tolerant and intolerant—tolerant when ideas are discussed in the field of thought, intolerant when those ideas are carried into the field of battle."

And furthermore: "This magazine is an intellectual gymnasium, not a contentious arena for militant activities; therefore, by mutual agreement, they [the editors] open the doors to anyone who has something to say, and they allow them enter with no restrictions whatsoever except those required by space and ... grammar. However, this newspaper is not a white flag for the gathering of parliamentarians from contending factions. It is simply a broader platform where all warring armies can post their respective orders of the day." Finally, riding the wavelength of a confused social anarchism with a decidedly anticlerical stamp: "We hate what is tepid far more than we hate what is cold. We prefer the oil of plebian fury or the medieval burning at the stake to the fat pale candles in the court of conciliation. (...) We reject only two things: the robes and wigs of senile librarians and the baby bottles and harnesses of graphomaniacs who are not yet weaned or who are just taking their first steps."

This terse and violently provocative tone was emphasized throughout the inaugural issue, whose contributors included, among others, Giovanni Molinari, Giuseppe Musso, Ernesto Valentini, Sara Field, and Onorio Ruotolo. (The latter praised futurism as "a new and fiery idea emanating from nine new suns in a battle between flames and radiance for the conflagration and rebirth of the world."). And finally, in a brief article, Giovannitti reiterated as a sort of unequivocal seal, printed entirely in italics:

Questo *Fuoco* non è una lampada da notte, né una bragia da scaldaletto per i pinzoccheri ed i baciapile del giornalismo alimentare della colonia. Tenetelo d'occhio e vedrete che tra non molto diventerà un incendio. È inutile quindi soffiarci sopra o versarci su delle bacinelle d'acqua lattiginosa da lavabi intimi. È inutile anche tirar fuori le grosse pompe d'incendio. Bisogna fargli largo e se si vuole isolarlo ci vuol della dinamite. Quelli che lo dirigono conoscono la fame, la guerra e la galera e non temono nulla. Sanno scrivere e sanno fare a cazzotti. Non li si può comprare, non li si può intimorire, non li si può adulare, non li si può prendere né per assalto né per assedio. Hanno la coscienza, la fedina penale e ... la tasca pulite e insistono arrestare ciò che sono. L'unico mezzo, quindi, per debellarli è quello di discuterli e di provar loro che hanno torto. Essi non rifiutano né discussioni, né duelli. Schifano soltanto che non sa usare né la penna né il bastone. Get it right.

[*Il fuoco* is not a nightlight or a warming pan for the coals of bigots and religionists of journalism who feed our colonies. Keep an eye out, and you will see that before long it will become a fire. It is useless, then, to blow on it or douse it with bowls of milky water from personal washbasins. It is useless even to call out the fire pumps. You will have to give it space; and if you want to isolate it, you will need dynamite. Those who know hunger, war, and prison firsthand have no fear. They know how to write and do battle. They cannot be bought, they cannot be intimidated, they cannot be flattered, they cannot be taken either by assault or by siege. They have their own conscience, they have no criminal record, they are honest, and they insist on being who they are. Therefore, the only way to defeat them is to debate them and prove they are wrong. They do not reject discussions or duels. They reject only those who not know how to use either the pen or a stick. Get it right!]

In an article titled "Why Am I a Futurist?" Giovanni Papini demonstrated and, in a sense, endorsed the programmatic para-avant-garde understanding, even amid the inevitable decline in tone and taste. Significantly, Papini's article appeared on the same page of that written by Giovannitti in which he outlines the agenda of the biweekly, whose main points are highlighted above.

In fact, besides Papini's initial presence in the journal, successive issues included other well-known Italian Futurists, such as Armando Mazza, Umberto Boccioni, Luciano Folgore, Paolo Buzzi, etc., demonstrating a staunch adherence to the themes and modes of expression particular to the Futurist movement.

Thanks to its interesting multidisciplinary structure, *Il fuoco* published the most heterogeneous critical and creative works. In the visual arts, it followed the energetic presence of Onorio Ruotolo—painter, illustrator, and, above all, sculptor—with contributions by important international artists of the day, such as Alice Beach, John Sloan, Charles A. Winter, Hy Mayer, R. Barns, Glinten Kampf, Stuart Davis, Art Joung.

Of these artists, Davis and Joung made a number of contributions, all under the banner of social radicalism, which was the central focus of the populist anti-capitalist and antiwar ideology of *The Masses*. Not only did *Il fuoco* use the same design and graphics as *The Masses*, it openly advertised the fact. In the Christmas 1914 special issue, we read: "*The Masses* is the only modern, open-minded, and militant magazine in the United States."

These illustrations, taken from *The Masses*, are distinguished by their satire, or sarcastic verve. I quote a few examples, both illustrated by Art Young, from the December 1914 and the January 1915 issues.

In the first, titled "WAR," we see two gorillas, one small and one large, in a jungle. The little one is saying, "Mama, don't tell me that those people killing each other over there are descended from us." The second, titled "The Perpetual Motion of Capitalism," is an explicit satire against capitalist exploitation of the working classes. Extraordinarily foreshadowing Charlie Chaplin's brilliant and polished performance fifteen years later in *Modern Times*, the drawing depicts a large wealthy man perched on top of a huge building (presumably an allusion to a large factory). On this summit, there is a sign reading "The High Cost of Living"; and the fat man, who is wearing an expensive ring on his finger, is dangling a long piece of string from his hand; the string extends down to the road where there is another sign reading, "Raise in Wages," that is, "raise our pay." On the ground next to the sign, a worker is bending down to collect coins from a change purse.

I have mentioned the biweekly's multidisciplinary aspect. In addition to graphics and illustrations, it published poetry, namely, by Italian Futurists and by Giovannitti himself, which is still completely unknown to the Italian audience. Another interesting figure among Italian expatriate writers is Antonio Calitri whose work would later be analyzed by Prezzolini. Giovannitti published essays, dramas, short stories, proclamations, reviews, and articles about sports, music, and variety shows. There were also some variously tendentious sections, beginning with one called "*Forno Crematorio*" ["Crematorium"] whose intentions were defined as follows: "*... rubrica di attualità in cui adageremo nel lenzuolo di amianto della fornace beccamorta uomini in vista, partiti, movimenti, istituzioni, etc., che sono morti moralmente di anemia cerebrale, di gotta o di elefantiasi e le cui carcasse, per ragioni d'igiene pubblica, vanno incenerite.*" ["... a regular column, and in its asbestos furnace we will place powerful men, parties, movements, institutions, etc. that are morally dead due to cerebral anemia, gout, or elephantiasis, and whose carcasses must be incinerated for reasons of public health."]

During the first nine months of the journal's existence, Giovannitti's influence was consistently intense; it published poems, essays, pamphlets, dramas, translations, and proclamations. Each contribution underscored the journal's inflexible socio-anarchistic position and vehement opposition to military intervention. However, in time, several members of the editorial board changed their minds and became increasingly in favor of intervention. The ideological contrast between Giovannitti and the editors came to a head in two issues: number 8 in May 1915, and number 9 in June 1915.

In issue number 8, Ruotolo published an editorial titled "*Anche Italia nell'immane guerra*" ["Italy, Too, In Enormous War"] in which he explicitly stated that he favored Italian intervention. Then, in the very same edition immediately following Ruotolo's editorial, Giovannitti wrote a long article titled "*Fiamme, faville, e ... cenere*" ["Flames, Sparks, and ... Ashes"], which was divided into several self-contained segments. In this article, Giovannitti clearly and sarcastically confirmed his pacifistic, anarchistic, and antimilitaristic position against the hypocritical American bourgeoisie and against any warmongering stance.

In order to reaffirm his inflexible antimilitarism, Giovannitti's article "The Deserter" ["*Il disertore*"] also appeared in this issue. The title of the article clearly and eloquently underscored his position in regard to the war.

This ideological contrast between Giovannitti and the journal's editorial board was evident throughout the issue and rendered even more contradictory when the editors launched a referendum asking the journal's readers to take a position regarding the war. And yet, the announcement did not seem to be a true referendum; rather, it was worded in such as way as to make it seem more like an invitation in support of the war. It read: "*organo di singoli, una ruota di trovatelli per tutti coloro che non hanno una anagrafata paternità intellettuale e che quindi si sentono sciolti da qualsiasi legame etico, sociale e spirituale (...), essenzialmente italiano senza essere patriottardo: è nazionalista senza essere guerrafondaio, ed è irreduttibilmente rivoluzionario nel senso che mira ad una transvalutazione di tutti gli elementi cozzanti della società, ardendo il vecchio, il consuetudinario (...), in una parola è l'organo nazionalismo giovane, fattivo irruente, battagliero e impertinente delle nostre colonie.*" ["*Il Fuoco* is an instrument of individuals who do not have an intellectual heritage; therefore, they are free from any ethical, social, and spiritual ties. *Il fuoco* is essentially Italian without being fanatically patriotic; it is nationalistic without being warmongering; it is revolutionary in the sense that its aim is the devaluation of contrasting elements in society by burying the old and the traditional. (...) In short, *Il fuoco* is an instrument of the new young nationalism—active, impetuous, bellicose, and impertinent to our compatriots."]

Giovannitti's final split from *Il fuoco* occurred in the following issue (June 16 - June 30, 1915). In an open letter dated June 10, 1915, Giovannitti highlighted "the irreconcilable conflict of political and social ideas" that had always existed between him as a "revolutionary socialist" and his friend Ruotolo as a "diehard nationalist." In this farewell letter, Giovannitti explained that the original philosophy of *Il fuoco* had been "to create a purely artistic and literary journal"; however, the unavoidable circumstance of the war has drastically changed these original intentions.

Nevertheless, if we read between the lines, we will find other reasons, perhaps more profound, such as the fact that Giovannitti was fully aware that Ruotolo bore the entire financial burden of the magazine; therefore, Giovannitti was not in a position to interfere with its agenda. More importantly, Giovannitti realized that the Italian-American public was not "truly educated"; for this reason, it was unable to benefit from the journal's purely artistic and literary qualities.

Giovannitti's farewell letter ends with a statement showing his usual noble and idealistic philosophy:

> A Onorio Ruotolo, che mi e fratello per la vita vada dunque oggi il mio saluto ed il mio augurio con la certezza che domani, dopo che questa violenta raffica di morte e di sterminio sarà passata, ritorneremo a lavorare insieme per il nostro sogno maggiore: quello dell' arte, la grande pacificatrice, la sola affratellatrice degli spiriti turbati ed irrequieti, quell'arte che lo ha destinato alle cime, a cui non mancherà di pervenire, quando la sua anima multiforme e tormentata avrà ritrovata la strada maestra della vita.

> [I salute Onorio Ruotolo, whom I consider a lifelong brother. I am sure that when this bloody extermination is over, we will return to work together on behalf of our major dream—that is, art, the great pacifier and the only fellowship of restless spirits. It is art that is destined to achieve glorious heights when its multiform and tormented souls will have found the main road of life.]

With Giovannitti's resignation, the subtitle of the final five issues of *Il fuoco* was changed from "Biweekly of Art and Literature" to the unqualified and explicit "Biweekly Nationalist." Visually emphasizing this change in direction, the cover of the first issue without Giovannitti's coeditorship appeared with a photograph of Gabriele D'Annunzio and the caption, "The Poet of the New Italy."

For his part, Giovannitti continued to reiterate his antiwar and antimilitarist position, which became even more intense following the tragic death of his brother, Aristide, while fighting on the front (August 20, 1915). Giovannitti then founded a new journal titled *VITA*; shortly thereafter, he wrote the drama, *As It Was in the Beginning*, which, according to Frank J. Cavaiola and Jerre Mangione, was a major Broadway success in 1917 (LaGumina 2000, 268).

As if to close an elegant circle begun in the first issue of *Il fuoco*, Papini published a poem in the journal's final issue titled "*Quattro belli occhi*" ["Four Beautiful Eyes"] (September 30, 1915). But how different this writing was from the effervescence of just one year before when his writing had an impudent and impetuous vitality; here, in this poem, there was a weary, nostalgic, and exhausted tone that reflected not only the demise of a periodical but, in essence, the demise of the entire avant-garde era.

The title of Giovannitti's new publication, *VITA, rivista dei nostri giorni* [*VITA, A Magazine of Our Times*], left no doubt about its scope. Everything of a utopian nature, including the imaginative and creative life, was summarily replaced with the myriad everyday problems inflicted upon the world by a war that would have no winners and no losers. Giovannitti was fully and painfully aware of this, even more so after the death of his brother, Aristide.

Let us peruse the pages of that periodical, which had a total of four issues (September 1915 to November 1915). The first three editions (September 1, September 15, and October 1) seem to indicate that Giovannitti had intended to publish a biweekly. The fourth and last issue appeared on November 1.

In the first edition, Giovannitti's editorial clarified the periodical's firm ideological position and the indomitable revolutionary socialism that supported its founding. I include significant excepts in the following passages:

> Questo giornale è l'organo di tutti i dissenzienti e gli irreconcialiabili, quelli che vivono ancora la vita profonda e intangibile della loro personalità spirituale e che vogliono ad ogni costo salvare i loro principi le loro passioni e la loro entità psicologica dal naufragio universale dei movimenti e delle ideologie, che la guerra va brutalmente preparando. (...) La guerra, infatti, esiste per noi come può esistere la peste; è una calamità che vogliamo combattere dopo averla studiata, invece di subirla supinamente.
>
> (...) Restiamo tenacemente aggrappati alla nostra dottrina rivoluzionaria a dispetto di ogni precipitar d'eventi (...) Siamo fermamente e incrollabilmente convinti, oggi più che mai, che la guerra non la vo-

gliono i popoli che sono costretti a farla, ma i governi e le classi abbienti che essi rappresentano; e crediamo con profonda sincerità che questo immane cataclisma lascerà intatte le condizioni di disparità economica tra i vari ceti sociali; che nessuna civiltà nuova e maggiore scaturirà da essa e nessuna barbarie sarà soppressa; e che la sola messe che i popoli ne raccoglieranno sarà una orrenda mietitura di cadaveri, di miserie, di debiti, di odi e di sciagure.

(...) Essa non ha per nulla modificata la nostra attitudine di ieri verso la somma totale di tutte le energie e i sentimenti umani che si compendiano nel nome di Vita. (...) Noi vogliamo restare anche ora che la guerra infierisce tutto intorno a noi, anzi ora più che mai, nel nostro magnifico sogno di solidarietà umana e di giustizia (...), perché in nessun altro momento della storia fu mai tanto necessario un ideale oltre e al di sopra dell'orrida realtà, per individualizzare gli uomini e farli vivere nell'intensità di se stessi, invece che automatizzarli sotto lo scudiscio di un'unica follia collettiva.

Per noi l'Internazionale del Lavoro non è ancora morta; se lo fosse bisognerebbe risuscitarla. E per fa sì che essa risorga bisogna che qualcheduno cominci a tendere la mano attraverso i mari e le montagne, che qualche generoso leghi alla baionetta il cencio rosso della solidarietà e della pace, e sollevi il fucile fuori della trincea. Cominciamo noi – diciamo noi qui fra gl'Italiani d'America ancora una volta la suprema verità. E la verità è una sola: grande, universale, intesa e compresa da tutti, eterna e indistruttibile: La Vita. Ecco spiegato il titolo e, col titolo, il programma di questo foglio.

[This periodical is the organ of all dissenters and all those uncompromising souls who still live a profound and spiritual life true to their nature, and who want, at all costs, to save their principles, passions, and psychological existence from the universal sinking of movements and ideologies, which the war is brutally effecting. (...) The war, in fact, exists for us as a plague; it is a calamity that we want to combat, after having understood it, instead of passively submitting to it.

(...) We cling tenaciously to our revolutionary doctrine in spite of any sudden and dramatic events (...). We are firmly and unshakably convinced, now more than ever, that the people did not want war, that they were forced into it; it was the rulers and wealthy classes that represent them who wanted war. And we sincerely believe that this terrible disaster will leave intact the conditions of economic disparity among social classes, and that no new civility will emerge from it, and no barbarism will be suppressed by it; and the only reward the people will enjoy will be the terrible harvest of corpses, misery, debt, hatred, and disaster.

(...) [The war] has not changed our former attitude toward the sum total of all human energies and sentiments epitomized in the name of Life. (...) We want to maintain our magnificent dream of human solidarity and justice even now that war is raging all around us— indeed, now more than ever (...) because at no other time in history was the ideal more needed, above and beyond the horrid reality, to individualize men and let them live in the intensity of themselves, rather than turn them into automatons under the whip of a single collective madness.

For us, the International Labor movement is not dead; if it were, you would need to resurrect it. And to make it rise again, you would need someone who would reach out across the seas and mountains, some generous person to attach the red rag of solidarity and peace to the bayonet and raise the rifle out of the trench. Let us begin, Italians of America! Let us again speak the supreme truth. And there is only one truth: great, universal, agreed-upon, and understood by all, eternal and indestructible: Life. This explains the title and, with the title, this journal's agenda.]

These passages speak for themselves; however, beyond a certain emphatic fervor, they are typical of Giovannitti's prose. They capture the full climate and antiwar beliefs that inspired anarchistic Italian socialists in America such as Carlo Tresca, Vincenzo Vacirca, Fortunato Vezzoli, e Flavio Venanzi, among whom Arturo Giovannitti was considered the most charismatic leader. These writers as well as others like them were the most frequent contributors to *VITA*, a journal whose mission was stated on the subscription page: "*non è l'organo di nessun partito e di nessun movimento organizzato, ma vuol essere all'avanguardia con tutti coloro che marciano con lo spirito moderno. È con le classi lavoratrici in tutte le loro battaglie, con le donne nel loro audace movimento d'emancipazione e con i giovani che in tutti i rami dell'arte e delle lettere portano l'alito vivificatore della modernità*". ["[*VITA*] is not the organ of any party or any organized movement; rather, it means to be at the forefront of all those who march with the modern spirit. It supports the working classes in all their battles, the bold women struggling for emancipation, and the young people active in all branches of arts and letters who are the life-giving breath of modernity."]

Faced with the monumental disaster of the war, Giovannitti's articles reflected on the precariousness of life: absorb it, be actively involved, bite it; in short, live it fully even those momentary aspects that might be crucial or worth pondering. The motto, printed in capital letters at the top of the first issue, read "DUM VIVIMUS VIVAMUS" ["Let us live as long as we live"], which intended, quite graphically, to underscore the journal's agenda, whose existence during wartime fragmented with every passing moment. The inclusion of a column titled "Asterisks," also edited by Giovannitti, corresponded exactly to this need. The column was structured for short fiery outbursts or reflexive fragments that laid bare Giovannitti's remarkable analytical ability as well as his profound *pietas*. He never abandoned that spirit of solidarity, palingenetic rebirth, or the thirst for justice by sharing and analyzing human suffering vis-á-vis the enormous atrocities of war. Here is an example of these "asterisks":

Il *New York Times* afferma che la Francia durante quest'anno di guerra da "infedele" che era è ridiventata cattolica. Non sappiamo se sia vero, ma in ogni modo è probabile. Finché la morte avrà dei terrori per l'anima umana (e nessuna morte è più terrificante di quella che incombe incessantemente sui campi di battaglia e non fa pensare mai ad altro, checché ne dicano gli esteti della guerra) finché essa non sarà la coronazione di tutta una vita laboriosa, fattiva e serena, la religione apparirà sempre come il supremo conforto. Non è concepibile che un ragazzo di venti anni, messo di fronte alle bocche dei cannoni non pensi a Dio e al paradiso.

[*The New York Times* reports that during this first year of the war, the 'infidel' France is once again Catholic. We do not know if this is true, but in any case, it is likely. As long as death is terrifying for the human soul—and no death is more terrifying than the one that hangs incessantly over the battlefield and makes one think of nothing else, despite claims to the contrary by the aesthetes of war—and until death is not considered the crowning of an industrious, active, and quiet life, religion will always appear as the supreme solace. It is inconceivable that a boy of 20, faced with the mouth of the cannon, does not think about God and heaven.]

L'idea di non vivere più non è riconciliabile con la certezza di non aver vissuto abbastanza. Non è concepibile che una madre a cui sia stato trucidato il figlio ancora adolescente si rassegni all'idea del distacco eterno. Dopo tutto vi è un lieve substrato di giustizia astratta e istintiva in questa recrudescenza di misticismo religioso; un'aspirazione subcosciente verso la perfetta retribuzione dei grandi torti subiti che viene dall'incapacità di rassegnarsi all'idea che i delitti della guerra sono al di là di ogni tribunale. In fondo è il senso primitivo della vendetta che riconduce Iddio alla ribalta dei popoli. Quando questa vendetta, che è poi la madre ripudiata ma sempre vigile della giustizia, sarà rievocata di nuovo all'unico giustiziere che può equamente somministrarla, il popolo, la religione si ritirerà ancora nelle penombre della superstizione e Dio abdicherà tutti i suoi giudizi in favore della rivoluzione.

[The idea of no longer being alive is not reconcilable with the certainty of not having lived enough. It is inconceivable that a mother whose adolescent son has been murdered can resign herself to the idea of eternal separation. After all, there is a mild and instinctive substratum of abstract justice in this resurgence of religious mysticism; it is one's subconscious aspiration to find perfect compensation for the great wrongs, which springs from an inability to accept the idea that crimes of war are beyond any court. In essence, it is the primitive sense of revenge that puts God at center stage. When this revenge, the repudiated but ever-vigilant mother of justice is recreated as the single avenger able to administer justice fairly, the people will relegate religion back into the shadow of superstition, and God will abdicate all his judgments in favor of revolution.]

These words echo the religious fervor of Giovannitti's adolescence when the then seventeen-year-old studied theology at McGill University in Montreal with the intention of becoming a Protestant minister. Of course, the young Italian from Ripabottoni would soon leave his studies to dedicate himself to endeavors that seemed far better suited to his temperament—literature, especially poetry and drama, social commitment, and social revolution. However that inclination, that religious spark, would always remain in Giovannitti's soul. It inspired his work to bring about a more egalitarian justice; and, in time, it gave him a profound sympathy for all exploited humankind.

From here, it was but a short step to the path of socialism, a purely humanitarian socialism. It involved remixing concrete ideas of commitment and social struggle; but at the same time, there were prophetic "visions" and good wishes for a new and better world.

Returning to *VITA*, there is no doubt that its basic agenda was the war as a recurrent and fundamental object of debate and, more generally, the deeds and misdeeds of American and European societies during those years. In fact, an article titled "*A proposito di atrocità*" ["About Atrocities"] was called emblematic of J.P. Warbasse, whose essence would have appealed to a "Free Society where human brotherhood and mutual aid" would be the dominant forces. In the same spirit, there were other articles, in particular, by the fiery Havelock Ellis ("*La psicologia dei tedeschi*" ["The Psychology of the Germans"]); Flavio Venanzi ("*La commedia diplomatica*" ["The Diplomatic Comedy"]); and Arturo Giovannitti ("*L'America Barbara*" ["Barbaric America"]). I would like to mention, parenthetically, that Warbasse, an active trade unionist in the Labor Movement contributed to the left-wing newspaper *The Nation*. This is the same publication that would be launched, thanks to editor Carl van Doren, a few years after Pascal D'Angelo, one of the most touching and significant figures in Italian expatriate literature. Van Doren wrote, among other things, the Introduction for D'Angelo's *Son of Italy* (New York, Macmillan, 1924), one of the most poignant and disturbing autobiographical documents about the history of Italian emigration to America. Warbasse was also to play a central role in *CO-OPERATION: A Magazine*, founded in 1917. Appearing in the top left of this magazine were these words: "To spread knowledge of the Cooperative Movement, whereby the people, in voluntary association, produce and distribute for their own use the things they need."

Here, we must mention Havelock Ellis (1859-1939), member of

the "Fabian Society" and well-known scholar of sexual evolution whose famous six-volume work, *Studies in the Psychology of Sex*, was published between 1897 and 1910. These volumes, which were the subject of heated controversy, were banned for several years.

The writer Flavio Venanzi (1882-1920) died at the age of 39, which inspired Giovannitti to write a touching poetic eulogy in a letter to Onorio Ruotolo. The letter, "The Death of Flavio Venanzi," can be found in a volume of Giovannitti's work, *Collected Poems* (Chicago, E. Clement, 1962 and New York, Arno Press, 1975, 102-109). Giovannitti would return the following year to write about his "lost brother" in the Introduction to a book titled *Venanzi: Political and Literary Writings* (New York, Venanzi Memorial Committee, 1921), collected and arranged by Giovanni Di Gregorio, another contributor to *VITA* and editor of the column "Old English Quarrels."

More than anything, however, it is Giovannitti's voice that appears most frequently and passionately in *VITA*—proclamations, invectives, apologies, observations regarding custom and society, chronicles and political reflections, poems, as well as special poetry dedicated to social matters, all as yet unpublished in volume form as are those he contributed to *Il fuoco*. (And when will such a collection be published?) Among all these texts, one that truly stands out is his poem "Il morte di mio fratello" ["My Brother's Death"], which he dedicated to his mother.

Following the example of *Il fuoco*, *VITA* also published illustrations of a highly subversive nature, for example, those of Robert Minor, Glinten Kampf, and Charles A. Winter—all dedicated artists or "rebels" who had been drawn to the socialist magazine *The Masses*. It is worth commenting on at least two of these illustrations.

The first is a work by Kampf that appeared in the third issue. High on a hill, there is a horse ridden by a macabre skeleton that is holding a bloody lance. Various corpses are scattered on the slope, and, in the foreground near the horse, a crying baby is curled into a ball. This direct representation immediately calls to mind the realistic socialist iconography of the Russian Revolution. The illustration's caption asks sarcastically, "United States: You called me?" Obviously Death represents the United States, which prevailed during this period of war. It should be mentioned that Giovannitti regarded Death as the personification of an evil war, and would, in various important and sometimes poignant writings, return to the subject in *VITA*. I am referring in particular to "*Le lettere della Morte. Lettera alla Vita*" (n. 1) ["Letters to Death. Letter to Life"]; "*La fine di uno scandalo*" (n. 3) ["The End of a Scandal"]; "*Ammutiniamoci!*" (n. 2) ["Let Us Mutiny!"]; and the aforementioned "*Il morte di mio fratello*" (n. 4) ["My Brother's Death"].

The other illustration, "The Awakening of Woman" by Charles Winter, was the cover for the fourth issue of *VITA*. In this illustration, there is a female figure standing by a wall and looking thoughtfully toward the city. In the distance, there are various houses and buildings. An old man and an old woman, apparently representing the tired and defeated workers, are crouched on the ground next to the woman. To the left of the woman's back and above the wall, we see a huge skull, behind which there is a great collection of faces. The explicit title of the illustration, "The Awakening of Woman," underscores the artist's awareness of women's conditions and their emancipation—a subject that Giovannitti considered in a long article at the beginning of the same issue.

This is a very important and broad article titled "Votes for Women," which I quote in full and annotate at least a few significant passages, for it is worth considering. Although he begins with a personal observation that he is in principle, and in keeping with his unwavering socialist position, a "staunch anti-electionist," Giovannitti says that the political vote is every citizen's direct expression of personal political intention. The vote "is to politics as belief is to religion. (...) Politics is direct and effective as much as religion is pure and sincere; they are both a practical and daily translation of spiritual concepts."

From here Giovannitti goes on to express his position in favor of women's suffrage, which is, in his opinion, necessary for two reasons: first, women want it, and second, they are entitled to it. Giovannitti argues that the right to vote is either a privilege or a right. If suffrage is considered a privilege, it is not in keeping with the principles of democracy; indeed, it is better suited for the ideals of an absolutist regime. However, if suffrage is a right, "then it cannot be limited by any restrictive qualifications of wealth, culture, or gender." Once we acknowledge the democratic principle that men and women are equally responsible before the law, in the name of what arcane reason, he wondered, are women prohibited from being allowed to debate, amend, and enforce the code itself?

Giovannitti continues his interdicting analysis by recalling that Christianity was the "first attempt at universal unification, designed to bring all of humanity to an equal and common spiritual ground (...) It would take a good eighteen centuries before this equality was brought from the field of theology to that law, that is, when the American and French Revolutions, which far surpassed Puritan reform in England, declared that all people are equal before the law. Socialism will be the final corollary of these two diverse ideologies into a single pure principle of equality, transporting it to its ultimate consequence of economic equality."

In anticipation of the eventual emancipation of women, Giovannitti underscores the socio-familial restrictions still imposed upon women in 1915. First, a married woman "must relinquish her name"; in addition, "the father has rights over his children regardless of the mother's wishes: for example, if they want to enlist in the army, emigrate, or even marry, the father has the final word." And again: "A married woman cannot recognize her own child from a former husband without the permission of her present husband, whereas a man can recognize 100 such offspring without consulting his wife."

Giovannitti gave recognition to more than 6,000,000 working women in America who paid taxes and contributed to the wellbeing of society on a level neither higher nor lower than that of men. He urged women to fight for the right to vote. In addition, remember that a long road toward emancipation was yet to be traveled even for former black slaves who had fought next to Lee and Grant.

Decades before the women's movement of the 1960s and 70s, Giovannitti dramatically rejected as "silly" the "hypocritical" belief that "a woman must be dependent on a man and is bound to family, motherhood, and the home fires." In addition, he rejected the prejudicial idea—"the shoddiest of all—[that] women are intellectually and physically inferior to men."

Finally, let us read, in its entirety, a passage that speaks volumes, at least in my opinion, about Giovannitti's ideological position and those preconceptions concerning the issue of women's rights that were so difficult to eliminate in 1915:

La verità cruda è che questi pregiudizi sgonfiati e privi di senso permangono soltanto per mascherare il fallimento morale e le umilianti condizioni dei maschi. Ogni pater famiglia, beato e beota, vi ripeterà con grottesca incoscienza che è lui che provvede ai bisogni della sua magione e che le sue figlie sono "ragazze per bene e di casa", mentre la realtà tragica è che le figlie strappate prima dei maschi alla scuola, si sono procacciato il pane e il companatico fin dai quattordici anni, risparmiando anche abbastanza per il tabacco ed il cicchetto di papà.

I sei milioni di donne menzionati più sopra non sono una prova formidabile che la donna è stata scacciata dall'ambiente domestico e gettata senza misericordia e senza riconoscenza nei traffici spietati delle competizioni economiche. In parecchi stati del Sud si va anche oltre; non solo la donna lavora quanto e più del maschio, ma la sua mercede è ipotecata dal padre o dal marito.

Il capitalismo ha distrutto la famiglia, ha consacrata la casa, ha infranti tutti i legami di autorità economica nei vari rami della parentela, ha livellato tutti i figli del popolo alla stregua dello stesso abbrutimento.

Solo la completa uguaglianza dei sessi, basata sul riconoscimento di diritti e di doveri unici ed assoluti, potrà con il tempo riportare gioia, pace e rispetto intorno al focolare domestico.

(...) Il mio lustrascarpe analfabeta avrebbe per innata fatalità biologica più perspicacia civica di mia moglie che potrebbe anche essere quella che mi sta dettando quest'articolo? Le tremila e più maestre della città di New York che istruiscono i nostri figli se ne intenderebbero meno di tasse e di tariffe dei tremila bananari che illustrano la mascolina 'genialità' della Little Italy?

(...) I nostri operai saranno maggiormente predisposti a risentirsi di un'altra indegnità codificata e sancita, quella costituzione federale che dichiara solennemente che "sono esclusi dal voto i criminali, i felloni, i pazzi, i deficienti morali e le donne". Capite? Le nostre madri, le nos-

41

tre mogli, le nostre sorelle sono accomunate in un documento storico ai delinquenti e agli idioti!

(...) Amico lettore, compagno che leggi, la tua scelta non può essere dubbia. Se non vuoi discendere, aiuta la tua compagna a salire.

[The plain truth is that these discredited and senseless prejudices only mask the moral failure and humiliating conditions of men. Each family *pater*, both blessed and beastly, boasts with grotesque ignorance that it is he who provides for the needs of his home and that his daughters are only good for taking care of the house. The tragic reality is that his daughters, snatched out of school before his sons, are his bread and butter from the age of 11, even saving enough money for Papa's occasional shot and his tobacco.

[If] the 6,000,000 women mentioned above are not formidable enough proof, [think of] the woman who is driven from her home and thrown without mercy and without recognition into the ruthless world of economic competition and trade. In several states of the South, [the situation is worse] not only because the woman works, and works even more than the man, but her father or husband has the right to claim her salary.

Capitalism has destroyed the family, consecrated the house, broken all ties of economic authority within the various branches of the family, and brought all the children of the people to an equal level of degradation.

Only complete equality between the sexes, based upon recognition of their unique and absolute rights and duties, may, in time, bring joy, peace, and respect to the home.

(...) Could it be that my illiterate shoeshine boy has, for reasons of biology, more civic shrewdness than my wife, who could also be the one dictating this article to me? Should more than 3000 teachers who instruct our children in the City of New York understand less about taxes and tariffs of the 3000 banana sellers who so eloquently illustrate the masculine 'genius' of Little Italy?

(...) Our workers are more likely to resent another codified and sanctioned indignity by the Federal Constitution, which solemnly declares that 'criminals, felons, the insane, moral morons, and women are excluded from the vote.' Do you understand? Our mothers, our wives, our sisters are united in a historical document with criminals and idiots!

(...) Dear readers who share these principles, your choice cannot be in doubt. If you do not want to degrade yourself, help your partner to rise.]

Perhaps this farsighted article, which is so full of common sense, would not suffice in and of itself to dispel the macho and anti-familial image that, in my opinion, too negatively and unfairly has affected and still weighs on the "man" Giovannitti. If we remember that this article was written in 1915, five years before the Constitution granted suffrage to American women, we realize its prescient and revolutionary importance.

In fact, attention to issues of a socio-political nature was always prevalent in *VITA*, but without overwhelming its purely literary aspects. Indeed, *VITA* published quite a few stories and poems, all edited by Giovannitti, which are still unpublished in book form. In addition to the articles by J.P. Warbasse, cited above, we find contributions by Flavio Venanzi, Fortunato Vezzoli, Vittorino Sbordone, the aforementioned Giovanni Di Gregorio, Charles Edward Russell, Roberto Di Tullio, William Knight or Guglielmo Knight [both signatures appear in separate articles], Jane A. Roulston, Vincenzo Vacirca, and columns of various types—about newspapers, magazines, books, social events, disputes, and controversies. Vacirca wrote a long article titled *Civiltà Inglese e Prussianesimo* ["Prussianism and English Civilization"] in which the Marxist author points out in his significant conclusion: *"l'inglesismo vale il prussianismo e che la pelle dei lavoratori dovrebbe essere considerata una ben ignobile cosa anche da noi , se volessimo farne tamburi su cui accompagnare i rauchi gridi di ' Morte al Kaiser! ' o di ' Long live England! ', o ' Italy ', o ' France '. La causa della rivoluzione operaia non s'affida né agli elmetti prussiani, né alle uniformi color Khakì (sic). Ma—lo disse quel... tedesco di Karl Marx—darà opera dei lavoratori stessi, internazionalmente uniti."* ["Anglicism and Prussianism are the same. And we, too, would regard the skin of the working people as something vile if we used that skin to make drums to accompany our raucous cries of 'Death to the Kaiser!' or 'Long live England!' or 'Italy' or 'France'. The cause of the workers' revolution does not rely on Prussian helmets or khaki-colored uniforms, but on the German Karl Marx, who will give these workers international unity."]

The final issue of *VITA* was late in going to press, and Giovannitti wrote an apology in that issue, saying, "Because of typographical errors, the publication has been delayed for days. To prevent similar incidents from occurring in the future, this issue is dated November 1, rather than October 15. From now on, *VITA* will go on sale on the 13th and the 28th of each month."

This promise would not be kept; there would be no next issue announcing, in capital letters, the "direct and special contribution" by Enrico Leone, who, in those years, was a professor of Economics at the University of Bologna and known for his clear opposition to the war.

Giovannitti was occupied with more pressing pursuits involving the campaign for pacifism. However, he did not forget that he was still an ardent Utopian and author who brought the two interests together. Although he wrote many heartfelt poems and plays that have now fallen into complete oblivion in North America, there is no doubt that his work aroused interest and enthusiasm during those years between 1915 and 1917. I recall two plays—*The Green Lantern* (written in Italian and published in *Il fuoco*) and *As It Was in the Beginning* (1916), which was performed on Broadway and was reviewed in major New York newspapers. The play was also translated into Italian and was staged at the People's Theatre in Manhattan on October 10 of that year winning great applause in the Italian community. Incidentally, it should be mentioned here that Giovannitti's work has never been published in Italy.

If this was perhaps Giovannitti's most splendid moment, it also marked the beginning of his gradual decline. The declaration of war on April 7, 1917 and the simultaneous weakening of the various factions and unions (also because of internal dissent), including the

IWW (Industrial Workers of the World), resulted in the direct elimination of dozens of newspapers such as *The Masses* and *The Proletarian* and the natural dissolving of others. The laws against "criminal syndicalism," espionage (Espionage Act, 1917), and sedition (Sedition Act, 1918) brought almost every struggle for social justice to a standstill. The arrest, in October 1917, of Giovannitti, Joseph Hector, Carlo Tresca, and Elizabeth Gurley Flynn for "anti-American propaganda" (that is, peace) and the subsequent arrest, four months later, of the entire Executive Committee of the IWW did the rest.

The sun was setting on an era of glorious revolutionary spirit, to which *VITA* had also contributed. It was the beginning of a new era of general reform, which would be supported by many trade unionists and socialist intellectuals from the first era.

The fifth Congress of the Italian Socialist Federation, held in Brooklyn in 1921, officially resolved its own dissolution. Giovannitti's dearest friend, Flavio Venanzi, had died the year before (February 27, 1920). Three months after that saw the arrest of Sacco and Vanzetti, for whom Giovannitti unsuccessfully held rallies, collected signatures, and wrote several articles. Although his critical and creative work continued to resonate intermittently throughout the next three decades, Giovannitti began his "complete and fragmented solitude," a term he used in a letter to his friend Vincenzo Di Lalla (Renato Lalli, *Arturo Giovannitti* [Campobasso: Rufus, 1981] 163).

It seems useful at the conclusion of this review of *VITA*, to present each issue's table of contents. And here let me express my gratitude to the Department of Rare Books and Microfilm at the New York Public Library for having permitted me to view and copy the rare, now unobtainable, issues of *VITA*:

NUMBER I, NEW YORK, 1 SEPTEMBER 1915

Arturo Giovannitti, *Dum Vivimus Vivamus*
Arturo Giovannitti, *Asterischi*
J.P. Warbasse, *A proposito di atrocità*
Flavio Venanzi, *La commedia diplomatica*
Arturo Giovannitti, *L'America barbara*

Havelock Ellis, *La psicologia dei tedeschi*
Giovanni Di Gregorio, *Our English Quarrels*
Alfonso Daudet, *L'assedio di Berlino*
Arturo Giovannitti, *Ode al sottomarino* (poem)
Arturo Giovannitti, *The Occupation of Rougemont* (from the first Act of *As it was at the Beginning*)
Anonimo, *Le lettere della Morte, Lettera alla Vita*
William Knight, *Il delitto e il delinquente*
G. Di Gregorio, *Note d'arte*
I libri del giorno, Tra giornali e riviste, La nostra libreria (unsigned columns)

NUMBER 2, NEW YORK, 15 SEPTEMBER 1915

Arturo Giovannitti, *Commenti della Quindicina*
Flavio Venanzi, *Il ramo d'olivo*
Robert Minor, *E ora sfamati, mostro!* (drawing)
Enrique Valdes Herrera, *Nel Messico rosso*
Arturo Giovannitti, *Ammutiniamoci!* (poetry)
Robert Minor, disegno per *Ammutiniamoci!*
Fortunato Vezzoli, *Contro un pericolo*
Vittorino Sbordone, *Come volano gli uomini*
Giovanni Di Gregorio, *Note d'arte*
I libri del giorno, Fra giornali e riviste (unsigned columns)

NUMBER 3, NEW YORK, 1 OCTOBER 1915

Arturo Giovannitti, *Commenti delal Quindicina*
Arturo Giovannitti (?), *La fine di uno scandalo* (signed *IL CORSARO*)
Tito Martelli, *I monatti della guerra*
G. Bernard Shaw, *La morte dell'artista*
Flavio Venanzi, *Verhaeren, poeta della vita*
Octave Mirbeau, *L'uomo di Diogene*
Glinten Kampf, *Mi hai chiamata?* (drawing, courtesy of *The Masses*)
Fortunato Vezzoli, *Per screditare la guerra*
Arturo Giovannitti, *Et tu quoque, soror* (Fantasia)
Charles Edward Russell, *Perché l'Inghilterra decade*
William Knight, *Materialismo e Morale*
Roberto Di Tullio, *Lettere del pubblico*
I libri del giorno, Fra giornali e riviste (unsigned columns)

NUMBER 4, NEW YORK, 1 NOVEMBER 1915

Charles A. Winter, *Il risveglio della donna* (drawing)
Arturo Giovannitti, *Votes for Women*
Flavio Venanzi, *Il pericolo futuro*
Vincenzo Vacirca, *Civiltà inglese e Prussianismo*
Emile Verhaeren, *La Germania e l'anima moderna*
Faber, *I becchini. Il figlio di papà* (drawing)
Arturo Giovannitti, *In morte di mio fratello* (poem)
Anonymus, *Per sfatare la leggenda*
Steinlen, *I senza patria* (drawing)
Joseph K. Griffis, *Il matrimonio di Zilta* (short story)
Jane A. Roulston, *The Books of the Day*
Guglielmo Knight, *Forza e Materia*
Lettere del pubblico, Fra giornali e riviste (unsigned columns)

∽

Always under the lens of this "archeological" research, we must at last resurrect the tragic experience of Pascal D'Angelo (1894-1932), on whom we will focus in the next chapter. Emigrated from the Abruzzo at the age of sixteen, D'Angelo found himself performing a wide variety of jobs, living in a railway car while teaching himself English at the price of unheard of sacrifices, with the help of a worn-out pocket dictionary and developing a poetic passion that in my opinion is unequaled in the history of Italian-American literature. When in 1924 he finally succeeded in publishing his autobiographical *Son of Italy* (1924), with an introduction by Carl Van Doren, this work was reviewed in the *New York Times Book Review*. This would be the high point in the writer's career, but the naïve and idealistic Pascal did not know how to take advantage of the opportunity. A few years later, consumed by fatigue and illness, he died in extreme solitude and poverty at the age of 38 (1932). His funeral and burial were paid for by friends and admirers, while his name and his work fell immediately into oblivion. Only most recently, thanks to a few courageous Italian and North American publishers, seventy years after his death, his work has been brought back into the light. Meanwhile, his name has disappeared completely from any directory, manual, index, or dictionary of American literature.

The case of Pascal d'Angelo, whose story, I realize, risks seeming like a heartbreaking film or a tearful novel of a disorderly crepuscular poet, is instead dramatically exemplary and perhaps even "justifiable" given the time, the xenophobic discrimination, and the many varied difficulties that Italian countrymen encountered at the beginning of the twentieth century.

What is not excusable is the incredible long silence into which writers like D'Angelo and Giovannitti have been plunged since their death. What is most unacceptable is that they have been forgotten by the very same Italian-American writers of today—and this is the most serious instance, although there are not many—who love to categorize themselves as "Italian-Americans." In this instance, ignorance and silence have become embarrassing and inadmissible.

I wonder if it is possible to attribute this silence *also* to a certain desire on the part of those who, having attained social prestige and wealth, *wish* to forget authors who testify, through their writing, to the most miserable and squalid conditions of Italian emigrants, as well as the suffering, hopes ("The Sun of the Future"), sacrifices, and pains that they left behind: things that, all in all, are better forgotten? To erase them from memory signifies, psychologically, to erase also the pages on which that suffering was written.

Is it not the primary and precise task of a scholar of Italian-American literature to raise those writers out of oblivion? And, before lecturing on the themes, ethnic, stylistic, interdisciplinary, hermeneutic, and "tribal" aspects of the current literary phenomenon, wouldn't it be better to start with a systematic examination of literary archeology (and justice)?

Given the times in which we live, with people rushing to burn themselves up within the society of spectacle, the past cannot be buried or derided. But, if the past is ever to be reexamined, especially the past that we have unjustly erased, it is not only to save literary validity and memory but also to enrich our volatile present.

CHAPTER TWO

Autobiography and Poetry
The Case of Pascal D'Angelo

But more sincere and dearer to my heart were the
tributes of my fellow workers who recognized that at
last one of them had risen from the ditches and quick-
sands of toil to speak his heart to the upper world.

—Pascal D'Angelo

The literary adventure of Pascal (Pasquale) D'Angelo (Introdacqua, L'Aquila, 1894-Brooklyn 1932), and all of the painful human drama it entailed (as mentioned in the previous chapter), risked passing under the radar of twentieth-century literary scholars—which is eventually what happened. The question of how to classify a poet like D'Angelo poses many difficulties (in terms of literary geography, without even touching on the pure and simple question of his identity), which is sadly the very same condition that unites the unfavorable destinies of virtually every expatriate Italian author in the United States.

The fact that these poets and novelists were at a disadvantage from the outset has impeded serious critical evaluation of their work. Indeed, they are often generically labeled "ethnic writers," which has resulted in their marginalization as literary "byproducts," mere side effects, of the hegemonic production of the country in which they conceive and compose their work. Their works are studied more as the collateral phenomena of cultural sociology and social anthropology (at times, even worse, as "picturesque" phenomena of a folkloristic, popular form of literature), than as actual literary works in and of themselves, objects that deserve the same footing as those of the natives. Nearly three-quarters of a century after the publication of his autobiography in 1924 (the only work D'Angelo published in his lifetime), deliberately written in English despite the myriad restrictions that beset him in '20s Brooklyn, *Son of Italy* has recently been republished by two small, though enterprising, publishing houses (Il grappolo editions, in Salerno, Italy; and in America by Guernica, edited by Kenneth Scambray, a scholar of Americo-Italian and Italo-American literature). The Arno Press (New York) edition of the book has been out of print since 1975 and can only be found in the collections of the best libraries.

Rather than being considered a natural component of American plurilinguistic expression, a phenomenology that a historian might call *letteratura aggiunta* has often been undervalued or regarded with a certain prejudicial eye, despite how well camouflaged it might be by the benevolent façade the North American literary establishment likes to maintain.

The transplant writers themselves, however, have unfortunately contributed (and, even to this day, continue to contribute) to their own literary ghettoization; too often have they transformed their own biographies as disinherited emigrants into the material of their literary work. Few expatriate writers of the first migratory wave manage to escape this rule, which is perhaps better termed "this temptation," that is, this impulse to self-confession that seems to compel them. The story is, however, different (as we saw in the previous chapter) for those Americo-Italian writers, whose autobiographical or para-autobiographical novels are not as bogged down in heavy-handed psychological conditioning. I would like to cite here a most exemplary case, *Umbertina* by Helen Barolini (1979; Italian edition, 2001) with its "storico e corale" tone (Lilli 2009, 9; "historic and choral"), in which the stories of three Italian-American women are stitched together by the thread of their common search for identity between America and Italy. Let us not forget that Barolini was and still is one of the most passionate scholars of the feminine sphere of the Italian-American experience (for a complete bibliography, see the appendix of this book).

In fact, the majority of these writers' narrative output (from Di Donato and Panunzio to Carnevali, D'Angelo and their successors Mangione, Tusiani, and eventually even Robert Viscusi) consists of autobiography. After pouring out their life stories, they seem not to have borne any ulterior urge to write purely inventive works. It is significant, for example, that other than Di Donato, who indeed continued to write para-autobiographic and semi-autobiographic narratives after *Christ in Concrete* (1939), all of the other aforementioned authors wrote only one narrative book, namely, their autobiography.

Once the burning desire to give a voice to their own existential experience as emigrants had been quenched, few ever desired or even considered writing other books. This single book became their spiritual baggage, an imaginative vade mecum that, at the same time, represented a vivid reality to be shared with their peers, traveling companions and descendents.

All but a select few are afflicted by this general predicament: I think emblematically of John Ciardi and John Fante, who are perhaps the only writers today whose work has plausibly earned a spot next to that of the greatest of their American contemporaries. But, in the case of Fante and Ciardi, we are dealing more precisely with "Americo-Italians," in the accepted meaning I explained in the previous chapter.

Here originates the limitation not only of critical and monographic exegesis, but also of the very ability of these autobiographies to have a significant impact on the production of "high" fiction in North America in the years spanning the 1920s to the 1950s, the period of novelists like Faulkner, Scott Fitzgerald, Dos Passos, and Hemingway. At this point the reader realizes the absolute necessity of evaluating these para-narrative works with critical instruments (sociology, history, economy, epistolography) beyond those traditionally associated with the study of literature.

And, on the other hand, what else could they narrate—these immigrants who were often semi-illiterate, hungry for work, and eager to dream—if not the difficulties they experienced in living color. Thus the vicious circle comes to a close, making the possibility of escape almost impossible. Yet, it is the only means one can hope to find redemption from physical, moral, and intellectual destitution.

It is precisely in a *cul-de-sac* such as this that we find a dreamer cultivating a fervid imagination. Pascal D'Angelo was the son of an Abruzzese shepherd who expatriated to America in 1910 (exactly nine months after Arturo Giovannitti and four years before Emanuel Carnevali) after he had hit rock bottom in the wretched existence he led in Italy.

Naturally the story is a bit different if we examine the genre of "poetry," in which, beyond the usual nostalgic self-pietism, one actually finds exalted moments of authentic poetry worthy of the same serious consideration afforded its hegemonic counterpart. The cases of Carnevali, Giovannitti, who was featured in the previous chapter, but also Pascal D'Angelo, and later John Ciardi and Felix Stefanile seem to me the most probing.

Returning to the abundant production of autobiographical and para-autobiographical novels by expatriate Italian writers in the United States, which have attracted significant critical attention in recent years (Boelhower 1982; Mulas 1989; Marchand 1991; Mangione-Morreale 1992; Martelli 1994; Franzina 1996; Gardaphé 1996; Tamburri 1991, 1998; Giordano 1999; Marazzi 2000; Durante 2001; for a complete list, see the bibliographic appendix in the back of this book), very few, in fact, go beyond mere sociological data, few aspire to a phenomenology that is genuinely literary, though they are still classifiable as such, *sub species casi.*

Pascal D'Angelo's autobiography, *Son of Italy*, belongs precisely to that literally exceptional category that historians use to denote a *literary case.*

I would now like to proceed with a reading from this book (all citations refer to the 1975 edition), which is truly exemplary and riveting in the context of so much Italian-American autobiographical writing from the 1920s to the 1950s, and still scarcely known either by connoisseurs of American literature—whom this work legitimately addresses—or by those connoisseurs of Italian literature, despite the modest resonance the book had in its day in Italy. See the contributions of Luigi Anelli (1924), Gabriele Candeloro (1925), and Giuseppe Prezzolini (1934, then 1950), as well as the renewed and certainly greater interest (but that today seems already circumscribed by time) that its publication in an Italian translation provoked in the last few years: take for instance, articles by Furio Colombo in the *Repubblica*, August 5, 1999; Pasquale Esposito in the *Mattino*, August

17, 1999; Oreste Del Buono in *La Stampa*, September 4, 2000; and Maurizio Chierici in the *Corriere della sera*, December 9, 2000. However, it was Generoso D'Agnese's ambitious article in the Italian-American daily newspaper *America Oggi* (December 27, 1998) that brought D'Angelo to the attention of Italians in America. The article is actually slightly presumptuous and contains several inaccuracies like that of suggesting that Pascal D'Angelo had been friends with Mark Twain (!), a case of wishful thinking if we consider that the year our little shepherd from Abruzzo arrived in New York was also the year of Twain's death.

In the very first chapters of the book a mild and mythic, candid and candied dimension emerges that characterizes both D'Angelo's way of narrating as well as his capacity to be surprised—first, in his childhood, recollecting the magic suspension of the world that surrounded him (rural life in small town Abruzzo), but also into his adolescence and maturity, recounting the brutal working conditions he experienced in America.

But this mythic dimension, external to the places themselves, (the Maiella, *montagna madre*, in many ways seems to represent its real and symbolic peak), provides a counterpoint to the internal environment Pascal inhabits in all of his candor ("ferocity has never been able to develop within me" [5]) with his family: his mother, his father and younger brother, in the most vile living conditions. They live in a leaky shack that they share with their animals: five sheep and four goats (and we should perhaps add the occasional nocturnal invasion of mice). All four of them sleep in the same bed. His life was marked by an implacable poverty that presents itself in its full disarming ferocity, even today, to those who go to visit this hovel, as I did in October 1999. In this dilapidated house, which remains today exactly what it was a century ago, and in the stingy stagnation of the surrounding countryside, dominated by the majestic silent mountains that tower over it, each day passes just like every other. It was natural for a gentle Abruzzese shepherd like Pascal to confront this reality with the attitude of the dreamer he truly was.

> We of the uplands of Abruzzi are a different race. The inhabitants of
> the soft plains of Latium and Apulia where in winter we pasture our
> sheep consider us a people of seers and poets. We believe in dreams.
> There are strange beings walking through our towns whose existence,
> we know, are phantasies. We have men who can tell the future and
> ageless hags who know the secrets of the mountain and can cure all
> illness save witchcraft with a few words. (9)

This is then his description of the magic of the place, in the countryside near Introdacqua, where one cold day in January 1894 Pasquale
D'Angelo was born (it seems fitting to restore his actual childhood
name). Phenomena like rain, snow, and wind had always governed
this country, isolated from God and from men, where, in part even
to this day, superstition and fear flourish (unforgettable the memory
of the old "wizard" who one day was struck by lightning—according to
Pasquale's mother, "by the fires of heaven"—during an apocalyptic
downpour), and so do popular forms of ancient wisdom, quintessen-
tially embodied, for example, in the figure of the beggar Melego, a
man of exotic voyages and various existential experiences, from
whom the young man will learn much more than he ever learned
from the decaying elementary school he attended in those days.
With great difficulty and uncertain success, they inhabit and extract
their sustenance from a most bitter land, which is rendered even
meaner and more ruthless by sudden droughts.

   This is the landscape, dominated by ignorance, prejudice, taboo,
and vain beliefs, that our young Abruzzese shepherd inhabited, ter-
rified, like the rest of the country, by the bizarre characters who pe-
riodically infest it. Here is the case of the vampire witch, deathly
frightening to the peasants, whose maleficent powers Pasquale and
his friend Antonio would attempt to neutralize by secretly pricking
her with a mattress needle (according to the ancient belief of the
place, sticking a needle into the leg or arm of the witch meant the
annihilation of all of her witchcraft). The whole situation builds to a
sort of "rural gothic" climax at the expense of a six-month old baby
who died of who knows what malady, but whose boorish parents
believe had been the victim of this particular sorceress. The story

ends in an actual "witch hunt" and a resolution that has nothing of the puritanical (thinking obviously of the pyres of Salem).

These are episodes of great intrigue written in a "poetic mode" (Gardaphé 1996, 24). Gardaphé evocatively recalls, in the epigraph to his critical study of D'Angelo's autobiography, a quotation from Vico on the "poetic primitivism" of primordial populations. The case of Pascal would then present an option for primitive oral culture in collision with the culture exquisitely expressed by the Anglo-Saxon literary tradition. I only agree with this assertion in part, inasmuch as I do not think that someone like Pascal D'Angelo ever had aspirations to become a *cantastorie*, or popular street singer. Quite the opposite (this emerges clearly over the course of his autobiography): he always had the high romantic poetic tradition of Keats and Shelley in mind, regardless of his ingenuous naivety. His is the authentic naivety of a true poet. I would even say that his *candor*, or rather his inclination to high literature (the English Romantics, but also Dante) and not to its lower forms (the popular tradition of *cantastorie*), permeates the book from start to finish, marking his work with an overall more intimate and profound seal.

In a land of tightfisted fertility fossilized by its archaic modes of existence, escaping to other worlds (mobility toward the exterior) seems to be the only possible alternative. This is what Pascal's father, by now completely spent, eventually recognizes in his son (who was at this point a young man of fifteen).

For the first time, he comes to understand the nature of the wound left by his fatal separation from his motherland. Here D'Angelo is very careful to gather in his autobiographical narrative (we are in chapter five, one of the most moving in the whole book) the range of emotions he felt, while still an adolescent, toward his father (who eventually decided to follow him) as well as toward an America that wanted to "deprive him" of his familial love ("At first I felt boyishly angry against this America which was stealing my father from me" [50]). But it is only for a moment that he must grit his teeth and be strong—the farewell scene with his mother is truly touching. *Navigare necesse est*, and, all things considered, the call of another world intensifies the driving motivation that pushes father and son to depart and, at long last, to tempt fate across the ocean.

D'Angelo sums up their long voyage on the *Cedric*, a steamship full of emigrants, in a mere two pages, which is very little when compared, for example, to the rich and animated passages that De Amicis, in *Sull'oceano*, had dedicated to a similar sea voyage 35 years earlier. D'Angelo places more importance on his experiences on American soil. He is concerned with what happened before and after his transatlantic passage, not with what happened in transit between the two poles of the "emigration" phenomenon. Totally foreign to him are the sociological, ideological, and cultural analyses underlying the trafficking of lives on board ship. He certainly did not have the culture or the instruments of social analysis with which De Amicis was so gifted. And certainly our author was unaware of De Amicis' existence as well as his work, including *Sull'oceano*, a book, as it has quite rightly been pointed out, "che ha avuto un ruolo primario e archetipico nella letteratura dell'emigrazione" ["that has played a major archetypal role in emigration literature"] (Martelli 1994, 108).

In fact, in terms of the author's empathy for what he is narrating and his ability to convey it to his reader, the narration only picks up steam again immediately after disembarking at Ellis Island.

It is April 20, 1920. Pasquale suddenly becomes Pascal. The deformed onomastic equivalent is the result of a linguistic pastiche presumably derived from the dialectal forms of his Italian workmates, who were predominantly from southern Italy, which introduces some of the phonetic thrusts that are characteristic of English inasmuch as they tend to simplify the orthoepy of a name in favor of something easier to pronounce (Pasquale > Pasqale > Pasqal > Pascal).

His first impressions are extremely arduous, unsettling, traumatic, among the most truly traumatic of those handed down to us by our emigrants. But their effect is also magnetic: the simple shepherd who, until the week before, had been accustomed to the metaphysical spaces of the immense green of the countryside and of the mountains of Abruzzo, where even the sea is only a mental hypothesis (Pasquale saw the sea for the first time in his life upon embarking in Naples), all of a sudden gets a taste, an initial full immersion into the magmatic, technological, dynamic reality of New York, a reality composed of cars, traffic, metro trains, metal, sirens, pneumatic hammers, smoke, vapor, exhaust pipes, engines, the mad coming and going of people of all sorts, commands and shrieks shouted in an unknown language.

> I grinned and turned startled at the sight of an elevated train dashing around the curve towards South Ferry. To my surprise, not even one car fell. [...] Chattering happily, we started to cross a broad street. All at once there was a terrific crash overhead, a car changed before us, two automobiles whirled around. Another car was bearing down on our group. [...] We climbed into a strange vision. The marvelous foreman spoke some words in an unknown language. [...] The foreman was anxious, pulling out a watch continually and saying that we had barely time to catch a train for our final destination. [...] What confusion greeted us at the station! We hurried through a vast turning crowd and dashed down toward a train. Almost before realizing it, we were speeding toward our destination, Hillsdale, where work was ready for us on the state road. I was overwhelmed, but pleased. (pp. 60-61)

What comes to mind, *mutatis mutandis*, is a whirling painting like *La città sale* that Umberto Boccioni painted in that very same vortex of time holding before his eyes a city, Milan, which was perhaps similar in many ways to the way New York in the 1910s would have appeared in the eyes of a dreamer like Pascal: a metropolis in full expansion, seething with life, brimming with sensations and colors, in which, incessant and ruthless, a whole teeming mass of people of the most disparate (and desperate) sorts: a multitude of aspiring workers, porters, laborers, bricklayers (more or less improvised), errand boys, diggers, demolishers, caretakers, longshoremen, but also cynical profiteers, delinquents, drunks, exploitation artists, prostitutes, and speculators. An unscrupulous and thankless society, ready to break the legs and arms of even the simplest and strongest manual laborer who happened to precipitate there from other parts of the world in search of a better fortune.

A metropolis that Pascal, once he has had the opportunity to become better acquainted with it after several years spent wandering far and wide with his friends, will later call both "attractive" and "repulsive" ("And we three walked on, wanderers in a magic show of forbidden splendor and beauty. And I thought of how lovely and yet repulsive this enchanted city was," p. 80).

It was a far cry from the streets paved in gold that a certain popular Italian imaginary had fantasized conjuring and mythologizing an America that was so far away! A famous, yet no less delightful, consideration comes to mind, which Terry Coleman inserted in his exceptional study *Passage to America* (1974, 207-208):

> It was an old superstition, sometimes half believed by the simplest emigrants, that the streets of New York were paved with gold. When they got there they learned three things: first, that the streets were not paved with gold; second, that the streets were not paved at all; and third, that they were expected to pave them.

This is the actual, harsh reality Pascal and his companions found upon their arrival in the "promised land." From Hillsdale to Tuckahoe, from Sparkshill to Poughkeepsie, from Ovid (New York) to New Branford (Connecticut), from Melbourne (Massachusetts) to West Pawlet (Vermont), the fellow villagers from Introdacqua suddenly found themselves working day after day as stonebreakers, shovelers, pickmen and waterboys, immersed in brutal fatigue from dawn until dusk, leveling and constructing roads and cattle-tracks, awful work hours and in atmospheric conditions, especially in the winter, beyond every limit of human endurance.

D'Angelo very capably describes, in just a few brushstrokes, not only his father, but even his teammates and traveling companions, who are fleshed out by their physical gestures, their reactions, and their individual characteristics: the strong and taciturn Matteo Rossi; Giovanni Ferrero, a carefree and incorrigible bachelor; Giorgio Vanno, strong, sly and smooth talking; Giacomo Gallina, who could have been a boxer; Andrea Lenta, robust as an oak tree, who also had a bit of an education; Antonio Lancia, who consoles his traveling companions with his beautiful singing voice; Mario Lancia, the foreman and the only one who has a smattering of English; and finally Filippo, Matteo's nephew, befriended by Pascal, who is the same age.

Theirs is a distressing life, rife with difficulties that hardly allow even the faintest glimmer of hope. Rather than take a turn for the better, the situation of these marginalized individuals goes from bad to worse with the passing of months and years. It is important to note here, on the sociological level, the communitarian concept of the "group." Our rustic Abruzzesi move as a group, they live as a group in shared (crumbling) surroundings, they go to work as a group, they move in groups from one job to another. It is not so much a question of feeling more protected; this is the embryonic stage of the first nuclei of Italian communitarians who, having come from the same region (at times even from the same town), eventually end up constituting the famous ethnic allocations of North America, which are still alive and kicking: Troy, Providence, Toronto, Philadelphia, Hartford, Boston, Chicago, Detroit, Brooklyn, Long Island, not to mention, obviously, the immense bustling hive that New York's Little Italy must have been in the 1910s and '20s (where we will shortly find Pascal), which is almost extinct today, as it has been absorbed by (the Chinese Community in) neighboring Chinatown.

Even in this situation of life at the limits of desperation, Pascal found a way to kindle his imagination and continued to dream, with streaks of authentic lyricism (several fully accomplished lyrical texts appear in the book), confirming the poetic allure that abounds in this autobiography. What follows are a couple of emblematic flashes of inspiration:

That night we were going home, piled in the trucks. Fresh was the breeze and calm the countryside. (69)

In the gloom, now, the windows began to glimmer around us; the muddy road appeared soft and misty, the fumes that coiled down from the factories became ghost-like. A couple of drunkards staggered past and went tumbling into a saloon. (80)

The stars were like exquisite, happy, living spirits giving their bright laughter to the silent night. A few were beginning to munch their food. The rest were moving about or waiting. In spite of the soft weather they all seemed to be in ill humor. (129-130)

And this is how they pass five long years in which the brutal, inhuman toil (and subsequent social marginalization) shows no sign that an end is in sight. We are by this time in the thick of a world war, and the United States suffers a period of economic crisis. The quality of life decisively begins to decline. They eventually hit rock bottom when as a group, at the end of their rope (living all together in a single, cramped room on Franklin Street in Little Italy, searching desperately for whatever job comes along), they fall under the spell of the promise of work in West Virginia offered to them by one of the usual unscrupulous shady businessmen. They arrive after a seemingly endless journey, tired, hungry, drenched with water and snow, in the harsh winter of 1915.

Among the jobs they had done until then, this one will take the cake as the coarsest, most thankless, most grueling of all. No critical comment can stand in the place of the blunt words with which Pascal (we are already two thirds of the way through the autobiography) evokes the conditions of raw survival and disgraceful decay he and his friends were forced to endure. A simple short excerpt from his description of the shack where they sleep in a heap, will give a sufficient idea of the situation:

The creaking and cracked floor was strewn with straw, which had fallen from the shelves or "beds." Straw covered our clothes and hair. The whole inside of the shanty with its forlorn occupants gave a picture of moral wreck and bitterness. We were pigs in our sty. (110)

A tragic experience that Pascal is able to relate with extreme narrative immediacy. The result is a tremendous portrait (and document) of the work conditions to which the common laborers—mainly

Italian emigrants—were subjected in those years; a portrait in which the ferocious exploitation of capitalism, cutthroat cynicism, and an absolute lack of human dignity loomed large.

It is an unrepeatable experience, which ends with the death of two friends, the serious injury of one of Pascal's hands (in the workplace there was no healthcare any kind), and a profoundly melancholic return to New York, not having received any pay in roughly a fortnight because, in the meantime, their employer had declared bankruptcy after working his laborers to the bone.

At this point (it is now 1916) the group falls apart. Some choose to return to the homeland, like Pascal's father, and others depart for other cities to start anew, if possible. This was an experience that, rather than discouraging Pascal once and for all, actually unyieldingly spurs him on, and that a short while later will ripen him for the arts, for music, and for literary creativity.

It is at this point that the generational difference between father and son is triggered: the latter's great leap forward and the former's disillusioned—though understandable—giant step back, which will leave the son, brokenhearted, to his own destiny.

Pascal was left to his own devices to confront a life that was still uncertain, though he had one resource that he intended to develop to the best of his ability: the English language. This was a tool that none of his friends had managed to master and that was a decisive indication of the anthropological, linguistic, and historical differences between the two generations.

The rest belongs to the legend of Pascal D'Angelo. But his was a long and agonizing apprenticeship: from his earliest passion for music (particularly for Verdi, after having attended an astonishing production of *Aida*), to the exhausting lexical practice stubbornly carried out over a small second-hand copy of Webster's dictionary; to his tireless haunting of the library (first the one in Edgerton, then the glorious central branch of the New York Public Library); the omnivorous devouring of mountains of books, first and foremost of poetry (Shelley is indisputably his deity); finally the extreme and "romantic" decision to dedicate himself exclusively to creative writing; it didn't matter if his attempts amounted to one failure after another.

With titanic perseverance and an unshakeable faith in poetry, Pascal stayed his course through the tortuous tunnel of the whole ordeal. The peak (or rather the low point) was the icy winter of 1922, one of the harshest that American meteorology has ever recorded. In order to save what little money he had left, he went to live in Brooklyn, in a decrepit little room, with neither kitchen nor heat, adjacent to a foul-smelling communal toilet. Water and urine often seeped into his room from under the door. On the crudest days, with the snow and the polar wind blistering outside, Pascal stayed in bed, rolled up in his coat that also served as a blanket; he had only the crusts of stale bread to eat, and, from time to time, a decaying banana. And yet, undeterred, he continued to write and to visit the editorial offices of newspapers and magazines, leaving poems for editors. One evening, returning on foot (!) from the New York Public Library (for those who don't know, it is journey of almost ten kilometers), in the full freeze of a snowstorm, he comes home to find his little room invaded by ice and snow: a couple of local hooligans had broken in through the window and taken a pair of his pants and some of his undergarments. His papers, his books and his bed were all drenched in dirty water. Pascal, the second coming of "Prometheus" (Boelhower 1982, 129), perseveres through even this latest in a long series of disasters.

He eventually writes a letter to Carl Van Doren, one of the editors of the important daily newspaper *The Nation*, in response to the literary prize it advertised. Driven by the force of desperation, the extreme and vibrant text of the letter appears in the final pages of *Son of Italy*. It is a letter, I would like to add, that is itself a poem and, at the same time, one of the most harrowing documents of Italian emigration to America.

This is no longer a letter written by an ex-shepherd semi-illiterate. It is the letter of a mature adult, who is not only fully capable of representing with dignity all of his fellow Italian expatriates in the United States, but who is also able to hold his own among the most upstanding and noteworthy citizens of the multicultural and multiracial America of the last century.

I can see no alternative than to present the letter here almost in its entirety (I apologize for its length) on which any comment would not only be superfluous but would also be in some way limiting.

To the Editor of *The Nation*:
Dear Sir:

I have submitted three poems "For the Nation's Poetry Prize" within in the established period [...]. I hope you will consider them from a view-point of their having been written by one who is an ignorant pick and shovel man—who has never studied English. If they do not contain too many mistakes I must warmly thank those friends who have been kind enough to point out the grammatical errors. I am one who is struggling through the blinding flames of ignorance to bring his message before the public—before you. You are dedicated to defend the immense cause of the oppressed. This letter is the cry of a soul stranded on the shores of darkness looking for light—a light that points out the path toward recognition, where I can work and help myself. I am not deserting the legions of toil to refuge myself in the literary world. No! No! I only want to express the wrath of their mistreatment. No! I seek no refuge! I am a worker, a pick and shovel man—what I want is an outlet to express what I can say besides work. Yeas to express all the sorrows of those who cower under the crushing yoke of an unjust doom.

There are no words that can fitly represent my living sufferings. No, no words! Even the picture loses its mute eloquence before this scene. I suffer: for an ideal, for freedom, for truth that is denied by millions, but not by the souls who have the responsibility of being human. For yesterday, New Year's Day, I only had five cents worth of decaying bananas and a loaf of stale bread to eat. And today: a half quart of milk and a stale of bread. All for the love of an ideal. Not having sufficient bed clothes for a stoveless room like mine, I must use my overcoat during the day. The room is damp—my books are becoming moldered. And I too am beginning to feel the effects of it. But what can I do? Without a pick and shovel job and without a just recognition?

[...] Please consider my condition and the quality of the work I submit. Then say if I can be helped without any expense on your part.

You can do—do something for me. Even in this horrible and inde-scribable condition I am not asking for financial aid. I am not asking for pity, nor am I asking for an impossibility. I only ask for a simple thing—a thing which you are giving away free. While you are giving it away free, why not see that it goes where it can help the most? I am not coveting the prize because of the money. No! But because it will give me the recognition that I cannot do without. If it's given to me I can go around to all editors, and I can say to them that I have been awarded "The Nation's Poetry Prize." When I say that, they will begin to accept them. [...] There is no writer who exists under such condi-tions. Let this prize break those horrible barriers before me, and open a new world of hope! Let this prize (even if it is an honorary one) come like as bridge of light between me and my awaiting future. Let me free! Let me free! Free like the thought of love that haunts millions of minds. If it's without expenses on your side then, give, give me an opportunity. Give me an opportunity before colds, wet, sleets, and many other sufferings will pitilessly distort my physical and mental shapes into a monstrous deformity. Give me an opportunity while it's not too late. [...] O please! The weights of duty crush me down and yet I cannot perform. I am not a spend-thrift. With a hundred dollars I can live five months. I am not asking an impossibility. Lift me, with strength of the prize, out of this ignoble gloom and place me on the pulpit of light where I to can narrate what the Nature-made orator has to say in me. (180-184)

The miracle occurs. A glimmer of hope finally flickers at the end of Pascal's existential ordeal. Thanks to his having won the prize and thanks also to Van Doren's intervention, the poetry of the *Pick-and-Shovel Poet* begins to appear in the best magazines. His work is recognized. Two years later D'Angelo publishes the book *Son of Italy*, with an introduction by the same Carl van Doren; and his work is written up in the *New York Times Book Review*, in the *Saturday Review of Literature*, in the *New York Evening Post*.

It is the high point of his career as a writer and poet. Pascal, be-ing the mild-mannered idealist he was, didn't know how to take ad-vantage of it. A few years later he fell ill and died in the extreme throes of solitude at the tender age of thirty-eight.

After decades of neglect it seems as though his work is now beginning (though still only modestly) to pique the curiosity of critics, mostly those interested in the sociology of literature and the history of Italian emigration to America. But we are, I repeat, only at the beginning.

We must remember that Pascal was essentially a poet, even though from the body of his poetic work we only have a small sample of his poems, many of which D'Angelo wanted to insert in *Son of Italy*, as further evidence of the inseparable tie between autobiography and poetry. As I draw my reading of D'Angelo to a close, I cannot help but linger a moment on his short *canzoniere*.

Much like his quasi-contemporary, Emanuel Carnevali, D'Angelo's muse was nourished by voracious though undisciplined readings of English poets and prose writers. Nevertheless, unlike the more refined and impetuous Carnevali, who forged useful relationships with some of the great American writers and intellectuals (among other things, he read, annotated, and sometimes even engaged polemically with their writings), D'Angelo's interlocutors were the poets of the past, in particular, as I have already mentioned, the English Romantics, whose works he read passionately.

In fact, D'Angelo's poetry is an ode to beauty, to the desire for the infinite, the ideal, the melancholic reverie, but without the poet ever forgetting, not even for a moment, his condition as an emigrant and his resulting, titanic struggle to survive.

Therefore, Pascal sees himself as having been entrusted, from the moment he begins writing, with a palingenetic mission: the poet has his role and his duty to obey his internal voice, despite any environmental hardship, and despite the language that is new, yes, but stubbornly studied and learned night and day, in the company of a Webster's dictionary, ever more tattered, and in the company of sublime masters like Keats and Shelley, masters who knew how to slowly illuminate him and give him the force necessary to persevere. It is a Promethean struggle, besieged by the persistent threat of poverty, which will bring the young Pascal, as we have seen, to abandon his workmates (after an exhausting experience as an unskilled laborer that lasted more than a decade; and *Son of Italy* remains, in this sense, one of the most disturbing documents), to withdraw to a wretched hovel in Brooklyn, and from there to launch "la sua sfida alla città, all'America e in particolare all'arte di comporre versi" ("his challenge to the city, to America and in particular to the art of composing verses"; Mulas, 1989).

For Pascal, the concept of poetry as a luminous and numinous spring; a ray of light that redeems the misery of the world, where the poet is "like an anchorite preaching his faith of light to space listening," well aware that he is "a ray that pierces through endless emptiness" (to quote a piece significantly titled *Songs of Light*).

Next to this yearning for redemption appears the myth of modernity and the frenetic proto-industrial city, the magmatic New York of the 1920s, the beloved and despised city; "a weird shadowy city," as he defined it in the eponymous poem. To this sprawling and all-engulfing metropolis, Pascal will dedicate *City*, one of the most vibrant poems of his small *canzoniere*, from which emerges a mobile and hallucinatory atmosphere that at times recalls Apollinaire's Paris (I think of the famous poem "Zone" that opens the collection *Alcools*, Apollinaire's masterpiece, published in 1913, about a dozen years prior to the advent of D'Angelo's poetry). Paradoxically, however, precisely (or even) amid the convulsion of the metropolis and the grueling conditions of his existence, Pascal never lost sight of his Shelley, his guardian angel, and, with him, the adolescent myth (or rather that of an eternal adolescence) that accompanies him. The figure of a boy significantly dominates more than one of D'Angelo's lyrics: in *Fantasio*, one of his most emblematic pieces, merging Beauty with Youth, he says at a certain point: "A fever of youth streams through my being / Trembling under the incantation of Beauty."

Pascal D'Angelo's poems are dominated by the contrast of dark and light: several of them even reference the latter in their luminescent titles. And it is possible that light is connected, unconsciously, even to the vivid infantile and ancestral memories he had of his mountains back in Abruzzo (an entire poem is dedicated to Maiella, "the mountain in a prayer of questioning heights"). And it is precisely this vivid luminous essence, mixed with a sort of airy grace

Luigi Fontanella

and filled with passages of visionary delicacy, that "compensate" for the vortex of inhuman labor. Indeed, with the exception perhaps of Arthur Giovanniti and Emanuel Carnevali, none of our other distant emigrant poets succeeded in capturing this essence with such active identification and in such suggestive, grippingly oneiric verses. The close of "Song of Night," so laden with resonances that recall the Orphic stature of Dino Campana (whom Pascal certainly must have read; resonances are also apparent in "Life in Life"), seems exemplary to me: "The earth is a blind wanderer, / Groping amid the unknown forests of time; / And with folded wings of splendor, calm and eternal, / The stars are innocent souls sculptured under the crypt of night."

Pascal's brief *canzoniere* concludes with a text significantly titled "The Last Shore," which I would not hesitate to place among his most poignant, and which, in my opinion, is right there at the same level as the best poetry being produced in Italy at the time. "The Last Shore" was published in the magazine *The Bookman* (September-February 1924-1925), one of the periodicals that had previously printed other poems by D'Angelo.

After this date, no other texts by Pascal are extant. He died on March 17, 1932 in extreme solitude and completely worn out by a life of great poverty. Nine days later, William Rose Benet commenting on the passing of D'Angelo in the *Saturday Review of Literature* (March 26, 1932), pointed out how the literary legacy of the writer from Introdacqua was essentially poetic in nature, and emphasizing, at the same time, how much stock he had so tenaciously taken in his own poetry.

67

APPENDIX

Select Poetry of Pascal D'Angelo

To Some Modern Poets
Your names are like decapitated giants
    bleeding black oblivion:
You are the frail voices
The indomitable rhythm of beauty writhes
    under the claws of your pens.
Your eyes are twin candles burning flames
    of yearning desire toward the high
    sacred altar of poesy.
All that you sought to attain has eluded you;
You have tried, and your day is passing.
Yet grieve not.
Much that charms is small and fleeting
To the greatness of eternity.
The earth is a tiny shadow tottering on
    the edge of death.
The moon is a throb of splendor in the heart
    of night;
And the stars are ephemera in the long gaze of God.
So grieve not
That your poems are the cold, fresh grass
    of a short Summer.
The flowers are few.

                        The Century 104 (January 1922)

Light
Every morning, while hurrying along River Road to work,
I pass the old miser Stemowski's hut,
Besides which pants a white perfumed cloud of acacias,
And the poignant spring pierces me.
My eyes are suddenly glad, like cloud-shadow when they
    meet the sheltering gloom.
After having been long stranded in a sea of a glassy light.
Then I rush to the yard.
But on the job my mind still wanders along the steps of

dreams in search of beauty.
O how I bleed in anguish! I suffer
Amid my happy, laughing but senseless toilers!
Perhaps it is the price of a forbidden dream sunken in the
    purple sea of an obscure future.

The Literary Review (January 21, 1922)

Midday
The road is like a little child running ahead
    of me and then hiding behind a curve—
Perhaps to surprise me when I reach there.

The sun has built a nest of light under
    the eaves of noon;
A laak drops down from the cloudless sky
Like a singing arrow, wet with blue, sped
    from the bow of space.

But my eyes pierce the soft azure, far, far
    beyond,
To where roam eternal lovers
Along the broad blue ways
Of silence.

The Literary Review (January 21, 1922)

In the Dark Verdure of Summer
In the dark verdure of summer
The railroad tracks are like the chords of a lyre gleaming
    across the dreamy valley,
And the road crosses them like a flash of lightning.
But the souls of many who speed like music
    on the melodious heart. strings of the valley
Are dim with storms;
And the souls of a farm lad who plods, whistling,
    on the lightning road
Is a bright blue sky.

The Nation (January 25, 1922; *Son of Italy*, 160)

The City

We who were born through the love of God must die
    through the hatred of man.
We who grapple with the destruction of ignorance
    and the creation of unwitting love –
We struggle, blinded by dismal night
    in a weird shadowy city.
Yet the city itself is lifting street-lamps,
    like a million cups filled with light,
To quench from the upraised eyes their thirst of gloom;
And from the hecatombs of aching souls
The factory smoke is unfolding in protesting curves
Like phantoms of black unappeased desires,
    yearning and struggling and pointing upward;
While through its dark streets pass people,
    tired, useless,
Trampling the vague black illusions
That pave their paths like broad leaves of water-lilies
On twilight streams;
And there are smiles at times on their lips.
Only the great soul, denuded to the blasts of reality,
Shivers and groans.
And like two wild ideas lost in a forest of thoughts,
Blind hatred and blinder love run amuck through the city.

            The Nation (January 22, 1925; *Son of Italy*, 162-63)

Songs of Light

1

The wind strikes the pyramids of silence
And they fall into fragments of glistening melody.
And drift beyond the forests and hills
Into sudden distant pyramids of gold.

The wind serpents around their glimmering
    pinnacles of silence,
And whirls off into outer blue,
And perhaps goes ruffling and panting
To where the loose-tressed maidens of space
Are floating on the winds of centuries.

2
The sun robed with noons stands on the pulpit of heaven,
Like an anchorite preaching his faith of light
    to listening space.
And I am one of the sun's lost words
A ray that pierces through endless emptiness
    on emptiness
Seeking in vain to be freed of its burden of splendor.

The Bookman (March 1, 1922;
Son of Italy, 155-56, second part only)

Whispers
When the azure hives of silence are filled
    with soft whispers –
Whispers of lovers that pass into faint twilights,
Whispers from the hazy distances,
    lakes and purpling palaces,
And the last drowsy whisperings of day –
And when Night half opens her deep,
    sorrowing eyes –
Eyes that gaze but see not, save beyond –
    beyond –
And the wind comes like an artist
Sculpturing the monolith of silence
    into a statue of whirring gloom,
And the black hives of stillness now quiver
    with crimson murmurings –
Then my subdued hearts swoons
With the silence of a flower that abandons
    itself in the embrace of spring.

For – Ah! what use is the jangle of words,
    or of thoughts, even,
When God is whispering?

The Literary Review (May 20, 1922)

Monte Majella
The mountain in a prayer of questioning heights
    gazes upward at the dumb heavens,

And its inner anger is forever bursting forth
In twisting torrents.
Like little drops of dew trickling along the crevices
Of this giant questioner
I and my goats were returning toward the town below.
But my thoughts were of a little glen where
        wild roses grow
And cool springs bubble up into blue pools.
And the mountain was insisting
        for an answer from the still heaven.

                    The Nation (October 11, 1922; *Son of Italy*, 23)

Song of Night
I am a thought hying under the outspread shadow
Of a winged dream, O Night!
Too soon will this great dream soar up into darkness,
With my being clutched in its talons limp and white.
Yet all existence lives gently in your shadow
O dream! O night!
The earth is a blind wanderer,
Groping amid the unknown forests of time;
And with folded wings of splendor,
        calm and eternal,
The stars are innocent souls sculptured
        under the crypt of night.

                    The Century Magazine (March 1923)

Night Scene
An unshaped blackness is massed on
        the broken rim of night.
A mountain of clouds rises like a Mammouth
        out of the walls of darkness
With its lofty tusks battering the breast of heaven.
And the horn of the moon glimmers distantly
        over the flares and clustered stacks of the foundry,

Uninterruptedly, a form is advancing
On the road that shows in tatters.

The unshaped blackness is rolling larger above the
thronged
    flames that branch upward from the stack with
    an interwreathed fury.
The form strolling on the solitary road
Begins to assume the size of a human being.
It may be some worker that returns from next town,
Where it has been earning its day's wages.
Slowly, tediously, it flags past me--
It is a tired man muttering angrily.
He mutters.
The blackness of his form now expands its hungry chaos
Spreading over half of heaven, like a storm,
Ready to swallow the moon, the puffing stacks,
    the wild foundry,
The very earth in its dark, furious maw,
The man mutters, shambling on –
The storm! The storm!

Son of Italy (1924) 75-76

Life in Life
I wander by the living field
Seekingof you, O unrevealed!
The tall oats bending in the sun
Like a golden glacier run
Toward the lane and stealthily
Are filled with earth's vast mystery
Of life in life.

Beyond the farmer's power too,
The harvest ripens. In the blue
The soul of wind, wild lyrical,
Is pouring forth. The miracle
Of Earth is massed along this lane.
The crows survey the heavy grain
And from the fringing bushes drop,
The boldest first, into the crop
Of life in life

And out upon the fields of love
A breeze that I am dreaming of
is passing in soft swaths and bends
The laden hearts to its own ends.
I feel that you are near to me;
My quickened steps are springing free.
Perhaps you linger there, to smile,
Confounding dogmas with the wile
Of one long kiss, beyond that turn
Where the golden fringes burn,
O unrevealed!

The Bookman 6 (August 1924)

Accident in the Coal Dump
Like a dream that dies in crushed splendor
    under the weight of awakening
He lay, limbs spread in abandon, at the bottom
    of a smooth hollow of glistening coal.
We were leaning about on our shovels and sweating,
Red faced in the lantern-light,
Still warm from our frenzied digging
    and hardly feeling the cold midnight wind.
He had been a handsome quiet fellow,
    a family man with whom I had often talked
Of the petty joys and troubles of our little dark world;
In the saloon in Saturday night.
And there he was now, huge man, an extinguished sun
                      still
    followed by unseen faithful planets,
Dawning on dead worlds in an eclipse across myriad stars –
Vanished like a bubble down the stream of eternity,
Heedlessly shattered on the majestic falls of some
                unknown shores.
And we turned slowly toward home,
    shivering, straggling, somber –
Save one youngster who was trying to fool himself
    and his insistent thoughts.
With a carefree joke about the dead man.
Snow began to fall like a white dream through

the rude sleep of the winter night,
And a wild eyed woman came running out of the
darkness.

The Bookman (September-February 1924-1925;

Son a/Italy [1924] 117-18)

The *Last Shore*
From the rocky haunts of birds
The ancient shepherd ocean
Is watching the faint herds
Of his endless motion;
In the black expanse of heaven
The bright stars gleam like tears,
And beneath is a great mist driven
Ah! Hope of years!
And under the mist each wave
Bears a heart that beats no more
That is stranded as they lave
The phantom shore

The ancient shepherd ocean
Is whispering "O cease!
O cease this soulless motion
And give me peace!"
Ah! there is nothing here but grief;
There is not the rest we need
Save where upon the reef
The dead hearts bleed,
And on the cheek of heaven
The bright stars trail like tears
While the mist is a grey hope driven
By the storm of years.

The Bookman (September-February 1924-1925)

CHAPTER THREE

Joseph Tusiani's Plurilingualism

*But I remember every falling night
and, with its darkness, every rising fear
deep in the tidal riddle of my thought.
I was not certain of the morning light
and, like you now, not sure of things most dear:
after this silent end of sunshine, what?*
—Joseph Tusiani

*Forse più pura e semplici risuoni,
all'orecchio non più ma solo al cuore,
per il contrasto che ti fa più dolce
e per l'incontro che ti fa più buona.*
—Joseph Tusiani

I have written more than once on the poetry of Joseph Tusiani (born 1924 at San Marco in Lamis, Foggia; emigrated to America in 1947). I will not in this occasion be able to avoid making reference to my previous work, but at the same time this is an excellent opportunity both to amend or enrich what I have already critically demonstrated and, when necessary, further elaborate certain thematic and stylistic aspects.

And so, it should be preliminarily observed that the poetic and poetological work of Tusiani spans his entire professional life and, even if it is "interspersed" with his translation work (which for Tusiani was inseparable from his own poetic output as it represents a sort of personal rewriting, especially in those instances in which his genius competes with that of the authors he held dear—something Marcel Proust once said comes to mind: "The duty and the task of a writer are those of a translator"). It represents a constant in his career as an intellectual, and this is apparent right from his earliest youthful experiments in the 1940s.

In fact, in 1943, when Tusiani was roughly eighteen years old, he made his precocious debut with the publication of *Amedeo di Savoia*, a narrative poem in free verse, under the auspices of his supporter, Father Ciro Soccio, who also wrote its critical preface.

In this little book, as in the others in the years immediately following (*Flora, Amore e Morte, Petali sull'Onda, Peccato e Luce*), all signed "Giuseppe Tusiani" (this is how the writer signed his books up to the middle of the 1950s), learned references are abundantly evident, many harkening back to Carducci, great expert of meter and prosody, or certain aulic D'Annunzian movements, or the Leopardi of the *Idilli*, or the Manzoni of the *Odi*. But along with this formative apprenticeship he began to nurture a sincere appreciation for the land of his birth, the devastation of which he had witnessed in the aftermath of the war. From the sight of such ruin, even if in aulic forms, as even Tusiani himself would later recognize, emerged "sincero almeno il primo impulso del giovane poeta verso tale condizione della sua gente" ("sincere at least the initial impulse of the young poet toward the condition his people were in"; Siani 1975, 14). This is where one finds the refined metrical skill that he derived from his intense readings of the Latin classics and from his having followed the exceptional scholar of English literature, Cesare Foligno.

Foligno is to have written a letter of presentation for Tusiani in the moment of his arrival in America; a letter that would have meant little to an intellectual as fussy, erudite, and volatile as Prezzolini. On this account, one reads the most delightful pages of Tusiani's autobiography, from the first of the three autobiographical volumes: *La parola difficile* (1988).

And so only in America did his poetry find a complete expressive voice and, paradoxically, only in precisely the very same English that he had so relentlessly studied in Italy and that he had so thoroughly eviscerated in assiduous readings over the course of the first year he spent in New York before he found an official job.

I turn the word over to Tusiani himself (I cite from an unpublished interview I conducted in May 1990, to which I will refer from time to time with the initials *IN*):

Dall'italiano classicheggiante della mia formazione liceale passai alla nuova lingua attraverso il romanticismo di Wordsworth, il poeta della mia tesi di laurea. Il mio trasferimento negli USA (1947) fu decisamente drammatico, se non addirittura traumatico. Conobbi mio padre, emigrato sei mesi prima che io nascessi, e da quella conoscenza scaturì, lenta e dolorosa, ogni linfa del mio nuovo mondo interiore. Quanto al fattore linguistico, sentii subito di aver messo piede, dirò, su un terreno vergine. Il bagaglio scolastico, di cui dovevo disfarmi, era tutto italiano; la lingua inglese non solo non mi aveva in alcun modo contaminato (forse non ho usato il verbo giusto) ma ero io a scoprirla e quasi inventarla gioiosamente nello studio dei classici, in quello studio paziente amoroso che mi avrebbe consentito il passaggio della conoscenza tecnica all'intimità creativa del nuovo idioma. (*IN* 1990, 1)

[From the classicizing Italian of my high school education, I passed to my new language through the Romanticism of Wordsworth, the poet of my undergraduate thesis. My move to the United States (1947) was decidedly dramatic, if not altogether traumatic. I met my father, who had emigrated six months before I was born, and after making his acquaintance, slow and painful, all the juices of my new interior world began to flow. Regarding the linguistic factor, I suddenly felt as though I had set foot, I would say, on virgin territory. The scholastic baggage, from which I had to liberate myself, was entirely Italian; the English language had not only not contaminated me in any way (perhaps this isn't the right verb) but I was the one who discovered it as though I had joyously invented it through the study of the classics, in that patient and passionate study that would have permitted the transfer of technical knowledge to the creative intimacy of the new language.]

His final consideration here is indeed corroborated in two volumes of poetry: *Rind and All* (1962), and *The Fifth Season* (1964). Tusiani is an extremely significant cultural and linguistic phenomenon. The two collections that constitute, together with *Gente Mia and Other Poems* (1978), a sort of triad of this poet's expressive maturity, were written in English. Among other things, one of the poems conceived directly in his adopted language, *The Return*, earned him the Poetry Society of England's Greenwood Prize in 1956: a fact, I would say, of historical as well as literary significance insofar as it was the first time that such a Prize was awarded to an Italian-American. The long poem, among the most touching of all Italian-American poetry, appears in the second volume of this triad and, in the author's own Italian translation titled *M'ascolti tu, mia terra*, in the volume *Mallo e Gheriglio e la quinta stagione* (1987), edited by Maria Pastore Passaro, who also translated *Gente mia e altre poesie* (1982).

Twelve years after the conferral of the Greenwood, another important prize, the "Alice Fay di Castagnola," came along to confirm the official recognition on behalf of the American establishment (the prize was a bit like the boutineer of the Poetry Society of America) of a "neo-American" man of letters who had not forgotten his Gargano origins in Puglia.

With his customary tact and measured sobriety, in just a few captivating pages of the *Parola Nuova* (Tusiani 1991, 166-176), he narrates the events of that scintillating evening of April 11, 1968 at the Plaza—where a host of poets participated, including several who had won the Pulitzer, from Anne Sexton (whom Tusiani befriended) to Richard Eberhart, Margaret Widdemer, Mark Van Doren, and Louis Simpson among others. This was only a few days after the assassination of Martin Luther King, whom Tusiani had met and interviewed in 1959 (the interview is available in the Veronese magazine *Nigrizia* [January 1960, n. 78]). That evening at the Plaza the great black leader was commemorated with a moment of silence. "Alla poesia di un nobile scopo," Lloyd Haberly said (it is still Tusiani himself who recounts the event), "egli ha dato commoventi e memorabili parole" ("To poetry with a noble purpose, he has given moving and memorable words").

To this day, these three books represent the central body of Tusiani's poetic work in English, which has been pubished in a great number of magazines (see the detailed bibliography compiled by Cosma Siani in the volume he edited *Two Languages, Two Lands. L'opera letteraria di Joseph Tusiani*, 2000); the volume presents the proceedings of a conference on the poet, held at San Marco in Lamis, May 15, 1999). To these works, two collections of poetry and a longer piece, also in English, should be added: *New Poems* (1983); *A Luxury of Light* (1989); and two years earlier the dense and controversial longer narrative poem *Cain: The Better Giver* (1987). Last but not least, I must mention his most recent efforts, beyond his works in dialect (which I will not address in this chapter)—*Il ritorno* (1992), written in Italian (I will go into further detail later), represents a meaningful return to his mother tongue and serves as the buckle to an ideal belt linking it, in its expressive instrument, to the poetry of his origin, and four other subsequent volumes, one in English, *Ethnicity: Selected Poems* (2000), and three in Latin, *Carmina latina* (1994), *Carmina latina II* (1998) and *Radìcitus* (2000).

Let us turn our attention to the central triad of works written in English, his *new* language (the adjective here is employed for all the force of etymological root) and a very frank linguistic means, though profoundly entrenched in his fecund humanistic hinterland. It is still with this that Tusiani's life blood was always nourished, as a poet and translator/rewriter. Again his work is best expressed in his own words.

> La mia esperienza globale di poeta e traduttore di poesia (non so come si possono scindere i due aspetti di un'unica attività creativa) io la vedrei concretizzata o riflessa in *Rind and All, The Fifth Season,* e, soprattutto, nella seconda parte di *Gente mia.* Perché? In qual modo? Non so. Penso che a un critico astuto non debba sfuggire, per esempio, il segreto estetico, anzi "latino," di una lingua inglese che si incontra e scontra con quella dei poeti della Poetry Society of America e della Catholic Poetry Society of America, di cui, nei miei anni più fervidi, fui, rispettivamente vice presidente e direttore. (*IN* 1990, 2-3)

> [My overall experience as a poet and as a translator of poetry (I don't know how the two aspects can be separated from what is one and the same creative vocation) I would see it realized or reflected in *Rind and All, The Fifth Season,* and, above all, in the second part of *Gente mia.* Why? In what way? I don't know. I think that an astute critic should not try to escape, for example, the aesthetic secret, or rather "Latin," of an English language that encounters and clashes with that of the poets of the Poetry Society of America and of the Catholic Poetry Soci-

ety of America, for which, in my livelier years, I served, respectively, as vice president and director.

In this, Joseph Tusiani seems in effect to summarize, perhaps better than other Italian emigrant intellectuals, the multicultural conglomeration that is fatally grafted onto every expatriate. With him, Ennio Bonea will later note: "l'emigrato di cui si fa simbolo, non è un semplice 'trapiantato,' ma un 'trasformato'; in lui, attraverso la sua poesia, "pscicodrama" dell'emigrato, è sintetizzata la storia culturale degli USA" ("The emigrant who becomes a symbol is not simply one 'transplanted'; rather, he is one 'transformed'; through his poetry, the 'psychodrama' of the emigrant and the cultural history of the USA is encapsulated in him"; Bonea 1982, 10). If it produces a natural enrichment that is reciprocal for the cultural anthropologies of both parties, then it would not entirely diminish the internal dichotomy that is always at odds with itself. This dichotomy is made up of suffering (nostalgia for the homeland) and oppression (the solitude and social discrimination endured in the new land). This is the very tension that has nourished so much poetry whether from the faltering foot of the first generation of emigrant Italian poets, or, better, of Italians *tout court*, who discovered that their adoptive home had a creative terrain of its own to offer, however uncultivated it might have been. Tusiani obviously does not belong to this sincere, albeit unrefined, cross-section. However, he still feels the issue of cultural identification and the need for creative release; and he feels it in all the turmoil that it implies. And he feels this in defiance of those who are closed up in their ivory tower, whom he snobbishly disdains (and disdained); for, amid great difficulties, many seek (and sought) to affirm this need for creativity, which was then, in the widest sense, the need for cultural improvement. There is an extremely efficacious and pertinent passage in his autobiographic essay "The Making of an Italian American Poet" (in the 1983 volume *Italian-Americans in the Professions*) that is worth quoting in its entirety, insofar as it illuminates, as best as one can, the problem:

So often and so wrongly has the so-called illiteracy of the Italian immigrant been mentioned that a word must here be said about a particular *sottobosco letterario* that no scholar has yet explored. I am referring to the poetic activity, in Italian and in the several Italian dialects, which for many years appeared in *Il Progresso Italo-Americano, La Follia, La Lucerna,* and *Divagando,* just to mention the major publications in the New York area. The birth and death—even the stillbirth—of hundreds of minor publications in Italian, in itself indicative of the intellectual restlessness of our immigrants, contradicts the theory of an absolute illiteracy.... Their poetry—it's true—was more often than not so poor and pathetic, so dim and devoid of the divine spark as to alienate any punctilious or supercilious "Aristarco Scannabue." Giuseppe Prezzolini, for instance, made havoc of what he apparently believed to be a threat to the awesome purity of the Tuscan *voce,* but he failed to understand that, by venting their emotions in the music of their vernaculars or in quasi-Italian (that is, often ungrammatical) quatrains, those "trapiantati" lived in the blissful illusion of not being completely such. He was also unable to recognize the innate genius or a race manifesting itself through people who made the most of their first or second grade of elementary education. And something else and far more important Prezzolini failed to notice from the ivory tower of his Casa Italiana of Columbia University—the semi-cultural atmosphere which, unknowingly, those "poetasters" had succeeded in creating for and around themselves.... Thus the poets of the Italian American *sottobosco,* whom literary Italy at best ignored, felt the need of establishing literary clubs where, in perfect mutual admirations and stimulation, those underprivileged pupils of the Muse (Sicilians, Calabrians, Apulians, Abruzzese, and even Tuscans) read and discussed their published and unpublished poems, and where entire chapters from *I Promessi Sposi* or Canti form *Divina Commedia* were recited by heart (Pane 1983, 10-11).

Certainly, the cultural baggage that Tusiani brought with him from Italy was much richer than many pathetic poets and poetasters of the first hour; nevertheless, he shared the very same pain of uprooting.

But his poetry was no longer tinged with sterile anger nor plaintive nostalgia. He himself clarifies the concept of nostalgia in a long interview conducted in November 1992 by the journalist and literary critic Franco Borrelli:

> Lei sa benissimo che per tutta la vita (con buona pace di Proust) noi ci portiamo dietro il tempo della nostra infanzia con tutte le sue fole. Nel caso dell'emigrato, poi, quello che Lei chiama "ieri" è l'unico punto di appoggio cui possa affidarsi chi in terra straniera non ha altra ancora di salvezza. Stando al suo etimo, la nostalgia altro non è che dolore o ansia di ritorno concesso all'emigrato è il ricordo e, attraverso il ricordo, il paragone col presente e, attraverso il paragone col presente, uno slancio verso il futuro. (Borrelli 1992, 24)

> [You know very well that over the course of life (*pace* Proust) we carry the time of our childhood with all of its follies. In the case of the emigrant, then, that which you call "yesterday" is the only point of support for he who is in a foreign land has no last hope of salvation. Staying true to the etymology of the word, nostalgia is nothing more than the pain or anxiety of return; but the only return, the only true return permitted to the emigrant is memory and, through memory, comparison with the present and, through this comparison with the present, momentum toward the future.]

The bitter and painful words on the expatriation of Nathaniel Hawthorne come to mind, which, however, Tusiani reverses in a greater hope for a future in which the "two lands, perhaps two souls" are able to coexist in some way (we will see it shortly in the important poem *Song of the Bicentennial*). It is worth recalling the Hawthorne passage, among the very first in America to have expressed the joy and the raw bitterness tied to expatriation to a foreign land. I cite John Ashbery (1989, 34):

> The years, after all, have a kind of emptiness when we spend too many of them on a foreign shore. We defer the reality of life, in such cases, until a future moment when we shall again breathe our native air; but, by and by there are no future moments; or, if we do return, we find that the native air has lost its invigorating quality, and that life has shifted its reality to the spot where we have deemed ourselves only temporary residents. Thus, between two countries, we have none at

all, or only that little space of either in which we finally lay down our discontented bones.

But, precisely, in Tusiani this lacerating dichotomy no long bears tinges of a nostalgic and solipsistic bitterness. Rather, it becomes a mirror simultaneously reflecting two souls that constitute, still and always, the same single soul that never ceases to interrogate itself with lucid and mature detachment. There is one section in particular in *Gente Mia and Other Poems* in which this self-inquiry finds, in the *secretum* of the poet, a particularly intense and emblematic moment, valid not only for Tusiani but for an entire generation of Italian expatriate intellectuals. It is in the fifth stanza of *Song of the Bicentennial*, the significantly liminal poem of *Gente Mia and Other Poems*:

> [...]
> Two languages, two lands, perhaps two souls...
> Am I a man or two strange halves of one?
> Somber, indifferent light,
> setting before me with a sneer of glow,
> because there is no answer to my plight
> I find some solace only in this thought –
> that maybe, just as this revolving earth
> must not proclaim your triumph all at once,
> I too must be, while waiting for my dawn,
> the night of my own self. (7)

These are verses of vibrant self-analysis that would have provided a comprehensive backdrop, in November of 1987, to the Conference of the American Italian Historical Association in Chicago, where Tusiani gave a keynote address on the very theme as the opening verse of this poem ("Two languages, two lands, perhaps two souls..."). His speech, which electrified the audience was followed by a presentation by Giose Rimanelli, another extraordinary emigrant (the speech he gave in response was titled "A Mesmeric Sculpture: Tusiani the Humanist"), and can be found in the volume in which the proceedings of the conference have been memorialized (Candeloro-Gardaphé-Giordano [1990] 1-8).

These verses, like so many others in this collection—probably the best of all of those written in English by Tusiani—of stylistic maturity; verses that demonstrate a definite (and definitive) adoption/acquisition of the English language, and the attainment, that is, of a glottological cultivation of the new idiom, operate on equal standing with that of an any actual American poet, despite a prejudice of long duration that has often weighed (perhaps still weighs) on Italian-American writers or Americans of Italian origin. At the hands of such a prejudice, many talented writers have suffered; one name out of the many that still awaits his "compensation" could be that of John Ciardi, whom I mentioned in the first chapter.

These verses, furthermore, like virtually all those that appear in this book's first section (we could call it the "ethnic" section—one of the poems is called "Ethnicity") that thus invoke memories, but these are never detached or passive moments; they know how to dialectically relate to the "occasions" that the poet from time to time experiences and interprets. And these occasions represent, in any case, moments in which our poet ceaselessly interrogates his surroundings as much as himself (see for example the poems "Ellis Island," "The Day after the Feast," "Letter to San Gennaro"). The very same section includes also *The Difficult Word*, a poem articulated in six stanzas in which Joseph conjures, with lucid observational ability, the adventure of his historic encounter with his father (who had emigrated before the poet was born), a man he had never seen before disembarking with his mother on American soil. In the poem, which would become the title of the eponymous collection (which is how, Tusiani, significantly, would have titled the first volume of his autobiographical trilogy), "tragedy and tenderness, emigration and filial love, intersect each other in turn" (Petracco Sovran 1984, 87); and the clot of so many years lived as a mere consequence in his father's eyes, a contradictory clot, suffered and incommunicable, in the end will dissolve cathartically in the name of love: "Let us (if faith begets but suffering) / forgive each other in the name of love: / even unnamed, a flame is war and bright" (14).

Certainly, always lurking in strong moments like this one, and even more where the sacred or supernatural component takes the upper hand, is the risk of falling prey to the emphatic or of resorting to overly bombastic eloquence. But, as a partial justification, rhetorical power is never an end in itself and represents the necessary complement (we could say the other side of the medallion) to Tusiani's poetry. Alfredo Galletti had already happily demonstrated this in his Preface to *Ode Sacre*. It seems opportune for me to extrapolate at least this brief annotation by the famous Italianist who succeeded Pascoli in his chair at the University of Bologna, and who also happens to be the author of a noteworthy volume of essays titled *L'Eloquenza* (1938):

> Il Tusiani è persuaso (e l'avvenire gli darà ragione) che—a meno di voler ridurre la poesia ad un'esclamazione o ad un singhiozzo, o, come vorrebbero certi estetizzanti, ad un'intuizione *ineffabile* (e perché ineffabile, del tutto inesprimibile)—poesia ed eloquenza sono inseparabili come il corpo e l'anima. Quando siano disgiunte, il corpo muore e il spirito entra nel regno delle ombre. L'eloquenza del Tusiani è tutta compenetrata di entusiasmo e di passione; il lirismo vi circola come sangue generoso in un corpo robusto, e perciò la sua eloquenza è poesia. (Galletti 1957, 9)

> [Tusiani is convinced (and the future will prove him right) that—without wanting to reduce poetry to an exclamation or to a hiccup, or, as certain aesthetes would like, to an *ineffable* intuition (and because ineffable, completely inexpressible)—poetry and eloquence are inseparable like the body and the soul. When they are separated, the body dies and the spirit enters the realm of shadows. Tusiani's eloquence is entirely permeated with enthusiasm and passion; lyricism circulates in it like generous lifeblood in a robust body, and thus his eloquence is poetry.]

In any case, that eloquent and archaizing emphasis is often redeemed by a strong, emotional depth whose lively accents of sincerity are at times moving (in the literal sense of the word) and can in no way not involve the reader. Several supporting examples can be found in many texts in the second section of *Gente Mia*—in my opinion the high point, together with the poems of *Il ritorno* (1992), of Tusiani's whole poetic output. I think of the suggestive "Nocturnes," full of grace and levity but also metaphysical restlessness. I think of "Ornithology: Footnotes One and Two," where he reaches a point of visionary sacrality. And I think of "For a Student Killed in an Automobile Accident," a poem laden with a tender, at times fantastic vision and participation, not detached, even still, from an Olympic equilibrium and a mastery of the expressive means that he had by then attained. The constant that runs through this entire section, as one critic has correctly noted, is comprehensively furnished "da un'ansia conoscitiva nella quale il ruolo della ragione è, felicemente, quello di pervenire al limite del razionale, per dissolversi nel mistero dell'inconoscibile e dell'impenetrabile che è il campo della poesia e del mito" ("by a cognitive anxiety in which the role of reason is, happily, that of crossing the limit of the rational, to dissolve itself in the mystery of the unknowable and the impenetrable that is the field of poetry and of myth"; Bonea 1982, 14). At least two examples: the second "Notturno," and the end of "For a Student Killed":

> Now if I fail to treasure this full moon,
>   imperial above
>   the river that is heaving with content,
> I know that when this final light is spent
>   the world I love
>   will also perish soon.
> So I am fondly following, with eyes
>   enamored and afraid,
> the last and easy languor of the night
> lest all I see grow suddenly less bright,
>   and the first shade
>   foredoom my paradise. (2)

> I do not know who was killed, Mary Jo—
> you or my dream, your life or my last faith.
> If I should ever love, how could I bear

that sound again, and then the whispered news,
and then the sight, and only then myself?
How could I weep if I should ever love?
And love, I know, is loss—it is the void,
cruelly green, around a lowing cow
lonely looking for her slaughtered calf,
it is the calling of a mother-bird
after the storm has felled her native oak,
it is my silence after all our dreams. (84)

Without forcing the comparison, and short of mentioning the resounding cases of Conrad and Beckett—in other words, to remain on Italian literary soil, after having been reborn/recreated in another language—one could say that on the whole in his work Tusiani accomplished what, for example, the Ungaretti who was active in France from '12 to '15, and then again from '18 to '21, had attempted in French, namely, to produce poetry that from a qualitative point of view had equal linguistic and literary dignity when compared with that of his French peers. Or rather I would like to highlight one particular aspect of literary ethnology that brings with it many benefits and great satisfaction, but also conditioning and prejudices that naturally arise in other geographical contexts (in our case there is an Italian intellectual who at the age of twenty-three, having only just graduated, emigrates to the United States and is able to magnificently master another language bending it, from an expressive point of view, to his own poetic creativity), which are palpably evident in Tusiani; prejudices, among other things, that still today are far from absent even among subsequent generations of emigrant intellectuals. This is what accounts for his terse English style, of great classical splendor. His mastery is the fruit of long *studium* that, when converted back into Italian (for example in translation), risks getting bogged down as a result of being transferred from its *new* linguistic state, to the "ancient" one he abandoned so many years before, except when, by truly extraordinary feats of magic, later on he lightens his touch, as is the case of the collection *Il ritorno*, which Tusiani wrote entirely in Italian.

In other expatriate writers, the expressive problem of language would have constituted an impasse. Our poet was in large part exempt from it. In many cases, Tusiani resolved the problem in extremely original ways: for example, by resorting to Latin, a language he uses in no fewer than seven volumes published to this day: *Melos cordis* (1955); *Rosa rosarum* (1984); *In exilio rerum* (1985); *Confinia lucis et umbrae* (1989); *Carmina latina I* (1994); *Carmina latina II* (1998); *Radicitus* (2000), not including, naturally, the numerous texts disseminated in specialized magazines (for a complete list, see the bibliographic appendix of this volume).

This is not the place—nor is it the task that I set out to accomplish—to analyze his Latin output, which by now, in quantity and quality, occupies a noteworthy place in Tusiani's body of work. I limit myself here to observing that his use of Latin has only grown more intense over the course of the last twenty years and that, after all, it could represent, in a subliminal key, the overcoming of that impasse: or rather a language used as a comprehensive instrument, unifying, liberating, sublimating. The following autobiographical reflections are very significant and illuminating in this regard:

Ho pubblicato, nel 1950, un volumettino di *nugae*, intitolato *Melos Cordis*, fittamente costellato di errori di quantità. Ma la *vis* poetica di quelle liriche fu scoperta da Josef Ijsweijn, dell'Università di Lovanio, forse il più grande latinista vivente, che a quelle pagine crude e scoppiettanti dedicò ampi saggi in latino e in finnico. A farla breve, ho pubblicato poi in tutte le riviste classiche d'Europa e America; ad Avignone e a Lovanio ho trovato prestigiosi editori per altre raccolte di versi latini, e, insomma, io stesso ho finito per prendere sul serio le *nugae* o *nugaelle* che mi ritornavano tradotte in più lingue. Sì, in latino, nella lingua pudica e solenne dei pochi, sono riuscito a dire cose che forse non avrei mai detto, o saputo dire, né in inglese né in italianto. Forse il latino è la "parola antica" di chi, avendo due lingue e due patrie, non sa quale di esse più gli appartenga o lo contenga. Indubbiamente esso è la base solida (e profondamente italica) su cui poggia la mia *ars poetica*. (IN 1990, 3)

[I published, in 1950, a slender little volume of trifles, titled *Melos Cordis*, densely constellated with errors of quantity. But the poetic force of these lyrics was discovered by Josef Ijsweijn of the University of Louvain, perhaps the greatest living Latinist, who to those crude and crackling pages dedicated vast essays in Latin and in Finnish. To make a long story short, I was then published in all of the journals for classical studies in Europe and America; in Avignon and in Louvain I found prestigious editors for other collections of Latin verses, and, in short, I myself ended up taking these little trifles or *nugaelle* seriously that came back to me translated in many different languages. Yes, in Latin, in the chaste and solemn language of few people, I managed to say things that perhaps I would not have said, or known how to say, in either English or Italian. Perhaps Latin is the "ancient word" of those who, having two languages and two homelands, don't know which belongs to them or contains them. This is undoubtedly the solid (and profoundly Italic) foundation on which my *ars poetica* rests.]

If Latin represents the constant and rooted foundation on which Tusiani's entire poetic residence rests, then his *ritorno* to the Italian language seems ultimately plausible. It is not by chance that one of his later collections will be called, precisely, *Il ritorno* (1992). This is a recurring term in the poet's affective toponymy. One could call it the key word that represents, broadly speaking, the comprehensive (and complex) linguistic unconscious of our author, both from a glottological-expressive point of view and from a broadly speaking Jungian-anthropological point of view: the telluric return to the motherland, wet-nurse and consoler of the poet's soul/body/time ("Usque ad telluris limitem" is the title of one of his most significant Latin poems). The psychoanalytic component in Tusiani's poetic opus demands to be studied, with the necessary critical instruments, in all of its complexity.

And so if his chthonic "return" to the homeland was the eponymous poem of 1956, thirty years later it would represent a return to his mother tongue: in short, a Tusianian koiné that proceeds forward and back again, circularly, from Giuseppe—to Joseph—to Giuseppe, or rather from Tusiani to Tusiani. Significant in this sense is the inscription that opens the book in question ("M'ascolti tu mia terra"), which ties back to a previous 1957 ode (published in Foggia in the *Quaderni de* Il Gargano, No. 5)—the Italian translation of the poem that won the Greenwood Prize. Equally significant is the initial poem of the collection, "Lingua materna," which from the somber obscurity of Plato's cave presents itself to the poet in the form a *return* to the Logos-Tempus of his origin. Thus, freed from simple para-nostalgic abandon, memory platonically becomes a return to ideas and, at the same time, an active exercise in illuminating the terrain he has traversed as well as the present moment of being and becoming in which he finds himself. This is the source of the restless, disenchanted attention the poet pays, in this book vibrant in existential interest, to the phenomenal reality that surrounded him. (I would note that all of these poems were written over the course of roughly three years, 1988-1991, which corresponds to the period the author devoted to correcting the proofs of his autobiographical trilogy.) A physical and metaphysical reality: and indeed this frequent slipping from physical to metaphysical (and vice versa) is one of the principle characteristics of "Ritorno": see poems like "Pioggerella" and "Idillio astrale." I quote this passage from the first of the two:

> A me parete
> tutte uniformi, gocce
> che, l'una dopo l'altra e sopra l'altra,
> caste cadete e calme,
> ma disuguali tutte, vi sospinge
> un ordine o un amore
> di cui non colgo senso.
> Immenso, chiamo immenso (altro non posso)
> il numero che siete; ma Qualcuno
> certo quel numero esatto conosce,
> e di voi tutte, ed anzi di ciascuna,
> sa veemenza e multiplo valore. (19)

In this magmatic movement we witness at a certain point an immersion of the senses: a warm, sincere sensuality here identifiable in a hidden female character who is a source of fantasies and phantasms, sudden sparks, as well as unassailable regrets and reconsiderations. *Ama se stessa, amando, giovinezza,* reads one of Tusiani's memorable hendecasyllables imitating Dante: a sort of memorable and universal scroll in which a vein of widespread melancholy inserts itself, namely that of blameless time, enveloping everything with its relentless grind. And I remember, though only in passing, that the central theme of "A Luxury of Light" is precisely the precariousness of time outside of time. Despite it all, Tusiani never ceases to interrogate himself on everything, on the nothingness of life, on his affections and his pleasures, on his hopes and delusions, knowing full well that although his interrogatives are destined to remain unanswered, they can nevertheless find, through Christian faith, a comfort that transcends history.

This book, valuable for its language and content, deserves to be admired beyond a shadow of a doubt for the formal elegance with which the verses have been polished, mostly hendecasyllables and *settenari*: an intense activity of knowing harmony and expressive grace, which, at times, verges on certain affected yet captivating cadences reminiscent of Góngora. "Luce riflessa" demands to be read in its entirety.

> Si umilia in alba l'inconsueto lume
> e già si esalta in giorno l'alba breve.
> Ma il raggio che son io,
> ed è sembiante angelico riflesso,
> come, se non vantandosi divino,
> può definir se stesso rilucendo?
> Creato in cielo, creo in terra anch'io
> se a vedermi riesco intimo ed integro
> nella singola foglia tutta vestita a festa
> o in un singolo implume
> dal primo raggio mosso al primo volo
> sulla nativa siepe.
> Altro motivo di mia vita ignoro
> o forse errava nel crearmi Iddio
> impicciolendosi in un filtro d'oro. (44)

Next to this register of the sublime, a sort of anthropomorphism through which the poet seeks to give an interpretation of the auroral sense of existence (the verses just cited demonstrate precisely this), there is still the whole question of "il recupero di un modo di fare poesia più discorsivo" ("the recovery of more discursive way of writing poetry"), as Pietro Magno notes in the preface, following models "che vanno dai *Sermoni* di Orazio alla 'Palinodia' e 'Al conte Carlo Pepoli' di Leopardi, che giunge qui a notevoli risultati, come *Lettera a don Dàmaso Alonso* e *Lettera a don Fernando Pessoa*" (Magno 1992, 12; "that range from the *Sermones* of Horace to Leopardi's 'Palinodia' and 'Al conte Carlo Pepoli,' producing here noteworthy results, like *Lettera a don Dàmaso Alonso* and *Lettera a don Fernando Pessoa*"). In the first there is among other things an intuition of a vague Keatsian flavor (I think of the famous *Ode on a Grecian Urn*), which also sounds like an inspired declaration of poetics. I cannot help but cite it:

> Forse, poeta, l'immortalità
> che noi cerchiamo è proprio questo sogno
> d'evadere dal limite intravisto
> in ogni nota o immaginata cosa:
> intravediamo, volenti o nolenti,
> noi stessi entro quel limite conclusi. (50-51)

In the second, dedicated to Pessoa, Tusiani engages in a sort of dialogue with the great Portuguese poet. At a certain point their supposed dialogue is transformed into a fully realized meta-textual discourse in which the allusive and illusive "game" of poetry is exalted. In this very self-conscious *includere*, poetry finds its meaning and final pacification: or that that of a Franciscan brotherhood with the world:

> Mi basta un gioco a illudermi e, pertanto,
> faccio con me giocare ogni sincera
> rima plausibile. (...)
> Abbiam tutti bisogno di una rima:
> trovo così un amico, anzi un fratello,
> se non in te, di certo in un ruscello. (53-54)

This oracular and solar poem is typical Tusiani. Here I must emphasize the frequent presence of the Sun, a real as well as a metaphysical presence that, now evasive, now more conspicuous, recurs throughout his body of poetic work. One example of many, apart from the many instances in *Ritorno*, can be found in *The Fifth Season*, in the initial piece in the volume of *The Fifth Season*, titled "Minima Theologica." I cite the opening line: "How simple is the dogma of the sun / when no theology of cloud makes your earth doubt" (3).

The "sacrality" of the objectives, which in the last instance addresses Tusiani's *poiesis*, does not negate the flesh of language, to use a Baudelairian expression, into which it sinks. This is how Tirsi and Titiro can explain themselves and at the same time transform those who "dormono / laceri tra cartoni e cenci luridi" ("sleep / ragged amidst cardboard and filthy rags"; 55), where the glittering, Babelic kaleidoscope of Manhattan becomes an immense, shining crèche. This is also how Poetry can be born out of extreme poverty and dejection, as an interior redemption, and the poet can yet again walk away from "inconsueto amore / a cogliere ritmo fiore" ("uncommon love / to gather rhythm flower").

Il ritorno concludes, as it should, with an "addio" to his beloved Puglia, which is redolent of a Calvalcantian *canzonetta*. The cycle comes to a close; the old man/child poet is now freely able to connect the sun to the cloud, the luminous silver to the dark lead of the olive trees, the obscure night to the morning's return that shatters the poet's perennial dream.

CHAPTER FOUR

Giose Rimanelli and the Never-Ending Journey

> *And this was really the way that my whole*
> *road experience began, and the things that*
> *were to come are too fantastic not to tell.*
> —Jack Kerouac, *On the Road*

1. PRELIMINARY BIOGRAPHICAL DATA

Among all of the expatriate Italian writers, Giose Rimanelli undoubtedly occupies a preeminent place, both for the length of his stay, which goes back close to sixty years from today, and for the interlinguistic depth his work has achieved. The last few decades have also seen the recovery (the reintroduction) of an author who broke onto the scene in Italy, in the beginning of the 1950s, with a debut as precocious as it was dazzling. In this chapter, I will reflect on some of his emblematic books, through which he thematically and formally filters, in more persuasive and evident ways, his long experience as a "fleeting" writer.

A nomadic figure of our literature, the "irrequieto e maledetto" Rimanelli—the epithets are his own ("restless and cursed"; Rimanelli 1979, 113)—seems in effect to embody again the subversive and dispersive, eclectic and multiform connotations of the variegated Italian intellectual diaspora of the 1950s.

Born in Casacalenda, Molise, November 28, 1925, Giose had a rather troubled childhood. Although his parents (Vincenzo and Concettina Minicucci) were of modest means, they still had effective (and affective) ties with the North American world: Concettina, though living in Molise, was a Canadian citizen, having been born in Verdun (in the province of Montréal) in 1905. She ended up in Casacalenda because her father Tony, known as Dominick, (also born in America, in New Orleans, in 1863) decided to return to his small town to start an umbrella business. Dominick's life story eventually comes to the fore in the 1959 novel *Una posizione sociale* (though the first draft dates to 1952), which was then republished in 1996 under a new Stendhalian title *La stanza grande*, a novel in which Grandpa Dominick is the central character.

In turn, even Giose's father, Vincenzo Rimanelli, has concrete ties to America: his father, Seppe, "un bastardo di un Leo Marinelli ebanista che anagrammò il suo nome e così creò, sia pure inconsciamente, un ben altro albero genealogico" ("a bastard of a Leo Marinelli, the cabinet maker, who anagrammed his name and thus created, even if unconsciously, an entirely different family tree"; Rimanelli 1979, 64), had already been in America for a while, more precisely in St. Paul, Minnesota, where he worked in the maintenance of the city's sewers.

At the age of ten, at the urging of his mother, a fervent Catholic, Rimanelli became a Franciscan seminarist in Ascoli Satriano. He wanted to become a missionary, he wrote sermons, studied Latin, Greek, Hebrew, French and ancient Provençal; his love for the troubadours of Provence would remain a constant over the course his entire literary life, right up to these most recent times that our poet has spent translating them into the Molise dialect.

Five years later he abandoned the seminary. We are in 1941. His adolescence was a period of "penitenza, ignominia personale, meditazioni e letture" ("penitence, personal disgrace, meditation and reading"; Rimanelli 1979, xvii), as he will later write. But it was also a period characterized by an array of polyvalent interests, travel and intense study, fundamental for his cultural formation.

After September 8, 1943, he goes to Venice where he first encounters the Venetian partisans, but he is arrested by the Nazi Schutzstaffeln (SS), in one of their roundups. After two weeks of imprisonment at Isola della Giudecca he manages to repair to Milan, where he is arrested again.

It is in this span of time, between 1944 and 1945, that he undergoes the crucial episode of his provisional militancy in the lines of the Republic of Salò: an episode born, ideologically speaking, of his juvenile confused state of mind (he will later say, "per debolezza e vigliaccheria, sentimentalismo e ignoranza" ("for weakness and cowardice, sentimentalism and ignorance") that in April 1945 will lead to his arrest again, this time by the "fazzoletti verdi" of Aprica, then by the Allies, who take him with other prisoners of war to the famous camp of Coltano, near Pisa, where he meets Ezra Pound. Here, he is locked up in a cage, and accused of high treason against his country. He manages to escape from the armored truck taking him to Naples, and, from the Cava de' Tirreni, he returns on foot to Casacalenda.

This brief but intense odyssey will provide material for his first novel *Tiro al piccione*, written in one fell swoop when he was twenty.

The postwar fury having passed, "morso da quell'aspide del nomadismo che rimarrà una delle costanti della sua personalità" ("bitten by that nomadic sting that would remain a constant of his personality"; Martelli 1991, xiv), Rimanelli refuses to leave with his parents for America (they end up definitively emigrating shortly thereafter with Giose's two brothers) and ends up spending all of 1947 wandering across Europe, traveling by freight train or hitchhiking through Switzerland, Holland, Germany, Sweden. He finally settles in Paris.

In the French capital he frequents existentialist circles (he makes the acquaintance of Sartre and Camus), he attends the classes of Gaston Bachelard, he plays jazz in a *boite* and makes friends with Boris Vian. But this brief bohemian phase lasts only a few months. He is forced to return to Italy. He lives (or gets by) as well as he can in Rome, passing most of his time cooped up in the Biblioteca Nazionale where he writes undergraduate theses for a fee. They are months of solitude and of extreme poverty, but also of frenetic study and of cultural enrichment that allow him to perfect his manuscripts, write his first articles for *La Repubblica d'Italia* (at that time edited by Ruggero Zangrandi) and forge solid literary bonds: Antonio Ghirelli (head journalist of the newspaper), Ugo Moretti, Corrado Alvaro, Carlo Muscetta and, above all, Francesco Jovine, whose secretary he becomes and who gives him precious advice regarding *Tiro al piccione*, contained, at the time, in an enormous notebook.

Finally the manuscript, revised and streamlined, manages to find its way, with Jovine's help, to the attention of Cesare Pavese (we are in the autumn of 1949) who agrees to publish it in Einaudi's "Coralli" series.

Unfortunately, the following year Jovine dies and Pavese commits suicide. The publication of *Tiro al piccione* is postponed also for ideological reasons. Rimanelli begins traveling again. He visits Brazil, Argentina, and Colombia; he also visits Greece and Israel, intensifying his journalistic activity.

The two-year period from '51 to '53 is propitious for Rimanelli. His name begins to become a "label" and his literary relationships expand to include the world of the theater as well as the cinema. He makes the acquaintance of Carlo Ponti and Mario Soldati; he writes for May Britt *La lupa* (from the eponymous short story by Verga) and for Anna Magnani, in '56, *Suor Letizia* (co-starring Eleonora Rossi Drago and directed by Mario Camerini). A few years later in Antibes he will write, influenced by the painting by Pablo Picasso, whom he met in Vallouris, the comedy *Tè in casa Picasso* (later published, in '64, in the magazine *Il Dramma*), the ballet *Lares*, in '65, and, in that same period, directly in English, *The French Horn*, a one-act play commissioned by the Actors Studio.

In '53 *Tiro al piccione* is finally published by Mondadori, and not by Einaudi, after a turbulent editorial adventure of which Sebastiano Martelli gives us a detailed reconstruction (Martelli 1991, xii-xvi). Elio Vittorini was the decisive intermediary. The novel was enormously successful. It was translated into several languages and eight years later Giuliano Montaldo adapted into an admirable film.

The following year it appears in America under the title of *The Day of the Lion*. New York's Random House was the publisher. For Rimanelli it could serve as an excellent calling card for his definitive move to the United States; a move that, however, in '54, he had no intention of making, despite the fact that he had just visited the country for the first time the previous year, an experience later recounted in his novelized diary *Biglietto di terza*.

Between '54 and '57, everything would seem to consolidate the artistic (and existential) position Rimanelli has attained: he is considered among the frontline authors of Mondadori's arsenal (the year after the publication of *Tiro al piccione*, he came out with *Peccato originale*, while *Biglietto di terza* was being prepared for press), he is the happy husband of Liliana Chiurazzi (their marriage takes place in Florence in '55 and two years later their son Marco is born), he takes several trips for both work and pleasure, and he continues to pursue his journalistic and cinematographic collaborations.

All of this, however, was to be derailed shortly thereafter and he would have to come to terms with the profoundly heretical, antagonistic, and intolerant spirit of any literary conditioning or hypocrisy (Roman, in particular), a spirit that was also narcissistic, ambiguous, mystifying, and in a certain way even self-denigrating, which is how Rimanelli's unconscious was formed and which will remain attached to him like a perverse icon that sprang from an *evil exhibited* over the course of his entire existence.

The facts are well known thanks not to just any old exegete, but to the account the author himself gives in the space of just a few tragic yet self-ironizing pages of *Molise Molise* (Rimanelli 1979, 139-148).

I am referring to an unfortunate collaboration with the weekly periodical *Lo Specchio*, for which he wrote a series of articles and reviews from '58 to '59. In these articles, he in tears to shreds many books and attitudes, placing a number of sacred literary giants of his time in the pillory, uncovering their dirty tricks, shameful alliances, secret societies, power plays, and other base actions with a taste for controversy and the most pungent provocation. But beyond his taste for a "challenge" and scandalous revelation—which, in any case, provide important information as to the literary habits of an epoch of Italian history, and perhaps the history of any epoch—these articles, signed with the pseudonym A. G. Solari, contain even "la storia della sua formazione, delle sue preferenze, dei suoi sentimenti dentro la società letteraria del suo tempo; oltre che come tentative di rompere il conformismo, la pigrizia, l'omertà che indubbiamente gravano sulla nostra letteratura contemporanea" ("the history of his formation, of his preferences, of his sentiments within the literary society of his day; beyond its importance as an attempt to break the conformism, the laziness, the omertà, or conspiracy of silence, that undoubtedly weigh on our contemporary literature"), writes Leonardo Sciascia (*L'Ora*, February 26, 1960) in a review of the volume *Il mestiere del furbo* (1959) in which Rimanelli collected these venomous articles, a book with which he will sign, in a literary sense, his own death sentence.

And yet, this book contains so much more than the author's personal idiosyncrasies; these are passionate pages about other authors that will be critically reevaluated only later. I am referring first and foremost to a writer like Federigo Tozzi, who was virtually an illustrious misunderstood outcast in the 1950s; but I also have in mind the penetrating pages he dedicates to the aforementioned Francesco Jovine, Cesare Pavese, and Rocco Scotellaro.

As a matter of fact, this book cost Rimanelli the harshest literary ostracism, additionally fomented by impartial factious ideologies (I refer the reader to Eugenio Ragni's excellent reconstruction of its historical and critical context [Ragni 2000, 37-96]). Hard fought and contested by too many factions ("I fascisti mi volevano fascista, i comunisti mi volevano comunista" ["The fascists wanted me fascist, the communists wanted me communist"]), blacklisted by now in indelible ink, Giose chose the path of exile. This controversial book, which prompted several publishers to put a price out for the author's head as if the mysterious writer had been a dangerous criminal, closed forever those "ineffabili, briosi, furiosi, intensamente creativi, ruggenti Anni Cinquanta" (141; "ineffable, spirited, crazy, intensely creative, roaring 1950s [Rimanelli 1979])

2. THE FIRST DEVIATIONS OF IDENTITY: *BIGLIETTO DI TERZA*

Rimanelli leaves Italy once and for all early February 1960. In his pocket he has an invitation to the Library of Congress's Coolidge Auditorium in Washington, D.C., where he will preside over a conference on contemporary Italian literature.

But this is not his first encounter with America. He had already had that earlier experience in the winter of 1953, when he went to visit his family in Canada. From that trip the para-diaristic pages of *Biglietto di terza* are born, which, first published by Mondadori in

1958, was reissued in 1998, exactly forty years later, by a Canadian publisher, Editions Soleil, based in Welland, Ontario, which lends the work a symbolic air of "restitution" to the land that originally inspired it.

Biglietto di terza (all of my citations refer to this new edition) is Giose Rimanelli's third title with Mondadori, but the first "novel" in which North American scenarios openly figure, and it follows by four years *Peccato originale* (1954). But the four years between *Peccato originale* and *Biglietto di terza* are deceiving, since by the end of 1954, the latter had already been completed although it had not yet been submitted to the publisher.

Effectively, the first quickly composed draft of *Biglietto di terza*, as per the author's explicit testimony, was jotted down between December 1953 and September 1954, which corresponds to the period in which Rimanelli was in Canada and he gives and immediate literary communication of his stay in this frayed narrative diary that moves, in a slightly Ginzburgian or, perhaps more accurately, in a Pavesian manner, between *narrated fiction* and *autobiographical memoir* (this explains the reason behind the quotation marks I put around "novel" above); where the term *memoir* here presupposes an effective temporal distance from his very *Erlebnis*, but an actual narrative whose artistic form already imposes a separation between recent life experience on the one hand and its reflections (its repercussions) in creative writing, or rather in life reinvented, on the other.

Upon closer inspection, this is a "technique" that reminds me of Giacomo Leopardi, but I could very easily go back as far as Petrarch, as both are poets much loved by Rimanelli. For example, I think of Leopardi's Canto "Il primo amore," in which the poet "historicizes" a contemporary event—that of falling in love with Geltrude Cassi, who had visited the Leopardi household from December 11 to 14, 1817—and its immediate repercussions in the poem, which he composed in the days that followed, December 15-16), projecting that experience into an eidetic dimension already detached, or rather, a lived experience and transposed into creative writing.

It is possible that it was also this oscillation in "genre" (diary?, journalistic account of his travels?, autobiographical memoir?, novel?) that the manuscript, once complete, delayed its finding an editorial home in its proper series and posing great difficulty to the editors at Mondadori in regard to its collocation. In his concluding author's note, furthermore, Rimanelli asks whether the ten months he passed in Canada weren't effectively too few to formulate an evaluation of this country of "singolare complessità" ("singular complexity"), and if, above all, not considering himself a "studioso scientifico" ("scientific scholar"), he had allowed himself to get, precisely, carried away too easily by personal "osservazioni di gusto letterario" ("observations of the literary sort"), excluding any definitive judgment on this immense country, as it must have appeared to him half a century ago.

Yet, confirming this oscillation, the author recounts in the same note a series of historical-social sources that he had used, in addition to the special thanks he extends to fellow journalists for various kinds of valuable advice he received from them. But then, to muddy the waters, he admits: "Molte storie che qui ho raccontato non sono vere, ma sarebbe ugualmente impossibile affermare che le storie narrate siano esclusivamente un prodotto della fantasia" ("Many of the stories I've recounted here are not true, but it would be equally impossible to say that the stories I've told are exclusively a product of my imagination"), which is an ambiguous statement that speaks for itself and that, again, leads back to that para-novelistic aura that I associated earlier with writers like Natalia Ginzburg and Pavese, and back to Giacomo Leopardi and Francesco Petrarca. The whole, really, demonstrates, as Sheryl Lynn Postman intelligently wrote, the intrinsically autodiegetic character (or rather relative to its very creative process) of a road novel like this one: "an autobiography presented in autodiegetic form as a history of a journey is, in essence, the history of a creative process, that of a writer who is evaluating through his own travels/travailles Rousseau's and Vico's lessons" (Postman 2000, 151).

It is time to proceed to a reading of *Biglietto di terza*: a reading that can't help but take the form of a running commentary (we are dealing with a "journey" after all) under the global sign of a deviation of identity, that seems in large part to constitute the macro-sign par excellence of the whole text.

The book presents a meta-textual frame, presumably written later, which Rimanelli must have felt was necessary, as though to give an introductory framing device to the story/account of his own personal travels and, at the same time, to lend it a comprehensive "coherence" that would serve to justify its novelistic framework. Obviously the term "meta-textual" here has nothing to do with the Italian neo-avant-garde (with *Biglietto di terza* we are at the beginning of the 1950s), whose earliest experiments were only carried out at the end of that decade. If anything, here we could talk about experimentation, which was never lacking in Rimanelli's work; however, experimentation must always be linked to the author's spirit of naturally eclectic curiosity (that from time to time will resound fruitfully with fecund and diversified allusions that range from jazz to the abstract painting movements of his time, up to the *Change* group) rather than to actual subversive militancy, as would arise a few years later, for example, with the *Gruppo 63*, which was completely foreign to Rimanelli.

Furthermore, the "metatextuality" we encounter in the first few pages of *Biglietto di terza* is entirely ensconced in the naturalistic theme of emigration as seen through the eyes of the *deraciné*, who turns the "journey" into a search for/into his own personal ubiquity-mobility-identity—a search well-served by a writerly allure so fluid, agile, with quick cuts, clean and concise, as though extracted and transposed directly from a notebook that we can easily imagine in the pocket of our "viaggiatore insonne" ("tireless traveler") like an inseparable traveling companion. Symptomatic, in fact, is his predilection for elliptical, paratactic periods with unexpected anacoluthons of the essayistic sort. To give you a quick example:

Io so la gioia di stare nudi sulla spiaggia, rotolati nella rena con l'onda che appena si pronuncia ai tuoi piedi. Ma quando c'è il sole alto e le cicale le immagini come gamberi nel buio fresco degli alberi più in là. Una spiaggia deserta ai confini del mare deserto, rincorrendo muti tempi della tua preistoria. Io so che si può essere colmi d'una stanca ebbrezza. Porti il tuo cuore aperto nelle mani. [...] I contadini avvertono con precisione, dentro di loro come un nido di vipere addormentate, il rancore antico che li divide dal mare. (15)

[I know the pleasure of standing naked on the beach, rolled up in the sand with the wave that just barely enunciates itself at your feet. But when the sun is high and you imagine the crickets like shrimp in the fresh darkness of the trees down the way. A deserted beach on the border of the deserted sea, chasing the mute times of your pre-history. I know that one can be overflowing with a tired intoxication. You carry your open heart in your hands. [...] The farmers sense within themselves like a nest of sleeping vipers, the ancient rancor that divides them from the sea.]

This instinctive "rancor" emerges vividly over the course of the days and nights he was forced to spend onboard ship, during the long crossing that Rimanelli synthesizes in two short chapters, entitled "L'uomo dalla salsiccia near" and "D.P.," in the first of which the unforgettable, realistic image of a man struggling with his sausage (who prefers to eat as much of it as he can and throw the rest into the sea rather than allow the customs officers seize it). This episode irresistibly recalls, *ante litteram*, a similar scene in a film that would come out fifteen years later (*La mortadella*, 1972, directed by Mario Monicelli), in which the protagonist, played by Sophia Loren, after having been stopped at customs in New York because she is in possession of a mortadella, prefers to slowly devour it rather than leave it in the hands of the zealous customs officers.

Although they risk falling prey from time to time to Verga's skiagraphic writing, the scenes and characters that populate the ship are ultimately believable and enjoyable, with descriptive passages of great happiness, with the ocean as a constant, somber, present (immanent), obsessive witness ("Questo mare, tu che sei vissuto sempre in montagna, ti fa impazzire" ["This sea, you who have always lived in the mountains, will drive you crazy"]). Again certain passages come to mind from D'Amicis' *Sull'oceano* (1889), a book that, as I wrote in the chapter on D'Angelo, can be considered the journalistic archetype for this genre. And it is a shame that Rimanelli doesn't linger a little longer on this period he spent at sea: the narration of his crossing is too brief and too few are the episodes he recounts. As was the case with Pascal D'Angelo forty years earlier, the writer was evidently more concerned with the place/world of arrival than with the fundamentally immobile and repetitive one onboard ship.

On the other hand, the "immobility" of the voyage heightens the "mobility" of the mind, which in the writing tends to coagulate in detached segments that illuminate from time to time situations and memories of lived experience, like the sudden flashes of a distant beacon or lighthouse.

It is at this point that the immense geography of Canada, white with snow, spreads out before the visitor's eyes. Such immensity and sense of awe inspire the traveler to delay describing it directly; instead, he skillfully depicts it through a dialogue between a traveler and a railway man who furnishes vague information and expresses himself with gestures that attempt to reproduce a sense of the infinite vastness of the country: "'Quando arriviamo?' [...] Disse: 'Domani forse, forse dopodomani, che ne so?' [...] Quanto è grande il Canadà?' L'altro fece una largo gesto con la mano, un cerchio, una parabola..." (30; "'When do we arrive?' [...] He said: 'Perhaps tomorrow, perhaps the day after tomorrow, how would I know?' "[...] How big is Canada?' The other makes sweeping gesture with his hand, a circle, a parabola...").

In order to reinforce the sense of the vastness that is slowly discovered, station after station, hour after hour, Rimanelli makes use in this phase of the book of a particular application of the polysyndeton precisely in order to suggest the effective progression of image-concepts that accompany (and are integrated into) the progressive sense of train travel, railcar after railcar, view after view, precisely, conjunction after conjunction.

Qui l'aria violentemente veniva a gelarti il volto, e qui anche i ferrovieri, bardati come minatori e con la lampadina elettrica sul petto, sostavano a chiacchierare in attesa del nuovo villaggio ove, prima che ferraglia stridessero, aprivano la porta e saltavano fuori [...].

[...] Ad una stazioncina saltò sui vagoni una mamma calabrese, secca *e* scura *e* alta *e* vigorosa di forse cinquant'anni... (33, italics mine)

[Here the air violently came to freeze your face, *and* here even the railwaymen, dressed like miners *and* with electric lamps on their chests, stopped to chat as they awaited the next town where, before the metal screeched, they would open the door *and* they would jump out [...].
[...] At a little station a Calabrian mother got on board, skinny *and* dark *and* tall *and* vigorous perhaps in her fifties...]

I think these brief annotations sufficiently introduce that sense of a deviating identity that I hinted at earlier and which constitutes the driving force behind *Biglietto di terza*, particularly evident, at this point, inasmuch as it is deduced on a train carrying *distinguishable and distinct* identities through an *indistinguishable and indistinct* reality.

In order to better explain my point, I want to consider for a moment the brief chapter titled "La mamma calabrese," which seems to condense, in the best way possible, the widespread effect of feeling out of one's element even between individuals who share a common destiny, thanks to which they are able (or think they are able) to recognize each other. A woman boards the train and wanders anxiously around inside, looking for her son Pasquale. She calls out for him ("Pasqualì, Pasqualì!") scrutinizing the "siepe di facce" ("hedge of faces"). Four men who go by the name of Pasquale present themselves to her, but none of them is *her* Pasquale. By now night has fallen and by night the woman accepts almost begrudgingly that "non si riconoscono i segnali e Pasquale non capisce u francise" ("the signs are unrecognizable and Pasquale doesn't understand French"). Shortly thereafter the train departs again with the Italian emigrants, as the woman continues to roam around on the station platform and watches "i vagoni scorrere, con occhi isterici" ("the cars of the train roll by, with hysterical eyes"). She never finds her Pasquale, who perhaps wasn't with the emigrants. Then the clean and cutting conclusion of the chapter: "Un italiano" says one of the men "sa lo stesso quando e dove deve scendere, anche se non capisce u francise" ("An Italian knows regardless when and where he's supposed to get off the train, even if he doesn't understand French").

Who's right? Is the Calabrian mother right when she says that "non si riconoscono the signs" ("the sign are unrecognizable"), or the man who maintains that "un italiano sa lo stesso quando e dove deve scendere" ("an Italian knows regardless when and where he's supposed to get off the train")? What is anyone able to recognize in the vast expanse where the signs tend to be fatally confused, as if to disappear in the infinity, which swallows them whole? Or does the emigrant perhaps actually possess an intuitive sense for people and places? Is it not perhaps precisely this short yet striking little chapter that brings into focus the sense of a certain kind of non-sense, determined by what I have called a "deviation of identity"?

The star beneath which this sign follows its own route is extremely mobile, eternally fleeting, much like "il passaggio" ("the journey") of these emigrants cooped up in a train crossing Canada: a gigantic monster, as though immobile, sunk beneath a perennial white blanket of snow. Again, fixity and mobility are intertwined until they create a sort of sublime osmosis in which the past (the memory of the places and people they are on their way to meet) and the future (which from the encounter with a new country one is able to divert into a perspective of what's to come) are mixed together, in the mind of the traveler, without a solution of continuity.

The symbol par excellence of this pro-gressing, of this neverending journey, is the train; a mobile symbol that slowly proceeds by losing itself and confusing itself with the diffuse whiteness of the snow, as though absorbed by it ("Il treno intanto s'era fatto del color bianco della neve" ["Meanwhile, the train turned white as snow"]); a train that travels toward infinity through infinity: an agonizing emblem of the very face of Canada. A little later we will see how this *atopia* (I use this term exclusively in its literal etymological sense of "no place") finds its greatest condensation, real and allegorical, in the city bus *Nowhere*, a bus that doesn't go anywhere, it is without a destination and without a destiny: an extreme, extraordinary symbol of this labyrinthine and limitless Canada. This is also where the sense of alienation in interpersonal relationships (the narrator immediately notices it) is accentuated by the linguistic slippage, which is even more complicated here, for there are three languages in conflict with one another: English, French, and the Italian of those who have only just arrived. This conflict can be traced emblematically—but also tragicomically—even within a single family, in which one brother speaks English, another replies in French, and the mother, who bridges the two, in Italian and in dialect.

This is how the image that I invoked a moment ago of the *Nowhere* bus truly becomes the symbolic identifier, not only of the geographic infinity of the Canadian landscape, but also, from within, of the objective intercommunicative difficulty, and therefore, the symbol of the solitude and of the planetary desolation in which its inhabitants wander about are reduced almost to ghosts of themselves. We read a passage, among the most exuberant, that for a moment made me even think of the disparate (desperate) sense of different lives/deaths the way Edgard Lee Masters somberly unfurled them in his *Spoon River*:

> Guardavo ora dal finestrino la fuga di case, la neve e il ghiaccio. Il ghiaccio, sotto le ruote, gemeva; e sul ghiaccio l'autobus slittava, ruggiva, si contorceva sfiorando spigoli di case, distributori di benzina, pali di fanali. Un'altalena. Era il primo pomeriggio e la città, sotto i fiocchi bianchi, pareva addormentata. Guardai uno per uno i miei compagni di viaggio, e anch'essi parevano addormentati, figure di sasso antico, anime di condannati che il Caronte sordo portava a Dite. Anche tre donne sedevano come affrante sui seggiolini di velluto nero, con espressioni morte sui visi. Una di esse, con capelli giallicci che le sfuggivano da sotto un cappellino di raso bianco a lustrini, teneva il volto nascosto in una veletta color tabacco dalla quale la sua bocca livida risaltava come una larga fessura ricucita. La sua mano stringeva quella di un uomo robusto, dalla pelle contadina, ed entrambi si sostenevano poggiando l'uno contro l'altra la testa. Alle scosse dell'auto i due sussultavano, si guardavano, abbozzavano un sorriso e tornavano a stare nella posizione di prima (78).

[Now I was looking out the window, the flight of houses, the snow, and the ice. The ice beneath the wheels groaned; and on the ice, the bus skidded roared, writhed as it grazed the corners of houses, gas stations, lampposts. A swing. It was the early afternoon and the city under the white snowflakes seemed to be asleep, figures of ancient stone, damned souls whom deaf Charon was ferrying to Dis. Even three women sat as though exhausted on little chairs of black velvet, with deathly expressions on their faces. One of them, with yellowish hair that was escaping out from under a little white satin hat with sequins, kept her face hidden in a tobacco colored veil from which her livid mouth stood out like a large sewn up wound. Her hand held that of a robust man with the skin of a peasant, and they supported each other by leaning the one against the head of the other. They were startled by the jolts of the automobile, they looked at each other, faintly smiled and, returned to their previous position.]

This is "il migliore e più profondo Rimanelli" ("the best and most profound Rimanelli"), as wrote Prezzolini, who was among the first to read *Biglietto di terza* (in the *Cittadino canadese*, March 7, 1959), and not the "didactic" Rimanelli, the one who every so often assumes—rather anachronistically—the role of the sociologist (see the questionable chapter "Le ragazze e noi"), but the one in which Rimanelli allows himself to go with the intermittent flow of epiphanic images that pass freely one after another as in an indistinct and unstoppable flux, which is very well suited, in fact, to the *indistinction* and *inarrestability* (or infinity) of a country like Canada, as it must have appeared to him fifty years ago, and the chaotic port of Montréal ("il più grande porto interno al mondo"; "the world's largest internal port") undoubtedly reminded him of Marseille, with "gli stessi marinari bretoni e baschi e francesi e irlandesi nelle taverne lungo i docks; le stesse donnine e lo stesso pianoforte scordato e il medesimo suonatore gonfio di birra; la stessa aria frizzante di fumo e zolfo e freddo e pesce in gelatina; e gatti randagi con pezze nero-oro sulla schiena, e neon impazziti, come per una sarabanda di carnevale" (109; "the same Briton and Basque and French and Irish sailors in the taverns along the docks; the same little ladies and the same out-of-tune piano and the same piano player bloated with beer; the same air pungent with smoke and sulfur and cold and fish in gelatine; and wild cats with black-gold patches on their backs, and insane neon lights, like those of the bedlam of carneval").

Yes, this is Rimanelli at his best and most profound. This is the one who knew how to collect that indistinct primordial matter that is at the base of the myth of the giant modern city, of the metropolis-in-formation, as writers before him also already knew how to intuit like Baudelaire, or, to remain within the theme of this book, Emanuel Carnevali. The great metropolis is a multifaceted, monstrous, sprawling city that naturally underlies the personal solitude (that is then also a consequence of isolation) of North Americans. Or perhaps, on the other hand (seeing that the situation is perfectly reversible), it is precisely this isolation that unleashes that sense of diffuse drunkenness and desperate happiness that the writer from Casacalenda encountered in the streets of Montreal, for Friday evenings they were (and I suppose they still are) inundated with people firmly set on enjoying themselves. In this sense the metropolis emanates an iridescent glow of frenetic, frivolous, global vitality (the likes of which the writer claims never to have found in any other city in the world), which stands in contrast to the white, asphyxiating monotony of his harsh workdays. A feverish whirlwind, extreme and to an extreme, from which you never know if you're going to make it out dead or alive ("... se esco muoio o non muoio ammazzato da un'automobile? [...] Due incidenti ogni cinque minuti... Ogni due anni il numero delle vittime aumenta di un quarto, più velocemente quindi del numero delle automobili," 121; "... if I go out will I or will I not die under an automobile? [...] Two accidents every five minutes... Every two years the number of victims increases by a quarter, quicker than the number of automobiles"), but, at the same time, necessary in order to recharge your internal vital "mechanism," only to find yourself ready to run wild again the next Friday night.

Another aspect that Rimanelli precociously emphasizes and destined to become in subsequent years one of the problematics most discussed among Italianists and linguists, especially in North America, is the particular idiolect contaminated by the Italians of America and by the Americo-Italians, which several years later he will proclaim in novels like *Detroit Blues*. By the early 1950s, the Rimanelli of *Biglietto di terza* was already aware of it, as evidenced by the fact that he appended a little glossary intended to explain some of the contaminated slang terms, most of which were (and are) created by the Italianization of their English equivalents; just as explanatory/didactic as was the final note, written in a Vittorini's spirit (I am thinking, in particular, of a book like *Il Sempione strizza l'occhio al Frejus*, an extremely controversial novel that preceded the drafting of *Biglietto di terza* by about a decade), which served as sociological support for Vittorini and Rimanelli in each of their storytelling practices, although in Vittorini, it was of a more manifestly ideological sort.

Naturally, here I refer to a specific "Italo-Canadian way of speaking" (which is the title of an entire chapter), which presents many analogies to that of Italian Americans, given that English is the contaminated hegemonic language. The effects that are obtained can also be involuntarily comedic; we find them in several passages that Rimanelli inserts between the didactic and the facetious over the course of his narration ("Sto in casa senza *stima* e senza *genitore*," one of his characters says at a certain point, which means "without hot water," or *steam*, and "without a doorman," or *janitor*; and another one will shout to him: "Non spogliare la grassa," linguistically mimetic of the English *Don't spoil the grass*). This dialogue, with its contaminated yet inventively colorful language, served Rimanelli among other things as vehicles for inserting more than a few scenes of the actual lives of the Italian emigrant community, rendering the story more lively and pungent, but always within the parameters of an enlarged and variegated geographic reality that remains that of Canada.

The journey that the narrator takes across the mythic land "up North," in the provisional company of a certain Peg Collins, serves to underline precisely the immense vastness of this country and the sense of *defamiliarization* it produces, with cities that have European names (London, Vienna, Verona, Paris, Dublin, Brussels, etc.), but whose inhabitants are not Londoners, or Viennese, or Parisians, or Dubliners, or Belgians, but simply and altogether Canadian:

Di Brussels, città immediatamente successiva, non riuscimmo a saper nulla. Ci dissero: "Si chiama Brussels perché si chiama Brussels come io mi chiamo Rob Mamie." "E vi sono, qui immigrati del Belgio?" Peg chiese. Rob Mamie alzò le spalle. "Belgi qua? Sentite, noi siamo canadesi e non belgi. Canadesi!" E ci piantò. (168)

[Regarding Brussels, the city immediately following, we were unable to find anything out. They told us, "It's called Brussels because it's called Brussels, the same way my name is Rob Mamie." "And are there any immigrants from Belgium?" Peg asked. Rob Mamie shrugged his shoulders. "Belgians here? Listen, we're Canadians and not Belgians. Canadians!" And he cut us off.]

Regarding Canada's intrinsic wandering (mixed with nationalistic pride), Rimanelli finally offers us one last formidable symbol: the *skidhouse*, or rather a self-propelled house, a house in transit: an extraordinary emblem of the nomadic character hardwired in the Canadian soul. We are in the period of the great crossings in search of oil. Entire families, entire wandering towns scoured Canada from top to bottom. They established the foundations for new villages, a few were merely transient, while others thanks to fortune and destiny would eventually become the earliest nuclei from which the industrial cities of Canada's future will spring. Rimanelli was an eyewitness of this reality-in-motion, with its constantly shifting identity, and he gives us a vibrant testimonial in this book.

And this nomadic lifestyle constitutes the last part of *Biglietto di terza*, particularly concentrated in the penultimate chapter titled "Viaggio senza ritorno." It is the longest chapter and also the one that is most exquisitely novelistic, which makes it stand out from the previous chapters, which contained mostly journalistic cues or historical/sociological annotations (for example those related to "miti e leggende indiane," or "Indian myths and legends"; there is even a chapter with this title, which seems to make it a didactic failure, as it is written in a descriptive vein, in contrast to the exclusively narrative style he generally assumes).

"Viaggio senza ritorno" is a dense chapter, almost a freestanding short story in its own right, in which one feels the presence of a novelist like Faulkner—the same Faulkner who thirty years earlier had flown across the North American sky as a volunteer in the Canadian Air Force; the same Faulkner whose *Intruder in the Dust* (1948) Rimanelli had read and annotated during his travels from Italy to Canada, which Prisco had given to him on the pier in Naples before boarding the ship for America; the same Faulkner who over the course of this first North American experience Rimanelli felt the urgent need to visit (in the meantime he had read important novels like *The Sound and the Fury* of 1929 and *Absalom, Absalom!* of 1936), seeking him out in his home in Memphis; the same Faulkner, finally, who published *A Fable* the following year (1954) with Random House, at the same time as Rimanelli's *The Day of the Lion.*

"Viaggio senza ritorno" is a fascinating and passionate chapter (in the manner of Tennessee Williams—yet another writer who could be paired with William Faulkner in the ideal genealogy of this chapter/short story), with a biting, vertiginous, vaguely Verga-inspired style of writing with sharp quick cuts, and with a pace now dilated, now suddenly attenuated. There are pages in this chapter that are more openly literary and inventive than the "novel" as a whole, where a series of characters like Lucia Messala, and Victor and Bill Foster remain fixed in the reader's mind for a long time.

Rimanelli's journey, like any true journey, concludes with a "return" (it is the first of many *nostoi* that we find in the multifaceted work of this writer): on the one hand, with an awareness of an enlarging of his anthropological "ubiquity"; on the other, a greater selective capacity in the matter of his own personal destiny. In no other place are geography and destiny derived from the same etymological root.

Furthermore, Canada is an uncompromising place; it is a place, Rimanelli says, where you can live only if you have truly cut ties with your past: "Il Canadà è bello perché vergine, selvaggio, disperatamente infinito... Io dico che tutti gli uomini che hanno patito torti, hanno sofferto l'usura della società e l'impostura del bisogno, dovrebbero venire qui per sentirsi liberi. Ma per restare in questa terra devi aver rotto i ponti col passato, e alle tue spalle, sulle tue rive lontane, non devi avere più nessuna voce che ti chiami. Diversamente il Canadà potrebbe diventare la tua pazzia..." (233-234; "Canada is wonderful because it is pure, wild, desperately infinite... I say that any man who has endured injustice, suffered from society's usury, and the fraud of poverty should come here in order to feel free. But to stay in this country, you must burn all bridges with the past; and at your back, on your distant shores, you can no longer have any voice that calls you. However, Canada could, on the other hand, become cause of your madness...").

With *Biglietto di terza* Giose Rimanelli wrote a short travel epic, just as, in those very same years, Jack Kerouac had written one in his *On the Road* (1957). With Kerouac, Rimanelli shares a sense of life as a constant journey (and learning process); the house of his soul is a *skidhouse* in perennial movement, like his irrepressible typewriter. And it is no coincidence that today, his last home is precisely in Lowell, Massachusetts, Kerouac's hometown, a few blocks from the house in which the author of *On the Road* was born and raised. His journey therefore—and its symbolic importance is powerful— concludes by returning full circle to where it began, only to start from the beginning all over again.

3. REFLECTION, SOLITUDE, POETRY

The second book in which Rimanelli's American experience is reflected is a collection of poems titled *Carmina blabla* (1967), written between the end of the 1950s and the mid-1960s. A self-ironizing title, *Carmina blabla* is also oxymoronic, given the two terms of which it is composed: the first is solemn and refined; the second— with its reference to idle chatter—undermines its "classicism."

Though Rimanelli only came to poetry later in life, it should not be considered secondary or "minor" with respect to those greater works in his narrative opus. (Rimanelli is by nature and by literary instinct a "narrative beast" among the most noteworthy I've encountered in the second half of the Italian and Italian-American *Novecento*.) Giose embarks on his journey into the realm of poetry as though acting on a need for internal reflection after his roaring years in Italy, in a sort of solitary, vaguely medieval *buen retiro*. Not by chance, the same year as *Carmina blabla*, he came out with the slender volume *Monaci d'amore medievale* (1967)—translations or rewritings of love lyrics by medieval monks and doctors and itinerants. It is a collection that contains "the most beautiful and sincere lyrics, now unruly and now ironic, now sinful and now parodic," as the author himself defined it. Luigi Reina wrote a couple of penetrating pages on this volume in a fully fleshed-out essay dedicated to Rimanelli's entire poetic output up to 1989, the year *Arcano* was published (see, of Reina's work, in particular, *Monaci d'amore medievale*, 80-88).

And it is in the context of this intimate collection, and in his rediscovered and renovated studies, that Rimanelli undertakes, among other things, university instruction, which will take him first to Sarah Lawrence College (1961), then to Yale University (1962), then to the British Columbia of Vancouver (1963-1964), and finally to UCLA (1965). Therefore, it represents a sort of break, though by no means an inert period, which will allow the writer to study his internal rhythms and reflect in greater depth on his life and his experience again. He does this through poetry, music (he writes blues, spirituals, little jingles, and Doric arias), and the visual arts (in this period of time he makes seventy-five oil paintings, seventeen tempera paintings, twenty pastels and over three hundred drawings). It could be said that our author's entire poetic output—his collections in Italian, English, and Molisan dialect include a dozen titles (roughly the same number as his narrative works)—was born of these states of reflection, solitude, experimentation, or pure abandon of the mind (even sober; for this final "disposition" I have allowed myself an emblematic reference to a book of sonnets, written in collaboration with the undersigned, playfully titled (but only playful to a point) *Da G. a G.: 101 sonnetti* (1996), a book that I will not discuss, just as I will not discuss many others published by Rimanelli, as I am here exclusively interested in just one specimen of his poetic experience, an important experience that remains, nevertheless, complementary to that of his narratives.

On the other hand, this period of reflection, in which Rimanelli feels the need to survey new and polyvalent creative forms, corresponds to a crucial phase in his professional life. In Italy he was blacklisted for base ideological motivations and literary envy as I indicated in the first part of this chapter. (Something similar happens in this same period to Giuseppe Berto, which however did not drive him to isolate himself abroad; Berto, among other things, was friends with Rimanelli, and in 1957 they collaborated in the production of an important television investigation of Southern Italy, the Mezzogiorno, as it is called, which aired on RAI from April 24 to July 3, 1958; and still, like Berto, it is characterized by a long conflictual relationship with the paternal figure: see the tender and biting pages of Rimanell's *Molise Molise* and those written in the appendix to *Carmina blabla*; by Berto see the whole first half of *Il male oscuro*, which was released in 1964.)

This is how the work of this author (once acclaimed, now, after the publication of *Il mestiere del furbo*, unacknowledged) from 1959 on was violently and systematically held hostage by the official Italian establishment, simply because its author—perhaps unique in Italy—knew how to make light of partisan servilities, of compromises, of group disputes and power.

It is possible (plausible) to suppose that it might also be his innate need to "transgress" that forces him to cling, though purely tangentially, to the ways of the neo-avant-garde, from which the writer will extract new juices for his own original and personal metalinguistic experimentation, which—hardly (if at all) present in his previous narrative work—becomes evident in his research (and in his work) precisely from the 1960s on, until it reaches its height in *Benedetta in Guysterland*, an extremely composite novel, written directly in English, which I will discuss later. And his metalinguistic experimentation will represent a point of no return in his fiction, though it is repressed in his poetic and memoir-oriented work.

Nevertheless, I would like to suggest that Rimanelli's encounter with the Italian neo-avant-garde in the early 1960s (I am obviously thinking of the Gruppo 63) is exterior, non only because by 1960 he was already living steadily in America, but also because that innate need of his for transgression and inter-linguistic experimentation was stronger than the need to turn to European models—but here, we must remember the magazine *Change*, one of the driving forces behind the French avant-garde, which published in 1972 the first chapter of *Graffiti*, a meta-narrative pastiche among Giose's most arduous and daring (to which I will return later)—can be traced to the draw of American pop art and jazz; it can be traced back to the "linguistic terrorism" of E. E. Cummings, to the schizophrenic-imagism of William Carlos Williams, to the totalizing, anarchic and pansexual autobiographical writing of Henry Miller ("for me the book is the man, and the book is the man that I am, ardent, obscene, turbulent, thoughtful, scrupulous, lying, and diabolically sincere"), to the turbid, ambiguous introversion of Nabokov; to the moralizing and crypto-Catholic intrigues of Graham Greene, and last, but not least, to the narcissistic and tormented longing for a happiness that will always elude those who lead the dissolute lives of F. Scott Fitzgerald's lost generation.

The list of references and "models" could continue, with the risk of piling them up in vertiginous reductions, which here, nevertheless, function as opportune indicators of the frayed and turbulent map of Rimanelli's opus and of his unwieldy, infinite creative experimentation. These markers also demonstrate the omnivorous intellectual curiosity of the author of the *Carmina*, who is never satisfied, but always open to the new, ready to evaluate and filter it through his own experience as a writer. It should also be added that the arrival of Rimanelli on American soil granted him the opportunity to allow, with greater breadth—we could even say with greater freedom—his intellectual restlessness to roam, his innate cultural curiosity, his personal sense of inquiry; and because America offered him a gaggle of aesthetic modalities, which, at that point in his professional life, the oppressive Italian atmosphere no longer allowed him to enjoy.

And so, America, in this immense country, Rimanelli leads a sort of "marginalized" existence at first (even if he was almost immediately involved in the activity of university instruction), immersed in fruitful years of study and research and writing, "macinando così più lavoro lui che mezza dozzina di 'contemporanei' messi insieme" (Moretti, 1967, 10; "churning out more work than half a dozen of his 'contemporaries' put together"). But his "marginality," his place on the edges of society, offered certain real privileges: indeed, it permits the "marginalized" individual a behavioral strategy that allows him to study the "center" without being seen or criticized. It affords him, in other words, forays and improvised raids into "enemy" territory, more or less like a sort of free shooter, or sniper, unencumbered by any cultural, moral, or pseudo-social obligation of any kind. The geographic and literary space, not to mention the expressive multiplicity that he discovers in his adopted country, affords him the opportunity to do all of this.

Thus, Rimanelli travels, studies, experiments, explores various creative media, drawing from his very own store of inventive malice, anger, fury, but also candor, obstinate persistence, unfulfilled curiosity, tendency to take risks, and taste for adventure. Above all, perhaps, his desperate, playful, even self-destructive desire to forge an identity for himself is constantly undermined, naturally consumed by a country like the United States, which is so laden with contradictions, so chaotic and centrifugal.

To his adoptive country Rimanelli offers a noteworthy, variegated, and cosmopolitan cultural contribution, which is without a doubt of the first order with respect to the Italian intellectuals who, over the course of the last century, expatriated to America. A contribution that found its expression in his numerous writings, cultural initiatives, and translations; or rather one that, on the one hand, was nourished by the new American culture, and that, on the other, spread an awareness of Italian authors and movements that had yet to reach the vast majority of Americans.

This is the articulated context that produced the poems that would eventually come together to form the *Carmina*.

Justifiably a "confessional" book, as the author himself defines it in an extremely useful note found in the appendix, *Carmina blabla* is an expression of the moments of that apparent "break" he made, or rather that reflection in which Rimanelli sought to establish *his* center and constitute *his* identity. The most immediate indicators of this are the obstinacy, on the part of the writer, in noting at the foot of each poem not merely the date of composition, but also the place and occasion in which each text came into being. In this there is a desire to legitimate the transitory nature of the *ubi consistam* in the ontological moment of one's own personal history; elevating the ephemeral to an absolute instant, because this is what the life of a writer is made of: living moment by moment his own existence with the awareness that any moment could be decisive. In short, making precariousness the fragile and robust law of our reason for being *hic et nunc* and of our daily routine ("Ragione di essere: / sesso e denaro. / E passa la vita correndo. / Passiamo la vita morendo"; "Reason for being: / sex and money. / Life passes at a clip. / We pass through life / dying," as a couple of his verses bitterly read in a poem sarcastically titled "Happiness").

And so, for the reader (and for the same writer who often writes in real time with respect to his objects of poetic inspiration), flashing before his very eyes, as in a film, now *à rebours*, now as in an uninterrupted tracking sequence, people, situations, and places in which those moments were experienced with reckless abandon—Detroit, New York, Washington, Palm Beach, New Haven, Vancouver, and, at times, even Molise. Since the thought of his homeland remained a constant for Rimanelli, he never forgets in this his itinerant mini-epic the love and conflicting ties that bind him to his roots. This explains why his paternal figure suddenly becomes the emblem of his ongoing grudge. The poem with which the *Carmina* opens, written in a neo-realistic vein but with modulations of blues in its iterative passages, bears witness effectively, yet sarcastically, to the grudge he bears toward his father, who also over the years was unable to forget "la millenaria sete patita nel sud" ("the age-old thrist endured in the south"):

L'Italia è una terra lunga
una terra lunnnnnnnga
come il mal di cuore
"l'Africa o l'America
ecco cosa ci vuole"

e sempre col ditto girava
quel globo di terra e di mare
per trovare la terra che ci vuole
Siamocresciuti nel buio
di un colco di terra che non basta
alla sete e l'Italia è una terra lunga
una terra lunnnnnnnga
da dimenticare
Ora è venuto in America
mette i bulloni alle macchine
Ha un giardino un garage le piante
tutta l'acqua che cuole negl'idranti
È diventato più giovane e esperto
più quieto più tondo un po' bolso
"L'America è fatta di acqua"
dice appena ridendo ai nuovi che vengono
ma pensa a quell ache manca al paese
(o l'hanno poi messa al paese?)
È alle donne scomparse che un tempo
pazienti modeste un po' strane
prendevano l'acqua coi secchi
al pozzo artesiano
L'Italia è una terra lunga
una terra lunga
una terra lunnnnnnnga
da ricordare (13)

Five years after the publication of this poem, another Southern Italian poet, who inevitably comes to mind in this instance, would also underline "con deciso impegno civile, mai smarrito nel corso di una vicenda umana ricca di affetti domestici e di virile partecipazione alle sofferenze e alle lotte degli umili" ("with decisive civic engagement, never lost in the course of a human adventure rich with domestic affective bonds and virile participation in the suffering and struggling of the poor")—these are the words of Giorgio Caproni excerpted from the official decision of the 1977 Viareggio Prize—as I was saying, another Southern Italian poet would similarly underline this ancient anger of rural society toward an endemic problem—the scarcity of water—that torments (and has always tormented) their land. The poet in question is Carlo Francavilla, a native of Castellana Grotte in Puglia, who died suddenly in 1986 and who today has been almost entirely forgotten. The poem to which I allude is significantly titled "Le terre della sete" ("The Land of Thirst"), written in 1972; it lends its title to the eponymous collection of poems (1977) and earned Francavilla the Viaraggio Prize for best first work. A few exemplary verses:

[...]
e dilagano i fiumi e i torrenti
sulle terre bruciate dalla sete.
E sempre torna a galla
la promessa tradita.
La terra chiama ancora
i figli discacciati
dalle case d'amore
incontro a nuove lingue,
seme disperso da mano nemica.

Rimanelli reflects on this grudge of their fathers and in part makes it his own, but only in part, obviously, because times change, and he experiences, for better or for worse, these changes viscerally—changes that are both social and psychological. His impassioned dialogue both in person and at a distance, with Corrado Alvaro, amply demonstrates this. It is precisely Alvaro, at least inasmuch as Rimanelli allows himself to divulge in 1955, who represents, in the eyes of his father, the tangible proof, in writing, for the reasons behind his distrust and his interminable inane protest. Giose wrote a touching and entertaining passage on the matter that is worth presenting here:

Con sé aveva portato pochi libri dall'Italia: trattati di agrimensura, qualche romanzo, dei giornali. In un giornale vecchissimo c'era un vecchissimo pezzo di Corrado Alvaro, intitolato *L'acqua*. Mio padre quel giornale se lo portava sempre in tasca, nella tasca interna della giacca. Quando aveva bisogno di ricaricarsi di odio, stendeva il giornale sul tavolo come un lenzuolo, e con la stessa intensa minuzia con cui un tempo girava il mappamondo prendeva a leggere il pezzo di Alvaro. Il giornale diventò presto un cencio lacero e illeggibile, ma egli lo custodiva sempre nella tasca interna della giacca. Quando lo zio Americano disse: "Ma è assurdo che in Italia non ci sia un acquedotto!" mio padre spiegò sul tavolo un giornale tutto nuovo. Disse: "Ti leggerò una cosa di sempre, che vale sempre," e cominciò a sillabare il vecchio articolo di Alvaro. Naturalmente lo sapeva a memoria, e il giornale spiegato sul tavolo gli serviva come prova di quanto stava dicendo. Questo pezzo di Alvaro, che ora figura nel volume *Itinerario italiano* edito da Bompiani, non è più lungo di due colonne di piombo, contiene 1800 parole, è stato scritto in una mezza giornata di grazia... e tiene imprigionata, per sempre, la vita di un uomo. Quasi ad occhi chiusi, mio padre sillabò le ultime parole del pezzo di Alvaro: "La notte l'acqua si lamenta compressa nei tubi e vuole uscire. E pensare che noi abbiamo cercato mondo anche per l'acqua." (Rimanelli 1979, 116-117)

[He had brought a few books with him from Italy: treatises on land surveying, a couple novels, a few newspapers. In one old newspaper there was an old piece by Corrado Alvaro, titled *L'acqua*. My father always carried that newspaper in his pocket, in his inside jacket pocket. When he needed to recharge his anger, he spread the newspaper out on the table like a sheet, and with the same intense meticulousness with which he once spun the globe, he would read Alvaro's article. The newspaper quickly became a tattered and illegible rag, but he always carried it in his inside jacket pocket. When his American uncle said: "But it's absurd that in Italy there isn't an acquaduct!" my father spread the newspaper out on the table again. He said: "I will read something eternal to you, something that will always be true," and he began to syllabify Alvaro's old article. Naturally he knew it by heart, and the newspaper spread out on the table served as the proof of what he was saying. This piece by Alvaro, which now appears in the volume *Itinerario italiano*, published by Bompiani, is no longer than two columns of lead; it contains 1800 words; it is was written in half a day of pure grace... and it holds a man's life forever imprisoned. Virtually with his eyes closed, my father pronounced the last words of Alvaro's article: "At night, water complains compressed in the tubes, and it wants out. And to think that we searched the world even for water."]

But Rimanelli's curious and restless temperament was unable, by his very nature, to accept or grow accustomed to the "statica pazzia" ("static insanity") of his forefathers, who were reluctant to understand (or even recognize) the industrial and technological advancements that had come to his motherland. The temperament of the artist, extremely receptive of the "new," is keen to seize from the American continent not only the "modernità dei tubi e degli irrigatori" ("modernity of pipes and irrigators") (related to the agricultural surveying the land that his father evidently held so dear), but obviously and above all the cultural ferment brought about by the new wave of pre- and post-war American literature: from Edgar Lee Masters and Scott Fitzgerald to Faulkner, Hemingway, Capote, Nabokov, and the poets of the Beat Generation, Giose's contemporaries. Vittorini and Pavese had also been believers in this new American literature (as were Sapegno, Muscetta, and Jovine, who were Rimanelli's earliest mentors).

Rimanelli's reception is manifest, above all, in his mastery of a new linguistic instrument, the English language, which the author knowingly employs, from the first years of his expatriation, in the effective expression of old resentments on the one hand, and a sense of having been ethically and culturally uprooted on the other— the schizophrenia of a statute of identity that is liable also to fail; nevertheless, he knows how to extract the literary juice and artistic sustenance necessary to thrive from such a perpetually lurking threat of failure. And, in fact, he will compose a good many of his poems directly in his new language: a fugitive's English that, like other writers of the past, he will mange to "rejuvenate," to make malleable and original precisely in the moment in which he models it to his inspirational needs and forces it to square up with his background. Very fortunately, in the afterword of the volume *Alien Cantica: An American Journey* (1995), the original nucleus of which was written directly in English in the same period as the *Carmina*, Anthony Burgess emphasizes this aspect: "Giose Rimanelli is one of those remarkable writers who, like Joseph Conrad and Jerzy Peterkiewicz and, among his fellow countrymen, Niccolò Tucci, have turned from their first language to English, and have set out to rejuvenate it in a way few writers could do who were blessed and burdened with English as their first language. In a sense, every writer nurses the desire not only to create new, fresh, original works of art but also to recreate the medium of language itself" (Burgess 1995, 145).

Mastery of a new linguistic tool also means conferring upon its poetic diction a greater *mobility*, as though an enlarged visual point of view were acting simultaneously in the development of the text: a pan-linguistic mechanism of which James Joyce had been a master or the Henry Miller of certain oneiric-visionary "pauses" we find in the *Tropics*; the latter is opportunely cited at the foot of one of this poems (*Ballatetta*, 22-23).

In Rimanelli this "gioco a incastro" ("puzzle") appears very frequently, almost to the point of leading to the fusion of registers, to their utter interchangeability. It is one of the characteristics of the structuralist play of the book, which thus lives in a continual alternation of the emotion/reflection that coincides with a satisfactory survey of the lexical energies inherent in Rimanelli's unbounded and spasmodic vocabulary, all of which is in service of a linguistic fever maintained constantly at high temperatures. Rimanelli continually supplants this centrifugal lexicon of his, with the flattering, sarcastic, and unscrupulous use of many rhetorical tropes among which prevail antiphrasis, alliteration, *calembour*, metonymy, epanalepsis, hyperbaton; thus probing a vast expressive spectrum: from the plebian to the sublime, from the specialized technical to the literary classical, achieving, at times, the allure of jazz or the lilting lament of the blues, or a pastiche of luxurious intensity.

Indeed, one rediscovers an expansive linguistic intensity a short while later (and at times in greater measure) in *Alien*, a book in which—as it has been acutely observed—"la tendenza alla varietà idiomatica e alla polimetria viene intrecciata alla tecnica surrealista dell'automatismo espressivo, nella successione orizzontale e sincronia dei segni verbali, a un raffinato virtuosismo sintattico-lessicale e a un insistito gioco metrico-stilistico" (Granese 1995, xxvi; "his tendency toward idiomatic variety and polymetry is intertwined with the surrealist technique of expressive automatism, in the horizontal succession and synchrony of verbal signs, to a refined syntactic-lexical virtuosity and to an insistent metrical-stylistic play").

Thus, high and low registers, the tragic and comic, appear simultaneously and, let us say, even ruthlessly from the moment that we realize that the author is always wide awake at the wheel ("the pilot is well in control," Burgess keenly wrote).

See, for example, the poem "Stil Novo" (31), in which Rimanelli places a series of short italicized and parenthetical meditations next to three little strophes, as though he were ironically adding a running commentary to his verses, as if he wants to streamline them and, in short, "reduce" them to "frivolous trifles." In the essay to which I have already referred, Luigi Reina correctly emphasizes this aspect by relating it to Rimanelli's dedication to Ciliegia (Sheryl) in *Arcano*, which is "ben più di una dedica: una dichiarazione di poetica. E un piccolo concentrato di estetica che introduce alla lettura della silloge. Perché veramente esser appaiono all'autore nugae" (98; "much more than a dedication—it is a declaration of his poetics as well as a small concentration of the aesthetic, which introduces the collection. Because they truly seem to be mere trifles to the author"): "Ciliegia, / caduta dal cielo / queste frivole cose / versi canzoni / prove riprove / di voce di suono / nella mia bocca di muto // Sono balze poi scogli / poi spiaggia poi nulla" (5; "Ciliegia (Cherry), / fallen from heaven / these frivolous things / verses songs / trials retrials / of voice of sound / in my mute mouth // They are cliffs then rocks / then beach then nothing // But sweet Love / is the comforter of night").

The technique of synchronic alternation (exposition/reflection) finds its greatest expression in *Graffiti*, which is only the incandescent detritus of an incredibly vast notebook, in part unpublished even to this day (but from which, as we will soon see, Rimanelli extrapolated yet another freestanding narrative fragment, *Detroit Blues*, entirely rewriting it), titled "La macchina paranoica," on which Alberto Granese has exhaustively written (Granese 1988, 168-215).

But behind the smoke and mirrors of the metalinguistic and plurilinguistic aspects of his texts, there is, returning to the *Carmina*, always the "return" to the self; and so here is the solitude after the party; the tormenting melancholy that mocks itself:

C'è un fiume domestico e largo
a reggerti il capo tra i palazzi
    Siamo partiti un mattino di questi
    con giacche e pastrani
    verso l'oriente
Pioveva leggero tra i palazzi
e tutto era chiaro cosciente.
[...]
Pioggia d'aprile, insistente
Così tu lasci che piova
    come ieri
    come oggi
        come sempre
        L'idea di un sogno ti sfiora
        e tu la rigetti nel niente
        Nella pioggia consumiamo le ore
    Ci resta l'ansia che dura
    la radio il giornale il drug-store
    Ci restano pallide ore
Perché non ci sono più avventure

(*Guardando l'Hudson*, 39-40)

Here, even in the midst of a serpentine seduction of Apollinairian memory, mixed with a few obviously D'Annunzian stylistic elements, the antiphrastic arrangement of such ballad-like elements becomes clear. But this reversal does not break the poet's dramatic *reflection*, that mixture so innate (and insistent) in him of an inexhaustible need for love, on the one hand, and the derisive, narcissistic irony ready to undermine him, on the other. Why—the reader could ask—does this dark tendency toward the self-destructive, this "maledettismo" ("self-damnation"), this desire to inflict pain on himself at all costs, this discomfort lying in wait that is always suddenly assumed, in the heart of a gratifying wellbeing that is right there within reach?

The "great need for death" is, then, literally, narcissistic, a necessary "perversion" in order to reset the scale, reach zero, that bottom of the barrel from which it is difficult to lift oneself up in search of a "new love." "Lazzaro," even if raised, will bring with him the burden and the awareness of pain existing in the world, on which he will still be able to laugh and play; but it will always mean *putting oneself at stake*. As for the laughter, it will be the tragic and mocking laughter of Mercuzio.

4. POLYPHONY AND HISTORY: *DETROIT BLUES*

Extremely close to Rimanelli's American experience is his novel *Detroit Blues*; although he wrote the first draft in the same year that saw the publication of *Carmina* (1967), it was not published until 1996.

It is an extremely centrifugal work that adds yet another tile to the complex fictional mosaic initiated more than a century ago with the same feverish draft as *Tiro al piccione*. Indeed, all of his work seems to have something feverish about it.

The "after word" that one finds in the appendix of *Detroit Blues* recounts, in part, the genesis of the novel, whose original nucleus can be traced back to the "pluriprospettico e pluridimensionale" organism (Granese 1988, 173; "pluri-perspective and pluri-dimensional") that is *La macchina paranoica*, a polyphonic narrative accumulation, from which Rimanelli will extract the novel *Graffiti*, and in which one also finds, under the title *Bella Italia amate sponde*, his diary that—written in Detroit during the torrid summer of 1967, under the duress of the race riots that shook the city—laid the foundation for *La macchina*, a diary that Rimanelli completely rewrote in recent years giving it the autonomous form of a novel that would come to be known as *Detroit Blues*.

This novel, as you may have already gathered from this brief introduction, represents the complex traffic of his mental and editorial workshop, which demands in its own right a philological and literary-historical study that would seek to situate the work in the context of Rimanelli's output as a whole. For the purpose of the present study, I am most interested in a specific reading of *Detroit Blues* with respect to Giose's American experience.

In the aforementioned "after word," Rimanelli establishes the external and internal poles of *Detroit Blues*; "external" in terms of the historical events that frame the novel (namely, the frayed diary of the time he spent in Detroit during the hot and humid July of 1967 when the African-American revolt broke out); "internal" in terms of the psychological repercussions that those events provoked in the mind of this intellectual Italian emigrant in America.

Put in these terms, the story could have taken the shape of an autobiographical novel. "Solo che *Detroit Blues*"—he says in the "after word"—"non è romanzo autobiografico, anche se giocato sulle tangenti bianco/nero in seno a una famiglia di emigrati molisani, con soggetto principale una strada che ospita bianchi di varia cultura e differenti origine etniche. Potrebbe essere definito un'indagine al microscopio nelle segrete maglie dei gravi problemi sociali e razziali che nell'intimo delle coscienze umane e all'aperto travagliarono la città di Detroit in quell'epoca, e travagliano l'America tuttora. Detroit è stata generosa con i miei ed è la loro tomba. Non ho antipatia per lei, ma nemmeno amore. Ciò nonostante la porto con me, è un importante tassello della mia esistenza. Ho capito il *suo* blues, il suo Motown Sound, e gli ho voluto bene" (206; "It's just that *Detroit Blues* is not an autobiographical novel, even though it is played out on the white/black tangents at the heart of a family of Molisan emigrants, with a street as the principal subject that houses whites of various cultures and different ethnic origins. It could be considered an examination under the microscope of the secret stitches of several serious social and racial problems, which in the intimate corners of human conscience and out in the open, afflicted the city of Detroit in that period, and continue to afflict the America of today. Detroit was generous to my family and it is their tomb. I harbor no hard feelings toward her, or, however, any love. Nevertheless I carry her with me. She represents an important stage in my life. I came to understand *her* blues, her Motown Sound, and I loved her"). And further along he specifies the nature of this narrative, when, in 1991, he decides to rewrite the diary in a healthy act of catharsis, "dandogli struttura autonoma di romanzo; una narrativa, comunque, secondo la tecnica che preferisce guardare all'esterno delle cose dall'interno di chi osserva, spronato anche dall'urgenza di riesaminare a distanza—come del resto fanno documenti, film, memorie e musica—i tragici e creativi anni sessanta americani che hanno lasciato un non trascurabile marchio in questa coda di secolo che sta per sbattere alla finestra del Duemila" (207; "giving it the autonomous structure of a novel; a narrative, therefore, according to his preferred technique of looking at the outside of things from inside the observer, spurred on also by the urgency of reexamining from a distance—just as documents, film, memories and music do—the tragic and creative 1960s in America that have left an indelible mark on the tail end of the century that is about to crash into the window of the year 2000").

This is then, at a distance of about twenty years, how the "external/internal" distinctions I cited above return in the "after word" and reconcile themselves in a perfect fusion in which historical truth and romanticized truth, fiction and memory, objective reality and private reality, are mixed together in that *unicum* that is, finally, Rimanelli's truthful and most profound narrative art.

I would now like to proceed, by means of a step-by-step analysis, to a reading of this novel, summarizing, first of all, its plot. I am grateful to Rimanelli who deigned to write a synopsis of it himself. I have to confess the two-fold reason that drove me to ask him to spell it out for me.

The first reason is egoistic: asking the author to "summarize" the vicissitudes or plot of the novel of his own creation has allowed me to avoid doing it myself and thus avoiding the risk of "summarizing" it in an all too personal way, given the extremely composite nature of the work. It is also true, and here I make amends for my weakness, that the task of the critic is first and foremost to "describe" a text; masters like Giacomo Debenedetti remind us of this fact. A book of essays, provocatively though significantly titled *Descrizioni di descrizioni*, by Giose's ingenious and implacable enemy, Pier Paolo Pasolini, reminds us of this fact as well.

The second reason is of a more subtle nature: to see, effectively, *which* phases of the story the author would be forced to privilege (and which phase would fade into the background) once he was forced to make a simple compendium of them; a little—though simplified a great deal—like the work of an ideal sieve used on himself: what remains and what is strained away. But here is the "parzialissimo sommario" ("extremely biased summary") as he himself called it, so kindly furnished by Giose:

Il professore di antropolgia Simone Donato (si occupa di macachi) riceve a Berkeley, California, dove insegna, una telefonata da Detroit, Michigan, dai suoi due fratelli più giovani, Saverio (veterano del Vietman, semi-invalido, e ora camionista) e Basso (fallito studente in medicina, fallito tennista professionista ma socio in un ben avviato negozio di armi e oggetti sportivi): gli comunicano di prendere il primo aereo, tutto è stato già pagato, ritirare il biglietto all'aeroporto, perché il "cugino" Larry è stato ammazzato. Larry Dope era figlio del noto chitarrista jazz Nebraska Dope, un indiano Omaha che tutti credevano negro, e di Adele Quency, ex priora in un convento di New Jersey, che saltò il muro avvampata d'amore per il Nebraska. Adele, nata a Detroit, era sorella delle gemelle Assunta e Assuntina che la madre, una Merola di Termoli, Molise, sposata al dissoluto avvocato divorzista Quency, portò in Molise, abbandonando il marito che si risposò. La gemella Assuntina sposò Cosmo Donato Rivosordo, padrone di barche, che si azzoppò durante una pesca di frodo sulle coste libiche. Da Assuntina e Cosmo nacque Simone, che venne mandato in un seminario a studiare, che poi abbandonò. Dopo la seconda Guerra Mondiale emigrarono a Detroit e la sorella Adele, l'ex monaca, fece l'atto di richiamo, pagò i biglietti e gli comprò la casa a Detroit, su State Fair Street e Gratiot Avenue, Saverio e Basso crebbero lì. Questi due figli sapevano abbastanza l'italiano, mentre Cosmo si esprimeva solo attraverso i proverbi del suo dialetto. Simone, invece, aveva fatto strada accademica se non soldi, mentre i fratelli questi li avevano fatti, insieme ad amicizie di commercio, anche se non del tutto pulite. Simone aveva conosciuto sia Nebraska Dope sia Larry ad un concerto jazz a New Haven, nel 1961, quando egli insegnava alla Yale. Larry, di colore scuro, ma più chiaro del padre e un po' vicino al colore marino, brumastro, di tutti i Donato—compreso Simone—era chitarrista/compositore in erba, ma di genio. Era tutto immerso tuttavia nei problemi politici, razziali, e lottava per questi come Martin Luther King e altri nei vari campus d'America. Si era iscritto a corsi di giurisprudenza ad Ann Arbor, e abitava "temporaneamente" al piano di sopra dei Donato, in soffitta. Cosmo non lo digeriva perché, per lui, era un "nero"; e neanche i vicini lo vedevano di buon occhio, eccetto due lesbiche della strada, che ricevevano tipetti d'ogni genere ai loro parties, e forse fumavano. Larry si metteva nei guai con tutti, anche con la polizia, perché secondo loro era un istigatore, e partecipava agli scioperi. Cosmo Donato Rivosordo infine lo cacciò via. Qualche giorno più tardi si venne a sapere ch'era stato ammazzato (e poi ritrovato spolpato nel fiume), dal gigantesco barista del Club privato di Grosse Pointe, il *Beowolf*, un ex nazista, in combutta con un altro abitante di State Fair, Cop Sorge, anche lui razzista, come quasi tutti in quella strada, che spesso leggeva Heidegger. Uno degli azionisti e member of the board era Basso. Il resto è thriller.

[The professor of anthropology Simone Donato (who works with macaques) receives in Berkeley, California, where he teaches, a phone call from Detroit, Michigan from his two younger brothers, Saverio (a semi-invalid veteran from the war in Vietnam, who is now working as a truck driver) and Basso (med-school dropout, failed tennis pro who is now a partner in a thriving arms and sporting goods store). They tell him to catch the first flight to Detroit, everything's already been paid for, he just has to pick up his ticket at the airport, because "cousin" Larry has been killed. Larry Dope was the son of the famous jazz guitarist Nebraska Dope, an Omaha Indian who everybody thought was black, and Adele Quency, ex-prioress of a convent in New Jersey, who jumped the wall, burning with love for Nebraska. Born in Detroit, Adele was the sister of the twins Assunta and Assuntina whom their mother, a certain Merola from Termoli, Molise married to the licentious divorce lawyer Quency, brought to Molise, abandoning the husband whom she remarried. The twin Assuntina married Cosmo Donato Rivosordo, a boat master who had been crippled during a smuggling operation off the coast of Lybia. Assuntina and Cosmo give birth to Simone, who was sent to study in a seminary, which he later abandoned. After the Second World War, they emigrate to Detroit and his sister Adele, the ex-nun, summoned her brothers, paid for their tickets and bought them a house in Detroit on State Fair Street and Gratiot Avenue, where Saverio and Basso grew up. While these two of her sons knew a fair amount of Italian, Cosmo expressed himself exclusively in his dialect. Simone, on the other hand, had made a career, if not a decent living, for himself in academia, while his brothers had made their money through their business friendships, which weren't always entirely clean. Simone had met both Nebraska Dope and Larry at a jazz concert in New Haven in 1961 when he taught at Yale. Larry, who was dark skinned, though lighter than his father and a little closer to the hazy, marine color of the Donato family as a whole—including Simone—was a budding guitarist/composer of great genius. He was nevertheless entirely immersed in the political and racial problems of the time and fought for them, like Martin Luther King and others, on various American campuses. He was enrolled in law school at Ann Arbor, and he lived "temporarily" on the floor above the Donato family, in the attic. Cosmo couldn't handle it because, to him, he was a "black"; and even the neighbors frowned on him, with the exception of the two lesbians on the block, who invited guys of all kinds to their parties, and probably smoked. Larry got into trouble with everybody, even the police, because he was thought to be an instigator, and he participated in the strikes. Cosmo Donato Rivosordo eventually kicked him out. A few days later they found out that he had been killed (his skinned corpse was found in the river) by the big ex-Nazi bartender at Grosse Point's private club, the *Beowolf*, with the help of another inhabitant of State Fair, Cop Sorge, another racist, like almost everybody else on that street, who often read Heidegger. One of the stockholders and members of the board was Basso. The rest is a thriller.

Here Rimanelli concludes his synopsis (written November 11, 1996). I could add, for the benefit of those readers who have yet to read *Detroit Blues*, that many other events are eventually grafted on to the outline Giose has furnished. After having arrived at his father's house in Detroit, Simone's introspective and detective-style investigations begin as he finds himself, since he is in Detroit, dramatically living through the racial problems that erupt in those years as well as the subsequent African-American revolts, from which he will eventually flee, mounting a (stolen) bicycle in order to catch the first available flight out, while at his back, grimly, between rebellion and repression, screams and gunfire between the rebels and the police continue to ring out.

We can now approach the novel in greater detail, starting from the title and its epigram:

The sun gonna shine in my back door some day,
The wind gonna rise and blow my blues away...

Two verses from an old popular ballad from the deep South, which seem to be just thrown haphazardly out there, really present an important linguistic clue: they announce the seductive allure, or rather the jazzy-psalmodic rhythm with which the novel is preparing to unfurl itself.

Jazz, as we know, is an African-American genre of music characterized first and foremost by its rhythm (it is the most important element that survives from African culture), and it also has a melodic matrix from improvisation and from a vocal and instrumental timbre characteristic of the popular songs from which jazz historically arose: work songs (those sung by black slaves), gospel and rituals (religious songs), and above all the blues: that is, popular songs characteristically secular, derived from the work songs of the slaves. The blues, an essential component of jazz, features recurring harmonic schemes and rhythmic formulas, and it is made up of melodies based on a tonal scale that often oscillates in an indefinite way between the major and minor keys, thanks to the presence of what are called blue notes, or rather notes that lend the blues a peculiar tonal indefiniteness, inasmuch as in a harmony in a major scale they will be lowered a half-tone, as though they belonged to the minor scale. Though this might seem like an extra-literary tangent, Rimanelli was, after all, a musicologist and composer. The importance of music in his work is widely recognized. The specific influence of jazz dates all the way back to the distant 1950s when he published *Una posizione sociale*, which also included a record by the Lambro Jazz Band from Milan, featuring his own original compositions. But here the epigraph, beyond its jazz rhythm, sets the tone for what might be seen as the overarching meaning of the novel, which is already implicit in the music itself: the base conditions of African Americans in the Detroit of the 1950s and '60s, their longing for liberation, their marginalization, their desperation that perhaps only music could (and still can) mitigate.

This is how the particular character of popular expression inherent to this type of music is related to the concept of a novel as a general fresco of an epoch and of the milieu characteristic of Detroit in those years. Charged with the task of transmitting this expressive polyphony is the language, Rimanelli adopts: a pastiche of Italo-English laden with charm. And here we touch immediately on an exegetical aspect, which in *Detroit Blues* is of central importance, and which I will explore in greater detail in a moment.

Another stylistic characteristic that runs windingly through the entire novel is that constituted by sudden shifts in tone and address detected in the narratorial voice: namely, the informal direct address adopted by the narrator every so often, which creates a reflexive detachment or a certain emotional distance from the protean narrative subject matter: a seeing, a seeing oneself, and a being seen that run simultaneously through the mind of the reader, who, though fully aware of the illusions at work in Rimanelli's house of mirrors, risks at various points getting trapped in the sap, no longer able to distinguish reality from its illusory reflection in the mirror.

It is the game of the double and its fleeting identification, already announced in the title of the initial segment ("Larry, chi?"; "Larry, who?"), which at certain points finds an extremely shocking representation over the course of the novel as the reader slowly comes to discover the striking resemblance between the protagonist Simone and Larry, "il bastardo di casa" ("the bastard of the house"), "lo scioperato Larry" ("strike-happy Larry"), the ambiguous Larry, the black sheep, and, above all, the temperamental musical genius who was barbarously murdered for racial reasons.

Regarding the informal direct address ("tu") as a narrative form adopted by the novelist to detach himself from his "divided first-person I," the protagonist who narrates the story, there is a whole line of extremely efficacious precedents. I am thinking of a couple of cornerstones: for example, the father of the *nouveau roman,* Michel Butor's *Modification* (1957) and Carlos Fuentes's *Aura* (1962). In *Detroit Blues,* the second person is invoked with reservation and is used only when the narrator feels the need to create a space between himself and the content of his narration, though it is seen through the eyes of the protagonist. One could say, in other words, that there is one Rimanelli who is doubled in Simone—the one in the story who acts in unison with the other characters— another Rimanelli investigator of History (this time with a capital "H") who places himself behind the character. He studies him, follows him like a bloodhound, investigates him, comments on his actions. Here too, though implicitly stated, the hardboiled element and extremely open, volatile character of the novel is apparent: it is obvious that it will never be resolved; it can never come to a close: the protagonist will in fact get married in other para-biographical novels (*Benedetta in Guysterland* and *Accademia*), as though recounting episodically the incessant continuum of the life of the novel as well as his life in the novel, and, at the same time, the incessant continuum of the novel in his life. The "finale" can only come with the end of the novelist's life *tout court*. From this point of view, the literally unsettling profound mechanism is set in motion in his most recent novels, written directly in English.

Returning again to his use of the informal direct address ("tu"), Rimanelli is only able to make discrete, syncopated use of it, also because he doesn't intend to transgress the character of the fresco that he is laying out. His novel could resemble a retable across which that investigative "tu" flashes like a lighthouse beacon, illuminating its innermost hidden recesses and clarifying the opaque implications that progressively trip it up. Indeed it is significant that over the course of many pages this "tu" is eliminated in favor of linguistic expansion and intermingling; however, it resurfaces just at the moment in which it resumes following the urgency of the facts, demonstrating not only the extremely complex nature of the novel— the temporal effects of its Janus-faced origin as diary/novel—but also the author's need to effectively render that objective detachment from the narrative voice (see the exemplary beginning of Chapter V and the various "repetitions" within it and following [35]).

Naturally, having gone down this dual-natured and intertwined road, in a manner of speaking, it can happen that the narrator allows himself to be led by the hand hither, thither, and yon where like a character behind the curtains shadowing (with that "tu") his Simone

making him his excessive "daemon," with risky relapses into manifestly self-indulgent pockets. In the end Rimanelli is the only one
who profoundly knows his double, his witty remarks, his weak-
nesses, his farsightedness, his moods, his *present memory*. Not in-
frequent in this regard are certain sudden autobiographical interjec-
tions (moments of great narrative happiness); extremely brief little
flashes, like spontaneous epiphanies in which gestures and recesses
of his childhood are illuminated (the seminary in Ascoli Satriano,
his maternal figure, his tormenting ambivalence with respect to his
sexual urges that he had either to repress or express, etc.). These are
fleeting moments, jolts perfectly assimilated into the pop-music pace
of Rimanelli's writing, which unravels gradually like a sort of novel-
ballad, entirely conceived in the semi-tones of a blues rhythm, aided
by a rhymed and schizo-morphic prose style.

In his prose, by means of an amalgam of extremely versatile
elements, he experiments with a vast array of rhetorical solutions:
from the refined to the plebian, from humanistic learning to the
memory of popular traditions transmitted to Rimanelli orally (represented for the most part by the conflictual father figure), which is
expressed by means of a Verga-esque technique, in his inclusion of
proverbs; Italianized English idiomatic phrases ("ho suonato un
campanello nella tua memoria," 82; which corresponds to the English idiom: "It rings a bell!"), and the constant slipping from the en-
trance and exit into (and out of) English, until he arrives at a dense
plurilinguism, that often spontaneously manifests itself as a natural
consequence of the discourse; a union (Italian–English–dialect–
slang) not to be understood as pure and simple commingling, but
precisely as a natural, fluid interference of one language within (with)
the other:

> Dalla Calabria alla Costa Azzurra e intorno alle spiagge a sud della
> Spagna hanno costruito e costruito condomini, alberghi, golf courses
> and roads have razed pine forests, flattened dunes, creando penuria
> d'acqua e incoraggiando gli incendi. [...] Well my friends, stavo pro-
> prio adesso passando per questa lovely city of yours perché la mia
> missione has a universal worth. (98-99)

[From Calabria to the Costa Azzurra and around the beaches in the south of Spain they built and built condominiums, hotels, golf courses and roads have razed pine forests, flattened dunes, creating a shortage of water and encouraging fires. [...] Well my friends, I was just now passing through this lovely city of yours because my mission has a universal worth.]

Here we have arrived at the central problem of the whole novel, namely, the particular language Rimanelli chose to write it in. But more than mere pastiche, a distinction so in vogue with the whole experimentalism of the 1960s, what we have here is a truly unique Rimanellian idiolect, given that the author does not limit himself to the simple interweaving of the two languages in the same sentence (Italian and English). His personal idiolect incorporates slang and dialect forms, conscious and unconscious Englishisms, popular sayings and proverbs, idioms, learned quotations, and phrases drawn from American slang. A little earlier I cited a few examples of this linguistic-syntactic-semantic fusion, which, from Chapter Thirteen on, seems to reach its highest concentration and is often shamelessly exhibited on the page.

Of this versatile amalgam it remains to be determined whether a voluntary willfulness underlies his eccentricity or if, rather, a metalinguistic automatism is behind it. I would be inclined to accept the latter hypothesis if I weren't already so familiar with the literally histrionic ability of Rimanelli's use of language. The problem is destined to remain open, especially when it comes to his rarefied way of capturing dialogue that he presents in fragments of just a few words:

"Savy might end up killed... like Larry. E noi con lui. Noi especially."
"Perché especially?"
"They call us *nigger lovers*."

"Well, he was pushing inside the truck a black boy, così disse Larry."
"E che vuol dire?"
"Quel camioncino è una ghiacciaia... His best food, *Black Magyk*, is sold frozen..."

"Voleva essere assassinato, Larry?"
"No. Ma io non predico, forse, che non esiste colored skin or white skin?" (1241f.)

Here, there is the risk of creating an effective incongruence especially for the reader who doesn't know either English or Italian. This last issue is a question of considerable importance, which I'm not sure if Rimanelli ever fully addressed.

Another problem he would have to address is the question of possible translations into other languages, which I consider to be nearly an impossible feat to accomplish. All of which brings us to another consideration: *Detroit Blues* is perhaps, indeed, the first actual novel by an Italian-American writer written for an Italian-American reader, just as *Benedetta in Guysterland* (published in 1993 though it was written many years earlier) is the first novel written, significantly, in English, by an Americo-Italian for an Americo-Italian readership.

Detroit Blues reflects the plurilingualism of the author and is, in fact, a novel written in a directly plurilingual way, inasmuch as its plurilingualism is not the result of an applied process (namely, first written in Italian, then alternated with English), rather, it is the result of a natural process cultivated over the very course of its creation, that is, organically in the midst of its narrative development, with effects not only of absolute linguistic interchangeability, but of natural semantic completion in either language, co-inhabiting by now naturally in the mind of the author-writer. It is significant that the novels written after *Detroit Blues* (*Benedetta in Guysterland*, *Accademia*, and *The Three-legged One*) were written entirely in English.

Linguistic cohabitation is so much more evident in *Detroit Blues* when both registers—something that occurs even more predominantly in the second part—are employed: either given directly in their continuum, or in English, followed immediately by the saying also in Italian. This operation is not to be confused with the Italianized English of our emigrants, the so-called *Italese*, to which scholars like Herman Haller (I have in mind his 1993 essay *Una lingua perduta e ritrovata*) and novelists like Rodolfo Di Biasio (alluding to his

1991 novel *I quattro camminanti*) have devoted much fruitful attention. This is not what Rimanelli is intent on recovering, but, as I said, he is more interested in the direct collage that a luxuriant interlinguistic and plurilinguistic fusion produces (Italian, English, dialect, American slang), at times not even objecting to certain particular idiomatisms that only an Anglo-Americanist would be able to catch. Here are another couple of examples, both with and without the approximation in Italian:

La filosofia di Jahbuch era a tutti nota, e forse era quella di tutti, anche della polizia. "These scum aren't people... We oughta gas these niggers—they're ruining the country." Questa feccia non è gente... Dobbiamo gassare questi negri—stanno rovinando il paese.

"[...] qualcuno mi ha detto oggi, al Museo d'Arte Moderna, che è finito il tempo in cui tagliavamo nel grasso. E ha aggiunto che it is Now meat and bone."
"E che vuol dire dire?" tuo padre chiede. Poi ci ripensa. "È come dico io, allora. A carne sóp'a l'sse luce."
"La carestia stringe, Cosmo. Laos, Cambodia, Burma, Vietnam, Cuba... Never trust anybody over 30, etcetera. E una donna ha detto, sempre al Museo, che life's a nightmare. Vai a letto col tuo corpo intatto, ha detto, e ti risvegli without your arms and legs."

"Detective? Ah certo! Le pistole sotto la giacca. Per questo stavate a spiare nella nostra casa e su quella strada? I'm going. Let me go!"
"Sorry, Prof!"
L'uomo coi baffoni poggiò la sua larga mano sulla tua testa, e la chiuse come in una morsa.
"Don't move!" Quindi la ritirò. Disse: "Spero che voi non vogliate veramente end up in quella bara, come vostro cugino, vero? Listen now, carefully." (122ff.)

And so this brings us to the last section of the novel, whose vertiginous crescendo must be underlined, at which point in the fiction a series of real episodes begins to appear, which the author is able to relive through a series of first-hand documents. Literary invention gives way to chronicle and history through narrative segments that resemble journalistic dispatches: in their tragic urgency they demand no ulterior narrative discardings. The narration grows anxious rhythmic, pounding, frenetic, like a long syncopated blues that accentuates its pacing slowly as the chronicling of the facts relative to the revolt of the blacks becomes more tense and intense, more strident and dramatic. At this point the "tu" ("you") becomes "voi" (second person plural "you all") as though by necessity, on the part of the narrator, of a choral vision of the whole, in which, among other things, the influence of cinematographic technique is not absent; I think, for example, of the so-called tracking shot, where the movie camera (analogous, ideally, to the eye and pen of the director-writer) follows in a continuous take the actions of the various characters in a scene. All of which, once again, serves the author's basic need to *expand* the expressive power of his language that remains the fundamental characteristic of this novel.

But, zeroing in on the conclusion, this multi-expressive expansion is still the means and not the final end of *Detroit Blues* (of course, these are the means to which Rimanelli's exegetes should return in order to comprehensively study his irregular writing machine). In Rimanelli the aspiration to interrogate the history he has traversed is profound, inescapable, whether as an attentive witness (who is also at the same time detached) or as an expatriate Italian writer in America in search of an old "patria" that no longer exists, as well as a new "patria" that does not allow itself to be easily adopted.

In the wandering of those who find themselves "perennemente fuoriposto" ("perennially out of place") even the concept of exile fails: it merely becomes the fundamental awareness of not belonging, and *Detroit Blues* could, indeed, be considered a novel of non-belonging, if it is considered exclusively on the basis of this reflection: the proof of which is found in the unsettling investigation into the identity of Larry, the character that acts as a counterpoint to Simone. While Simone investigates Larry, the investigator investigates himself at the same time, in a narrative arabesque that often has something of the detective novel.

But Rimanelli's other soul, that of the passionate research scholar, brings him to reflect on the past (as well as recognize his reflection in it) in order to better understand his own personal history in History. Above all, when history forcibly erupts into the writer's life at a certain point, with all of the impetuous violence connected to the centenary vexations the blacks in this country have suffered, he is profoundly shaken by it. At this point the private mixes with the public; the public brutally invades his private life. Rimanelli, who had lived through that torrid July of 1967, but also the following decades, knows, in rewriting that feverish diary, how premonitory those upheavals in Detroit were, for example, with respect to the even more tragic events of 1968, the year in which Robert Kennedy and Martin Luther King were assassinated. He knows that those years and those events changed the face of America forever. He also knows, finally, contrary to the feeling of not belonging that he also possesses, that these were not years lived in vain: they *belonged to him*, they belong, that is, to a past that cannot be eluded, but, if anything, reexamined and reinterrogated in order to understand its (as well as his own) errors, omissions, joys, and illusions.

5. On Rimanelli's Exoteric Narratives

It will be clear, having come to this point in the chapter, that in the vast and chaotic body of Giose's work, those literary pieces he wrote directly in English, from the 1990s on, occupy a privileged place by now undeniable, and represent the creative plurilingualism of this cosmopolitan writer. He is Italian, American, Italian American, Americo-Italian, Ur-Canadian, and Molisano (on this topic I use these geographical genealogies in order to emphasize the parallel linguistic ancestors who informed first diachronically, then synchronically his work): Italian and English and French and Italo-American slang—which makes its first appearance between 1953 and 1954, the year that Rimanelli completed a draft of *Biglietto di terza*—and even Medieval Latin, and, last, but not least, Molisano dialect, a sort of ideal buckle on the belt of his literary biography that binds Rimanelli to his native land. Not only does this cosmopolitan output attest to his plurilingualism, it also demonstrates the existence of his formidable writer's mechanic shop that worked on, and continues to do so to this day, multiple cars at the same time, or, if you will, only on one car, until he forces it to become "paranoica" ("paranoid"), intended in the literal and allusive sense: I think again of the title of Rimanelli's personal Zibaldone, to which I have referred on numerous occasions in the previous pages, titled *La macchina paranoica*, from which Rimanelli has from time to time excerpted various clips, rewriting them, and presenting them in stand-alone works.

I also want to clarify that all the conjunctions I used above to link the languages that Rimanelli has put to use over the course of his career are to be considered, rather than simple conjunctions, full-fledged hendiadys that serve to express a single concept, namely, Italian; but there is English; but then there's Italo-North American slang, but then also Molisano dialect, etc. etc.

Just such an extremely complex and stratified process has brought Rimanelli in recent years to the creation of an idiolect all his own, though it is also the fruit of a dense hybridization. We just witnessed it in the reading of an exemplary novel like *Detroit Blues*, in which this idiolect resolves itself in a dense linguistic amalgamation in which all the various formal registers combine in a single uninterrupted continuum.

A writerly organism, therefore, that, seen as a whole, suddenly seems to be of difficult collocation and fruition as a result of its experimental and pluri-perspective nature. And it is foreseeable that Rimanelli's future exegetes will debate among themselves Rimanelli's many faces pulling his work in one direction or another; one that pulls toward the shores of a realism that is painted in neo-decadentist colors and thus establishes a connection between the novelist from Calenda and the great tradition of naturalism and Euro-American post-decadentism (from Gustav Flaubert to Thomas Mann and André Gide; from William Faulkner to Tennessee Williams to the cultural hybridization of Nabokov, but even to Verga, Tozzi, Svevo, Alvaro, and Pavese in the Italian tradition); the other, in turn, that pulls toward the shores of an exasperated para-avant-garde experimentalism mixed with the desecrating verbal game that has its matrix in Lewis Carroll and continues then through Joyce, Pound, Burgess, with discardings, contaminations, and excesses that can even be traced back to Dadaism, the Beat Generation (Kerouac's nomadic literature, for example), from the musical suggestions of Edgard Varèse, John Cage, and from the vast and variegated North American season of jazz and blues.

In fact, since the scene has shifted to the United States, we should also keep in mind the influence of Pop Art (which I have already mentioned above) and the rhythmic idiom of certain black writers (like Ralph Ellison), that finds its two most representative archetypes in the emotional expressiveness of Richard Wright and in the syncopated gait of Langston Hughes.

I realize at this point of my treatment of Rimanelli's work that the backfill of all this cultural geography may seem overwhelming, but filling this gap responds precisely to the demands his output in English (and not only in English) makes of the reader who has an Italian as well as an American perspective. It should not be ignored that at this point in his life Rimanelli had lived in North America, although for more than fifty years his permanent residence often has been interrupted by more or less frequent travels, and that the novels written in Italy, though foundational for his opus, account for no more than three: *Tiro al piccione*, *Peccato originale*, and *Una posizione sociale*, whose title was later changed to *La stanza grande* for the second edition. The first draft of *Biglietto di terza*, though it precedes the latter of these, had indeed been written, as we have seen, between Canada and the United States.

So after *Biglietto di terza*, excluding *Una posizione sociale*—whose narrative, in fact, depends on research conducted in the United States, particularly in New Orleans, the birthplace of his maternal grandfather Tony (Dominick) Minicucci, where the famous massacre of eleven Italians occurred in 1891, the massacre that would later come to be known as "The New Orleans Lynching," that Dominick had witnessed—all of the following novels, and at this point we can even add all of Rimanelli's poetic and critical work (with the exception of *Mestiere del furbo* of 1959), was written by Rimanelli in large part outside Italy, which is to say, in America.

This work can therefore rightly be inscribed—if it must be "catalogued" as a whole—under the rubric of exotic literature, or, even better, exoteric, or rather, expansive, "external," not enclosed in a restricted space but open, centrifugal, evident. I use the term "exoteric" as the opposite of "esoteric," which indicates instead something "internal," something "reserved" for the few, something "hidden."

His is not only, after all, an "ex-patriate," but literally an "expanse" literature, namely, one that departs from situational circumstances in order to expand beyond. This is the source of his character, which has been called cosmopolitan, nomadic, and of the frontier ("border writing"), as Fred Gardaphé happily argued, stating that just one culture is not enough for Rimanelli, who, more than an Italian or an American or an Italo-American writer, is a border writer, a tradition that unites writers like Kafka, Nabokov, Borges, and Gabriel García Márquez (Gardaphé 1996, 112). Last but not least, this is also the source of his plurilinguistic character, which has such illustrious precedents; the cases of Pound or Joyce or Beckett or Nabokov are again extremely opportune, obviously beyond any particular product and any single modality and any specific expressive ideology.

It is, to be sure, within this mobile epicenter of exquisite postmodern manufacture that we should collocate his first two American novels, *Benedetta in Guysterland* and *Accademia*, whose initial drafts date to 1970 and 1975 respectively.

6. *Benedetta in Guysterland:* The Caricature Effect of a Collage-Novel

The genesis of *Benedetta in Guysterland* has already been thoroughly documented in a valuable 1995 essay by Romana Capek-Habekovic, an attentive reader of Rimanelli's work, who presents an abundance of references and a richness of details, in large part furnished by Rimanelli himself (Capek-Habekovic 1995, 35-58). Taking her extremely useful work as my point of departure, my goal here is then to enter deeper into the structural and compositional nerve center of this novel, while seeking at the same time to illuminate a web of intertextuality that her reading has suggested to me over time.

Written in Albany, New York, in October 1970, *Benedetta in Guysterland* fully reflects the linguistic revolution of Rimanelli's writing that had already been thrown into a state of alarm by previous experiments that herald it in a most unequivocal way, experiments I have already sufficiently addressed. *Detroit Blues* is, along with *Graffiti*, the most evident example. And it is worth mentioning again the fact that the first chapter of the latter novel was published in the French translation of Lucrezia Rotolo and Jean Paris in the May 1972 issue of *Change*, which also just happened to be exclusively dedicated to linguistic and structural studies on James Joyce. The names of these two translators subsequently appear in *Benedetta in Guysterland* (230-233) in one of the "reports" Giose requests from various international writers and scholars, undoubtedly one of the most illuminating of those he solicited and received at the time, and that he duly collected and mentioned in an appendix, a further confirmation of the composite (as in a mosaic) and metatextual character of this novel.

Machine e montage and *Opera buffa*—the titles Rimanelli gave to the note he sent Jean Paris on this occasion and to the chapter published in *Change* respectively—give us preliminary clues as to how we should read this novel; a novel that is in large part driven by precisely the mechanisms of the assembly, disassembly, and reassembly of pre-existing writing, and the general idea of a ludic and burlesque work.

The double procedure of "montage" and "burlesque," proceeding from a spirit of self-conscious literary experimentation, is furthermore underlined by the author himself in the peritext, here crudely present, but which has always constituted a fundamental characteristic of the metatextual narratives of our author:

A collage for sure. [...] This is a research book. In literature, a research book is a critical book most of the time. Never a novel, however. Instead I wanted to do a novel based on research, hence on language. I wanted to tease my mind. I wanted to tease your mind. I can't say, therefore, like Flaubert, "*Madame Bovary c'est moi.*" This *Benedetta* is a worldly creature. We all contributed to her creation. (214)

Thus, literature as a game and the game of literature; playing provocatively with words and turning them into a game, with the author putting himself at stake in the game. A concept of *mischief* and *delight* typical of all the historic avant-gardes, which, however, as we will see shortly, dawns in faraway lands (having its certain archetypes in Laurence Sterne and Jonathan Swift) and arises even in Italian writers, in the wake of writers like James Joyce and Wyndham Lewis (the first Italian names that come to mind are those of Palazzeschi and Landolfi, though they are so different from each other and, of course, also very different from Rimanelli).

It is interesting to note that the concluding phrase of the above-cited passage calls *Benedetta* "a worldly creature," with an obvious pun on "world" and "word": Benedetta as a worldly/wordy creature, or rather pertaining to the world of words and to the words of the world.

It is, in my opinion, precisely in acknowledging this fact that we can detain it, capturing it ideally on one of those momentary pins, the butterfly-writing Benedetta represents, both as an elusive character, who continually slips the grasp of the reader who is poised to catch her, and as a mercurial, *liquid* creature made of nothing more than words.

This is the source of the *caricatural effect* of the novel, which is the global icon under which it can be inserted, on the one hand, and, on the other, the natural, necessary use, on the part of the author, of other writings in order to construct it (just as one would assemble a playful puzzle piece by piece), or rather of writings other than his own.

The final peritextual solution then seems perfectly consequential. Having virtually exempted himself of his responsibilities, having been "absent," the writer will eventually ask others (his readers) for a report or final judgment on an artistic technique *à la* Duchamp that

146

saw its *artifex* having the time of his life on the other side of the glass the entire time:

> I don't know if I know. This is why I asked for a report. Though knowing that I know every line of the book, its composition, the end-result that I hoped to achieve, still let the others tell me what it is all about. (214)

7. THE VERBO-MENTAL PUPPET THEATER OF *BENEDETTA IN GUYSTERLAND*

A temporal-linguistic outburst and a verbal-mystificatory game pushed to the max, in fact, seem to constitute from the beginning of *Benedetta in Guysterland* the most relevant expressive aspect. What we have here is a sort of spontaneous act of verbal creation, also often provoked through lexical deformations in the same word. "I have a mind to confuse things," the authorial voice says at one point with shameless candor. This is then how, as though spilled carelessly onto the page, words intertwine with one another through rhyme and assonance, as in a little verbal-mental puppet theater, frenetically changing costumes with each other, and thus reciprocally bringing something of themselves to bear on the others they gang up with. The following is a series of excerpted examples whose phonic alliterative game can only be appreciated in the original:

> Pressing my nose to the window pane, hiding the pain (37)
> In the room filled with the soft wisper of the fan and the subtle throb of a drum (37)
> And sent me upstair, in the past. Just a narrow room with naked neon blasts. (44)
> Pursued by visions of hell. You can tell it, by the smell (44)
> Pheromones are really sort of airborne hormones (44)

In these examples, the linguistic overturning occurs not only on the basis of any single alliteration, but penetrates even the semantics of the text with a strong deviation from the norm and a decisive upsetting of any expectation. The whole is determined by means of a capricious act of the will, and thus serves the "dada" spirit evoked in the title of the first peritext *For-a-word* (a play on *Foreword*) that immediately preceeds the story: "As dada rock gets worse, outdoor micro-boppers get better" (27).

His decision to resort to the non-sensical casuality of a Dadaist matrix fits perfectly in the context of the composite, mosaic framework of *Benedetta in Guysterland*. We find the recipe in one of Tristan Tzara's seven sulphurous manifestos, *Manifesto on Feeble Love and Bitter Love* (Tzara 1964, 51-61), where in order to construct a Dadaist text Tristan Tzara provocatively recommends that the words be cut from an article in any old periodical, and that they then be extracted one by one at random from a bag in which they have been placed and "delicately" shaken. This technique will be recovered several decades later by William Burroughs, who, along with Marcel Duchamp, is still to this day one of the most audacious experimenters in radically altering the compositional material of literary and artistic production. The whole is dispatched with extreme liberatory intentions in which freedom, play, and provocation are interchangeable synonyms ("I love words. Not mine, not anymore. Because liberation is at the corner of your mouth. Why plan a plot, then? The afternoon is a narrow sheet of light wind," *Benedetta in Guysterland*, 29). Where the statement: "Liberation is at the corner of your mouth" seems to irresistibly echo Tzara's "thought is formed in the mouth" (written entirely in upper case in the *Manifesto* in question, 53).

The "words" that the Dadaist leader told us to extract from any old newspaper or magazine, Rimanelli draws—essentially with the objective of formal diegesis in mind, which reflects his Anglophone education—from "Esquire," the magazine that launched Pietro Di Donato and was also read voraciously by Rimanelli in his formative years. *Benedetta in Guysterland* is dedicated to this very magazine ("This work of random lines is dedicated to my best English prep-school teacher: *Esquire* mag"). At point n. 5 in the appendix (which presents 22 points for clarification), the reason behind this unusual dedication is explained (in which beyond *Esquire* two other dedicatees are mentioned: Guy Talese "for having suggested this work" (an allusion to the fact that some of the characters and situations were inspired by his reading of Talese's *Honor Thy Father*, passages of which had appeared in *Esquire*) and finally Pietro Corsi for having "saved him from destruction"):

> I learned English from *Esquire*. An Italian antifascist thinker, who died in prison a long time ago, once told his children that the best way to learn a foreign language is to start translating it, word by word, with the help of a dictionary. That man was Antonio Gramsci. I welcomed the suggestion, and when I turned *Esquire* mag was near at hand. It happened many years ago in Italy, on a crowded beach after the war. For years I exercised by translating bits of articles from that magazine. (223-224)

A pluri-perspective first-person narrative voice addressing another interlocutor (for all intents and purposes identified as Joe Adonis) seems to constitute, both dialogically and autologically, the novel's central axis. It consists of a para-diaristic narrative voice (the diaristic framework will figure even more predominantly in his next novel *Accademia*), identifiable as that of Benedetta; a voice that roams in the realm of a "grand present" in which past moments and future projections flow freely. What we have here is an implacable river that moves with extreme mobility in a sort of continuous round trip from the mind to the page and vice versa: "These thoughts live in my mind as they appear on paper, muddled and, as I only know too well, unorganized" (40).

Therefore, a full-fledged mental *parlerie* simultaneously spills out onto the author as well as the reader, who finds few points of comparison in any other writer in the Italian twentieth century: the first example that comes to mind is Palazzeschi's *Piramide*. They are the effects of the collage-novel and of the linguistic and inter-nominal intermingling (Gela Gelaturo; Muscolini / Musolini; Al Scorpione / Al Capone; Lu Cane / Lucky Luciano; etc.): a "linguistic mosaic," as Fred Gardaphé has intelligently written in the Preface, of whose parodic nature, which so permeates the entire novel, there can be no doubt.

And it is above all through the exercise of parody that Rimanelli exorcises "the obsessive fascination" of the Mafia by defamiliarizing it from all traditional stereotypes tied to Italo-American gangsterism, with comic linguistic effects, *mutatis mutandis*, that in certain moments call to mind even the irresistible parody of *Pépé le Moko*, just as the unrivaled Antonio de Curtis gave it to us in 1949 in *Totò le Moko*, directed by Carlo Ludovico Bragaglia, where the actor throws himself into continual linguistic acrobatics as a Neopolitanized ".Algerian."

It is from here that the complex sense of pantomime or theatrical burlesque springs forth, which proceeds through continuous accumulation (the third chapter is truly a ludic-linguistic tour-de-force) in a syncopated pop rhythm, made of scraps and snippets, boutades and provocations, sudden stops and sudden starts. Thus, results a schizo-morphous narration, highly alliterative, that does not distain, in any way, the allure of jazz, within which the words dance together, with their rhymes, assonances, and chain link of crisscrossing references, those that Freud called "ponti di parole" (Freud 1973, 200-201; "word bridges").

Such writing, made up of many kinds of writing, or rather a kind of writing that makes light of itself, cannot help but take up antiphrasis as its principal rhetorical trope that so perfectly serves it. Antiphrasis is the trope that consists in saying the exact opposite of what is intended either ironically or euphemistically; and therefore, in this case, Rimanelli employs it as a sort of self-reflexive parody of the very language he uses. Linguistic self-parody creates, thus in this way, within the narration, a whole series of references-echoes, intended not only to provide a bubbly phraseological rhythm internal to the Rimanellian page, but also to lend it, on the whole, the tone of a ballad of quasi-epic proportions, if we allow "epic" to enjoy a popularizing semantic, or rather something of the "grandiose" that is, however, also at the same time "playful" (a stellar example is Rabelais' *Gargantua*, which, among other things, Jean Paris proposes as a point of reference for the name *Guysterland*: "Guysterland refers to Rabelais' Gaster episode, the monstruous meals being translated, here, into those wonderful sex scenes," 231). In the initial peritext it is Rimanelli himself who defines *Benedetta in Guysterland*, more than once, as a "ballad": a post-modern ballad, of course, that utilizes all of the mass-media instruments and broadcast mechanisms of contemporary popular culture.

This ballad or "psychological fable" recalls in part—as I mentioned above—that of Lewis Carroll's *Alice*, while turning the terms on their head: there "una bambina che racconta la favola del suo strano viaggio in un mondo adulto" ("a little girl who tells the story of her strange journey into an adult world"), here "Benedetta è un adulto che racconta la storia della sua vita in un mondo feroce di bambini, ovvero di uomini immaturi, ossessionati dal sesso e che giocano a fare i gangsters" (Gardaphé, cit., 114; "Benedetta is an adult who recounts the story of her life in a ferocious world of children, or rather of immature men, obsessed with sex and who play at being gangsters").

In *Benedetta in Guysterland*, the story is painstakingly concocted in the form of a long "confession" made up of the fragmentary and digressive perorations of the narrating character (Benedetta), who recounts to us all of her wanderings and misadventures. Her life story boils down to a struggle between mobs of gangsters, her imprisonment, various ruminations or reflections or flashbacks or oneiric projections that accompany her (for example, her relationship to her parents; with her mother Venerea, and most of all with her father Joseph). And finally her liberation that has all the ingredients and modalities of a comic ending.

8. THE EFFECT OF "OVERCROWDING" AND OF "EXCESSIVE REALITY"

Benedetta in Guysterland is a novel overflowing with revelry and symbolic places (that return in *Accademia*) like Nabokov County, Hawthorn, Appalachia ("land of the Mind"), Anabasis (where Benedetta's college/collage stands—a place of extreme passions and masturbations), Paliermu, la Gaia Scienza (the bar situated beneath the room in which Benedetta is locked up, an obvious parody of Nietzsche), and of real and usual characters like—beyond those that I've already mentioned—Zip The Thunder (a deformation of Zeus the Thunderer, *capo dei capi*, boss of all bosses, Benedetta's captor), Willie ("dead because the guys did not like the way he used to talk," 72), Hester (his wife, " the trapped housewife," 121), Fosco Fiaschetti (another boss, head of a mafia group, and, apparently, Joe Adonis' lieutenant), Holiday Inn Sinclair ("a typical patriarch, friend of the fetus and oppressor of the child," 128), Crystal, also known as Crystal Baby, who according to Zip is a "beautiful musician: she knows everything Madame Pompadour knew" (151).

And so a crowd of characters and places that combine to create the sense of a dilated fairytale in which desecration and mysticism, tenderness and cynicism, playfulness and eroticism, continually alternate with one another, often in long interior monologues, which in the second half of the twentieth century found their moments of greatest density in the mature narrative of Giuseppe Berto, but whose archetype for Rimanelli remains James Joyce. And from Berto (above all, in the erotic and moralistic dimension he insists upon, as though still in conflict with a father figure) Rimanelli then definitively distances himself because Giose knows how to masterfully insert into his narrative a sort of ironic post-modern falsetto—a category entirely absent (and foreign) in Berto—with the result of accentuating and distorting the parodic effect with which *Benedetta in Guysterland* is imbued. Chapters XII and XIII are culminating moments of this metamorphic linguistic paroxysm, which does not distain resorting to the theatrical. "Change is what makes us alive," one of the dialoging characters will emblematically state.

This is the effect of *overcrowding* or *excessive reality*, or even, if you will, thinking of Marinetti, of an intentional theatrical *exaggeration*, within which interlocutors like Boot and Sissy, and even Zip, overtly become pure mental inventions. Their performances, often overflowing with punch lines in which free linguistic play has a way of unleashing itself with greater agility, contribute to the sense of alienation in which the reader begins to get increasingly lost among the multiplication of the author's mental mirrors. It is as if he places at the reader's disposition a whole series of explanatory openings or factual references that, though departing from his *Erlebnis*, are dilated to paradoxical dimensions. A broad example is found in Chapter XIX, in which Rimanelli reflects on campus life at the college in Anabasis:

Yes, a place where vast expanses of time beat in your head like the steady roll of a snare drum. It is easy to feel lost, swimming in time among the everchanging, evermoving collages of leaf shadows, patterened on lighter green grass. The college is a place of extremes... (133)

A place where paradoxically the young people, though they have to forge their own cultural identity, are often sucked into a chaotic vortex and become victims of inconclusive foolish ambitions, tragic depressions, apparent sexual liberations, and ruthless power games. And the protagonists of this multicolored world are the various professors, hermits, nymphets, lesbians, pederasts, and overworked politicians, all acting within a hypocritical and puritanical academic respectability. This is a chapter that constitutes a clear anticipation of *Accademia*, a chapter/pamphlet written in a tone sarcastic and paradoxical, tender and ferocious.

The reflexive and monologuing tone gloomily accentuates itself more and more in the last part of *Benedetta in Guysterland*, until it reaches anxious moments of full-fledged verbal automatism, interrupted only here and there by para-theatrical passages. Language, Rimanelli seems to warn us, is like an achieved state of loss: we delude ourselves into thinking that we use it to communicate our thoughts; instead, the words that are supposed to clarify them, only render them incomprehensible. "Abbiamo solo questo sporco linguaggio con cui non capire" (174; "we only have this filthy language with which we cannot make ourselves understood"), the author will say in one brilliant intuition. Words are drops of water that drip uninterrupted down the great glass of life in which we reflect ourselves and, beyond which, we delude ourselves into seeing its drops on the other side.

9. DISTANCE, DIVERSITY, DIVERSION

The aforementioned traits of gloominess that Rimanelli seems to throw down on this page, casually or with mocking carelessness, are, nevertheless, only momentary. The author does not neglect the primary and ultimate end that drove him to write this novel, and that decisively drives him to write at all: "Why bother writing?," he asks himself in the last peritext (Chapter Six, 224). And he responds (to himself): "For the difficulty of it, I guess, and the fun of it. Writing as play may also mean writing as a source of lifestyle." It is a very important declaration that lies at the root of everything Rimenelli the experimenter achieved in the 1960s and '70s (and beyond): writing for fun and having fun writing, or rather di-verting himself through writing and distancing himself from the creatures of his creation. It is necessary to insist on this crucial aspect regarding which, from the theoretical and methodological point of view, I refer the reader to something I wrote on "play and literature" (Fontanella 1992, 151-158). For now it is sufficient to recall that in the famous distinction on the game played by Roger Caillois, or rather on *Agon* (enjoy-ment as competition), *Alea* (enjoyment as chance), mimicry (enjoy-ment as imitation or mimesis), and *Ilinx* (enjoyment as vital motivat-ing force), it is above all to these latter two categories that Rimanelli's novel legitimately belongs (Caillois 1967, 42-48).

I explored enjoyment as imitation above when I revealed the collage nature of *Benedetta in Guysterland*, which avails itself of the contributions of other writings. Here "mimesis" should be under-stood as the distancing of the author, or rather as the concealment of himself. Though participating in the game, the author is the mys-tery guest, whom Joyce calls the "unidentified guest," similar, in short, to one who anonymously crashes a big party, participating with the greatest pleasure without being recognized, without ever being iden-tified.

The other category delineated by Caillois is *Ilinx* or rather en-joyment as an extremely mobile, vital, and vertiginous driving force. As it turns out, this category will effusively pervade the novel, culmi-nating with a particular concentration in the last chapter.

The liberation of Benedetta will significantly correspond to an accentuated, *literally explosive* verbal liberation. The pistol fire of the various gangsters is also the tropological transposition of the ver-bal gunfire and fireworks of the author. The whole thing climaxes in a sort of *burlesque* or conclusive hullaballoo, which recalls that of

Detroit Blues, with the difference that here in *Benedetta in Guyster-land*, the dynamic of the actions are articulated in parodic verbal-mental dimension, while in *Detroit Blues* it is the result of a tension with a historical backdrop that actually existed and perhaps still exists to this day. And again: while in *Detroit Blues* the author is unable to *detach* himself from the story being told (he will reiterate in the appendix his intention of re-examining those historical events—the racial clashes of '67 on the eve of the assassination of Martin Luther King—which he had personally witnessed), in *Benedetta in Guysterland*, words act more like so many scattered pieces of a puzzle that demand to be assembled and capriciously disassembled: a toy that must be invented by reinventing the reality to which it belongs.

An alchemical and mercurial novel, *Benedetta in Guysterland* (effectively, *a liquid novel*, the structure of which Tamburri also discussed [1994, 477]) remains in my opinion one of the happiest and freest moments in Rimanelli's narrative world, in which the language of a novel becomes a novel of language. Language/desire that distills in a liquid form the very words themselves, as in transparent water/air, in order to dispatch them to other meanings, where a bite into an apple, can behave in such a way as to transform itself magically and playfully into a kite.

> Then, well. What's a word? An apple. And an apple? A thirst to bite. And a bite? A kite. (247)

10. *ACCADEMIA*

His penultimate narrative piece, written directly in English is *Accademia*, the first official announcement of which we find in the autobiographical chronology of *Molise Molise* under the title *Gli accademici*.

The original manuscript of this novel, much larger and more composite than the edition published in 1997 by Guernica, was called *The Three-Legged One: A Glossed Novel* (now available from Bordighera Press). It is not my intention to linger on the variegated period of gestation and subsequent reduced reformulation of *Accademia*, which would require a study of its own, and this is not an opportune moment to do so. Therefore, I will proceed to a reading of the version of *Accademia* that found its way into print, revealing first of all its para-diaristic framework ("The aim is not to remember but to save what I do not know in the moment that I know what I am not saving"), or rather conceived as a self-analytical excavation.

Some of the place names in *Benedetta in Guysterland* reappear here, like "Anabasis" (the town in which the events narrated in *Accademia* take place), "Nabokov County," "Appalachia," etc. But with respect to *Benedetta in Guysterland*, this new novel wants to put forth an epochal fresco. The novel's propulsive center is the life of an apparently calm and controlled American college. During the late 1960s or early 1970s, a myriad of issues mixed with one another, which lumped together sex and violence, equal rights for gays and lesbians, transcendental meditation, Woodstock, the fanciful, libertarian instances of "flower children," and, most of all, a sense of global happiness (that was, however, only apparent), and planetary solitude: a synthesis of the desperate vitality of those years.

At the center of this chaotic memorial bundle we find the reciprocally destructive relationship of a couple, Lisa and Simon Dona; the former, volatile and perverse, the latter, moralistic (I use the term "moralist" thinking of a writer like Flaiano).

The entire story is gloomily dominated by the presence of Death, which the first-person narrator establishes as a sort of cruel and self-destructive ballet:

> At the age of twenty came the resurrection after death in the Italian Civil War. At age thirty-five came my resurrection in America, after death in my native Selimo. And now, on the threshold of fifty, comes the new shattering blow that draws near. I am so conscious of witnessing myself dying it inebriates me with a new life. (31)

Here, it is not difficult to make out in the "Selimo" an anagram for "Molise" that is a reference to that anonymous signatory of the "confession" (Anonimo Selimano = the anonymous man from Molise) made by the narrating-narrator to Dr. Ralph Pepin of whom Riman-elli speaks in the appendix.

And it is through this male-female relationship that he weaves, on the one hand, the various senses of punishment the man inflicts on himself—who relates to his partner as both tormentor and vic-tim—and, on the other hand, the playing out of these perverse and ritualistic games between them, in a web of intricate ambiguities and morbid perfidy.

In short, a game of massacre from which emerges all the varie-gated, fatuous frivolity of a certain American mundane-intellectual-istic-bourgeois milieu, within which a true capacity to love and the drive to authentic passion seem to be forever lacking.

Accademia has Nabokov and Flaiano as its guardian angels, ideal points of reference; but it is entirely original is its meta-textual drive, made up of fragments from Lisa's diary (which occupies virtu-ally all of the second part of the novel), at times more erotic than others, but also pervaded by a subtle misogyny; diary from which—among other things—one infers bits of Giose's own autobiography, who intermittently allows himself to be taken by the hand, especially as the tragedy and the humor of the piece grow more exasperated and his self-indulgent dandyism is unable to counterweigh the sense of profound solitude that persecutes the narrative subject.

This treacherous game of love and death, internal to which sui-cide is considered the supreme form of self-criticism (100), seems therefore to constitute the central axis on which turns the bitter para-biographical story of *Accademia*. And it is precisely when solitude is reflected naked to itself and is revealed to itself (and to the reader) that the most persuasive and sincere pages of this novel are found, those, that is to say, that are stripped of the intellectualizing reflec-tions and digressions that are at times as didascalic as they are af-fected.

Furthermore, beyond the categories of "*troilismo*" and "voyeur-ism" (128-130), which play a fundamental role in the sexual dynam-ics of *Accademia*, a noteworthy introspective component emerges from the diaries, nourished precisely by the ménage à trios, insti-gated and desired by Lisa as an alibi for herself.

Also noteworthy is the symbolic dimension that accompanies *Accademia* and that finds its metaphorical culmination in the "murder" of Simon at the hands of two women, who bleed him to death: and in so doing fully serve his character, the one who "perceives reality in symbolic terms, attaching great importance to details" (137).

Accademia is, after all, the jagged story of a desperate love affair, garnished with sarcasm, perfidy, and nihilistic games of reciprocation. The last chapter of the novel, written through a wide-angle lens (vaguely in the Kerouac vein), is a continual alternation of past and present, as in an ideal panoramic that, among other things, confirms the cinematic framework of this endless and inconclusive work. In this sense, the final Pavesian bluesy signature is tormenting:

> Every thing comes to an end and everything starts all over again.
> I love the rain. (152)

Accademia is Giose Rimanelli's most "American" novel. In it his linguistic play seems to me neither as free nor as transgressive as *Benedetta*, full, as it is, of an intellectualizing and erudite *bruire* that stifles the parodic element present in *Benedetta in Guysterland*. *Accademia* is also the more bitter, tragic, and desperate novel of the two, which, however, also (and still) wants to debate and meditate on desperation as in an extreme ritual from which there is no hope of escape. In this sense *Accademia* is perhaps an even more problematic novel than *Benedetta in Guysterland*, a "romanzo fantastico a chiave" (roman à clef "fantastico"), as has been justly noted (Avarod 1998), which is in some way even more ambitious. And certainly future Rimanelli scholars will not be able to avoid it both on the basis of the dense literary referentiality it contains (Zenophon, Shakespeare, Carlo Gozzi, Freud, Jung, Nabokov), as well as on the basis of the comparative reading that necessarily demands to be performed against the original manuscript (*The Three-Legged One*), which here, constrained by space and scope, I have not been able to address.

11. EMIGRATION AS MEMORY, ART, DESTINY

> Quel caleidoscopio che intanto ora guardo, è quel barile
> di vino che ora quasi vuoto rotola pian piano giù per la
> stretta scala della vita, perché questa vita si restringe in se
> stessa ormai, ne conto le gocce rimaste cercando di fare
> un ultimo "paradigm" sul *dove, come* e *quando* del bevuto
> per infine poggiare la testa sulla pietra e dormire. Ma ri-
> cordo che in nessun luogo al mondo sono veramente ri-
> uscito a dormire più di qualche ora, dopodiché richi-
> udevo il libro nello zaino e riprendevo il cammino.

Rimanelli's most recent book (with respect to the moment in
which I am concluding this chapter) is called *Familia* (2000), a book
of emigration memories. The subtitle reads precisely just this: *Memoria dell'emigrazione.* In it the author reflects on himself and through
an uninterrupted stream of consciousness, memorial flood, records
the balance of a life, of his life as a writer. It is a work of restless,
yearning self-reflection that allows him to clarify—*à rebours*—his literary biographical journey. I would like, in concluding my discussion of Rimanelli, to proceed to a reading of this book that is in
many ways exemplary of an entire generation of expatriate Italian
writers, capable at times of illuminating the sense and the deep fur-
rows yoked to the Italian intellectual diaspora.

In the meantime, this section's epigraph is immediately useful to
my purposes—beyond its immediate, touching reception—in introducing this volume, which, broken into three segments, seems to
echo that triad of *where, how, when* contained precisely in my epigraph above.

The first segment, which Rimanelli calls "libro," a practice derived from his appetite as an impassioned reader of medieval and
humanistic texts, bears the title *Nonno Jazz* and refers to "emigration as memory," the first step in the itinerary of memory (the first
allegorical figure Rimanelli delineates is that of the "step" or *passo*),
composed of three distinct moments, each autonomous from the
other but united by the same theme: that of the family as a nucleus
that emigrates from one place to another (in this case from Molise

to North America), dragging with them the intact casket of the past and the open book of a future to be experienced in its entirety.

Already from these preliminary indications, the reader understands his personal memory will continue to flow, rooting itself in historical memory, sewn together with a connective thread along which the writer's zigzagging words stream (proceeding forward and backward).

Protagonist of the "first step" is Giose's maternal grandfather, Antonio Minicucci, aka Tony "Slim" Dominick (whom we met in the first pages of this chapter dedicated to Rimanelli's biographical intervention; we then encounter him again in the novel *Una posizione sociale*, also known as *La stanza grande*). Only here, in *Nonno Jazz*, Rimanelli delves deeper into the "romanticized" memory of Dominick, to study, with the scrupulous accuracy of a scholar, the historical, social, and cultural background of the geographical area in which (and of which) Tony was both participant and eyewitness: the Louisiana and in particular the New Orleans of the period straddling the end of the nineteenth and the beginning of the twentieth centuries; a chaotic city that would give rise to, and from there propagate like a contagious disease, jazz music, Dixieland jazz, from Dixie, with a particular reference to Louisiana and the city of New Orleans. The figure of Grandpa Dominick, with his trumpet that he plays whenever he wants, is like an icon that seduces the reader's attention with charismatic charm.

As in a silent film, the other ancestral characters on the trunk of his family tree dance like flickering projections across the screen: Seppe Rimanelli (his paternal grandfather) with his wife Maria Giuseppa Melfi, and, of course, his parents, Vincenzo Rimanelli and Concetta Minicucci (Concettina "Squeeze" Minicucci) who, born in Montréal in 1905, as we have already seen, was brought from Canada to Italy in 1913, only to expatriate there again at the end of Fascism, the regime that had always impeded her family from returning to North America (or more precisely, it had allowed her to leave Italian soil, inasmuch as she was born in Canada, but *without* her family).

These are years of "affliction and sacrifice"—key words, which for Rimanelli, brand like an indelible mark the first generation of emigrants. "Redemption," on the other hand, will be the key word for the following generation.

To the rhythm of the *bamboula* (referring to a sort of little drum struck with cow bones, and, by extension, to the eponymous dance) here then open as in a throbbing slice of life and adventure, bloody racism and mafia, exaltations and vexations, all-consuming passions and overwhelming lacerations, Bourbon Street, Congo Square, Franklin Street, and other legendary places of old-school New Orleans. It is here in these very streets and in these very squares that the author, with lucid and analytical archival research, mentally traces his grandfather's steps. This is also where the initial symptoms of Dixieland Jazz appear in its primordial form, which would soon spread, like a leaf seed on the wind, to other cities like Detroit, New York, and Chicago. In fact, in Chicago in 1915 the historic first record in this genre would be cut by the Original Dixieland Jazz Band, composed of a group of white musicians directed by Nick La Rocca (La Rocca's name should be remembered alongside other legendary founders like Buddy Boldew, Bunk Johnson, John Robichaux, Jack "Papa" Laine, and the "confrères" of La Rocca, Leon Rappolo and Tony Sbarbaro). And it is in these pulsating pages that the beat of the *bamboula* slowly seems to transform itself into the same insistent rhythm of writing and dance.

But Rimanelli never forgets that this sprawling city had provided the backdrop to the cruelest and most ignominious massacres in the history of Italian emigration to America (in particular for those who came from Sicily). We are in March 1981, following in the footsteps of an attentively executed study by Mario Rimanelli and Sheryl Lynn Possman, *The 1981 New Orleans Incentive and U.S.-Italian Relations: A Look Back*, published in 1992). Giose traces the feverish moments of the racist massacre in which public and private are inextricably intertwined in a continuum constantly in flux; though they deal with bloody events that ultimately do not directly pertain the author's personal biography (in fact, they occur in a period that he had "perceived" as a young man through the fragmentary fairytale stories of Grandpa Dominik, who had lived through them, though he was never directly involved). They produce in him a specular effect, with pronounced psychological repercussions, so much so that he felt the need, the urgency, to re-evoke them with historical tenacity and emotional participation, dedicating to them an entire chapter.

More peaceful but also more subtle is the task he set for himself in the second "book," *Core càre*. The subtitle of his second section, which rightly and strategically occupies the central part of *Familia*, is *Emigrazione come destino (Emigration as Destiny)*. *Core càre* is the stylistic method Rimanelli excavates from the living memory of a passage from a letter his father sent to his mother (unfortunately this epistolary correspondence has been lost, along with other precious documents), "durante il loro clandestino corteggiarsi" ("during their clandestine courtship") (...core càve è a tèrre mije s'è uenìte a fatejàme"). It must be said right off that this section was anticipated by Rimanelli in one of the more interesting *Quaderni sull'emigrazione*, edited by Norberto Lombardi of the Nicola and Giulia Iannone di Isernia Foundation. The volume in question, titled *In nome del padre*, with an excellent introduction by Lombardi, collects three life stories tied to the emigration of the three anthologized authors: Michele Castelli, Torquato Di Tella, and Giose Rimanelli.

Here too, in *Core càre* the reader finds himself before a triad of key words (*esilio, ritorno, destino*), that animate the pages of this sinuous and singular segment. It should immediately be said that Rimanelli is most convincing when—casting off his cultivated and pedantic robes, which gives a lot of space (at times, perhaps, too much) to socio-historical information and research and very little to the actual lived experience itself (a defect, or rather, an excess of "embroidery" that one often finds in his other works that oscillate from essay to narrative—he abandons himself to the memorial flux of the narration, presenting the reader with a series of flashbacks and fragments of his childhood and adolescence: phases of fundamental existential formation, like his adolescence in Seminario, that will then later contribute to his *Weltanschauung*, as well as to the very imagination of the narrator. I think of those episodes conjured with such natural narrative felicity, like those of his father's periodic flights. (Quite rightly, Lombardi has pointed out, in his introduction to *In nome del padre*, that in *Core càre* "prende un rilievo inconsueto la figura del padre, che nelle opera più o lontane era collocata in penombra e considerata secondo un profilo critico" ("he depicts in an entirely new way the figure of his father who in earlier works had occupied a place in the shadows and was presented in a critical light," and I would also add in a tone that is decisively antagonistic). I also think of other equally enjoyable episodes, like the time he did some pole vaulting with his classmates over the Cigno, the river outside town (the prize/meal at stake: frogs which they would roast and eat together, that is, everybody except the one who came in last). I also think of that most tender episode of the famous (and expensive) 48 Omega shaving brush that Giose gave to his father, which was later passed back his son, who still uses it to this day as an *object d'affection*, and he turns it into material for his writing. I cite only a couple of these red-hot splinters that *mobilize* themselves in the mind of the reader, where they stick.

His particular fascination with self-presentation, or rather what Rimanelli himself calls "il fascino di rappresentarsi" ("the fascination of representing oneself"), constitutes the chief sum of his writing style. I draw your attention to the following passage, which resonates decisively like a full-fledged declaration of the poetics behind his narrative art.

[...] Definisco il "fascino di rappresentarsi," quella diretta o indiretta autobiografia che si avverte in quasi tutti i miei scritti, ciò che—anche genericamente parlando—si identifica con etnicità ed etnografia in quanto l'autobiografia opera un po' come l'etnografo che fruga in ciò che è nascosto e latente nei linguaggi, nelle culture che a un primo contatto appaiono opache, ostiche quasi, per rivelare poi alla fine lo splendore dei caratteri: il discorso, la dinamica. È più o meno, questa, in corrispondenza con (o è essa stessa?) la nozione pitagorica dell'oblio, della superficiale apparenza dietro la quale si cela la nascosta realtà. (89)

[... I define the "fascination of representing onself," that direct or indirect autobiography that is evident in almost of all my writings, that which—even generically speaking—is identified with ethnicity and ethnography insofar as an autobiography operates a bit like the ethnographer who probes what is hidden and latent in those languages and cultures that upon first contact seem opaque, almost impenetrable, in order to reveal then in the end the splendor of their characteristics: the discourse, the dynamic. This more or less corresponds with (or is it the same thing?) the Pythagorean notion of oblivion, the superficial appearance behind which the hidden reality is concealed.)

Core càre is therefore its incandescent and rational nucleus, made of flights (backward and forward through time), of adolescent discoveries that are still reflected in the quickly ripening soul of the author, sudden agglutinative attenuations of his brooding mind, and even for that matter of continuous "growth" operating right down to the writer's final vital drop. In short, the whole thing in the incessant motion of a constant coming-and-going between past and present, or perhaps it would be better to define it as the movement of a Past-Present that is also a Present-Past, which in a labyrinthine way constantly intervenes in the globalizing dictate of this book, with both a centrifugal and a centripetal effect at that same time.

This last annotation is particularly pertinent to *Giose e io (Emigrazione come arte),* the third section of *Familia,* that consists of the revised text of a theatrical piece titled *L'arcangelo e il ragazzo.* Here the author, as though in his own kaleidoscopic "secretum" dialogues with himself and with the multiple "branches" of his personality he has disseminated over the course of his "voyage," or rather, with the many facets of his real and projected existence, of which he gives an account through its theatrical reflection. For me its theatrical debut was unforgettable. Giose was there with his friends and others from his region (I would like to here remember at least Sebastiano Martelli, Carlo Jovine, Renata Debenedittis). It took place on December 21, 1998 in the "M. Pagano" Auditorium in Campbasso, under the excellent direction of Pierluigi Giorgio and the extremely talented Claudia Pescatori in the role of Lares, also known as "the flower woman."

I mentioned above the centrifugal and centripetal effect of this book—in fact, one of the primary characteristics (if not the main characteristic) of *Familia* is precisely its circular trajectory, where departure also means return, and return does not mean staying, not in any permanent sense, a per-manence, because other duties call, other voices encourage him to depart again. "Rest" is only ever momentary. And although these pages are filled with the melancholy of farewell, or rather, the awareness of a "time" that is no more, inasmuch as it has passed, it is also true that time as an end in itself cannot be forgotten or planned or prolonged, given its unfading mobility.

Rimanelli the man and artist, as pure energy and movement, lives and works in a time that is continuously mobile, where past and future mirror each other. Thus, unhinging the usual terms in the temporal exchange of ideas and of his *phantasmata*, the hidden entity takes form, as through a dilatation of one's field of vision, which is a different way of bringing into focus the pain and the mystery, the whole and the void of existence.

From this distance, categories like "exile" "expatriate" "one-way" "round-trip" disappear. Being deprived of membership to a specific place becomes, on the contrary, in a true writer like Rimanelli, *membership to all places*, whether real or imaginary. Rimanelli knows, in his heart, that his irreducible *Heimat* exists in a world eternally in motion, which is also the motion of the world. Novalis has already expressed this very sentiment in a splendid intuition in his *Ofterdingen*: "I often feel now that that my fatherland breathed into my thoughts colors not ephemeral and that its image has become a singular sign of my soul, a sign that I divine more and more, the more profoundly I understand that destiny and soul are two names for the same concept."

The image of a "patria" becomes, thus, "an ubiquitous place where one is always at home, because home and writing always go hand in hand." Having understood this omen, having intuited its entire ontological and sentimental importance, was no modest feat for Rimanelli. Finally, the true and final foundation of his nomadic-autobiographical-narrative-poetic writing resides precisely in this undertaking. The tropic essence of an eternal birthplace (of precisely a Heimat), so intimately connected to the erratic Giose, transforms soul and destiny into words that describe the same reality and a single, unique concept.

CHAPTER FIVE

Alfredo de Palchi's Life and Poetry

> [...] *ma sei rattenuto*
> *malmenato sulla cassa rovesciata*
> *e ti sgozza l'intelligenza*
> *mentre il sangue ti sballotta* [...]
> —Alfredo de Palchi

1. SOME PRELIMINARY BIOGRAPHICAL FACTS

First of all, I wish to explain the reasoning behind the title given to this last chapter, dedicated to Alfredo de Palchi, an Italian poet who expatriated to the United States almost fifty years ago, on whom Italian critics have produced a remarkable bibliography, though it is circumscribed, broadly speaking, to the first decade of his career. The first scholar to address his work was Glauco Cambon in 1961, followed by Vittorio Sereni, Giuliano Manacorda, Marco Forti, Silvio Ramat, and many others. (I refer the reader to the bibliographic appendix of this volume, the first of its kind on this author.) This bibliography quickly diminished in favor of that which was accumulated, or rather nourished, in the United States. It can constitute, for the reader, an initial methodological hint; a sort of litmus test capable of immediately highlighting, in an unequivocal way, the inseparability of the two substantive nouns found in the title of this chapter ("life" and "poetry").

In few other poets of modernity is the nexus between life and poetry so tight, so direct, so fatally necessary as it is in De Palchi, and obviously here memory runs straight to the stellar models of Baudelaire, Rimbaud, Campana, Ungaretti (these are the first names that come to mind; poets much loved by Alfredo, who certainly more than others made the same connection and nourished it; but I think also of writers closer to him in terms of their life experiences, like Emanuel Carnevali, Arturo Giovannitti, Giose Rimanelli—"irregular" writers, subversive and nomadic, who have partly shared the biographic/poetic experience of a *deraciné* like De Palchi, although in different ways in ideologically very different times (by which I mean literary ideologies).

Sonia Raiziss had nevertheless already applied this very dichotomy to our author on the occasion of the publication of his first "American" book—though it was also new to the Italian audience who was already familiar with De Palchi's work.

The book in question is *La buia danza di scorpione* was released in 1993, though it was composed more than forty years earlier in Italy. I will explain later the sense of that "American" in quotation marks, as well as the enormous chronological hiatus from its composition to its publication when it comes time to discuss his earliest poetic foray in greater detail below.

Beyond having been De Palchi's principal English translator, Sonia Raiziss is an excellent exegete of his work. She was also his partner for many years. It should be made immediately clear, in order to avoid ambiguity, that Alfredo has always conceived and written his entire body of poetic work in Italian, even though he has resided more than two-thirds of his life outside of Italy: first in France (from 1951 to 1956), then in the United States (from 1956 to the present), with brief and occasional visits to his homeland. His trips in recent years have been longer and more frequent.

Before jumping right into a reading of his work, I will follow, propaedeutically, the biography of this poet, who in my opinion is among the most gifted and singular in the history (if a comprehensive history will ever be written) of Italian expatriate writers in America.

De Palchi was born on December 13, 1926 in Legnago (to be more precise in Ponte de Legnago, in the province of Verona) to a father who, though they had met, would never legally recognize Alfredo as his son (a certain Giovanni Sandrini), and to Ines de Palchi, who was born in 1903 and died at a ripe old age on February 17, 2000 in Feltre (Belluno).

He spent his childhood in an extremely poor family environment. He attended elementary and secondary school (the latter with an interruption before earning his diploma) in Legnago. Looming large over his adolescence was the figure of his maternal grandfather, Carlo de Palchi, an infamous local anarchist with anticlerical convictions. To this day Alfredo still vividly remembers one of his more frequent witticisms ("I preti mangiano la carne cotta nell'acqua," namely, "Priests eat meat cooked in water"), which would eventually become a verse in one of his poems, sarcastically alluding to the prestigious position of the clergy.

More than anyone else it was this very grandfather who succeeded in encouraging his grandson to gradually take an interest in art, in literature (his first indelible poetic encounters: Giosuè Carducci, Ada Negri, and most of all Angiolo Silvio Novaro), in music, in politics and in culture in general. For the pure mnemic-autobiographical pleasure of it, one of the convictions that had rooted itself in the mind of young Alfredo when he was in elementary school demands to be reported here. It is a typical, infantile "myth" that his imagination would have nourished, namely, the myth of the "beauty" of poets. Poets were thought of and imagined not only as purveyors of beauty, but also as actually being beautiful and physically seductive. A tenderly narcissistic myth that would soon be shattered, when, a little later, De Palchi happened upon the physical portrait of Leopardi, just as he has been handed down to us by his contemporaries and posterity.

Carlo died in 1941. His funeral procession, in a rather Fellinian way, consisted of only his grandson Alfredo and a mangy dog that did not even belong to the family. His figure will be conjured again by the poet in two later lyrics that are rough-hewn, yet of a noteworthy expressionistic realism, in his volume *Sessioni con l'analista* published by Mondadori in 1967.

These were the years of the dawn of the Second World War. Alfredo, who had a fairly good inclination for all things mechanical, worked in a mechanic's shop. He would later work as an errand-boy for the electro-domestic company Riello. He would promptly give his wages to his grandfather in order to contribute to the financial well being of the family. Years later in *Sessioni con l'analista*, he will unwillingly channel this point in his life: "A 12 anni / meschino nella

169

tuta lurida di grassi / per motori e nafta / consegno 5 lire / la setti-
mana—domenica compresa / nella busta troppo larga al nonno / anarchico / mangiato dal cancro" (99; "At 12 / shabby in dirty overalls
greasy / with motor oil / I consign 5 lire / (weekly—Sunday included)
/ in an oversized envelope for my anarchic / grandfather / wasted by
cancer" [105]; all translations from *Sessions with My Analysis* by I.
L. Solomon).

In the fall of 1942 he moved to Milan with his mother Ines.
With the war by now in full swing, they lived in an apartment near
San Babila. They both worked very hard—his mother as a cleaning
lady at a hotel in Via Washington, and Alfredo, who was by this
time almost sixteen, at a laboratory specializing in mechanics.

In the summer of 1943, upon returning to Milan after a visit to
Vercelli to see his aunt (Ines had a younger sister, Bruna, who lived
there; and two brothers, Nereo, who lived in Villa Bartolomea (Verona), and Guido, who lived in Paris), they come home to find their
entire apartment block demolished by an air raid. They are forced
to return to Legnago.

Between 1944 and 1945 a crucial event occurs that will dramatically change Alfredo's life forever. He is implicated in an obscure
political assassination plot. The murder, in Angiari, in December
1944, of a Veronese partisan (Aurelio Veronese, aka "il biondino"),
was the work of a certain Carella (or Carrella), a fascist and leader of
the national rail troops. The affair will be evoked later in broken
and relentless verses, in a dark crescendo as in a nightmare that is
never truly resolved, in the eponymous section of *Sessioni con
L'analista* (118-120).

Though completely unconnected with the murder, De Palchi
was accused and tried. At the bottom of the whole thing lies the fact
that in the winter of 1944, impelled by other more experienced af-
filiates and by an insipient (illusory) enthusiasm, he temporarily en-
listed in the *Brigate nere* (Black Brigades), at that time under the
leadership of Junio Valerio Borghese. A gesture of political ingenu-
ousness for which seventeen-year-old De Palchi paid dearly, and
which, *a posteriori*, in light of historical reality, he certainly shared
with more than just a few other stray youths of the time, many sup-

porters of the fascist Republic of Salò among them. Recall Giose Rimanelli (who is virtually De Palchi's contemporary) and his emblematic *Tiro al piccione* (1953).

As a matter of fact, his case was heard in Verona in June 1945 and had the air of a witch hunt, the dust of which still does not seem to have settled even today at a distance of more than half a century (just look at the most recent squalid, sporadic attacks of any hack journalist or fanciful "*operatore culturale*" in the *Basso veronese* press, unfounded attacks that were stirred up again on the occasion of one of De Palchi's visits to Legnago in the spring of 1998). Hastily tried, despite the perorations of his appointed lawyer (a certain De Voto) demonstrating the absolute innocence of the accused, De Palchi was condemned to life in prison (the public prosecutor had pleaded for the death penalty!), while the top management of his brigade, from Junio Valerio Borghese down, had effectively been condemned to execution by firing squad.

Thus, De Palchi embarks upon his odyssey, constellated with harsh reproaches, humiliating false accusations, incontestable injustices, and ruthless torture endured in various prisons; not to mention the endless barrage of judicial appeals that, on the one hand, managed to reduce his unjust period of detention with the result he was finally released once and for all in the spring of 1951, and his complete innocence was contextually proved four years later (the definitive reversal of the sentence occurred in 1955, at the Court of Assizes in Venice, and De Palchi, with the assistance of lawyers De Marisco and Arturo Sorgato, was entirely absolved of ever having committed the crime); on the other hand, these events inevitably left their mark on the life (and destiny) of this poet.

De Palchi was first sent to prison in Venice, then to Regina Coeli in Rome, then to Poggio Reale in Naples, then to the Penitentiary in Procida (where he stayed from 1946 to '50), and finally to/ Civitavecchia (from 1950 to '51). And although prison was a devastating blow that must have exhausted him, it was also a coming-of-age experience; and, paradoxically, it even provided him with the stoic energy to resist, to react, to read, to study, to reflect, to grow, and, last but not least, to write his poetry as a real *homme revolté*.

It is impossible, therefore, to embark on a reading of his work, especially if one intends to do so diachronically (as I intend to do this chapter), without taking into consideration the atrocities he endured, inasmuch as the poetry he produced is steeped in them.

Alfredo wrote his first poem in Poggioreale when he was not yet twenty years old. I say "he wrote," but the verb expresses only euphemistically the furious act of scratching those early trifling verses into the wall of his cell.

Shortly thereafter, in the Procida penitentiary in the winter of '46, he completed his singular poetic apprenticeship. Chained to a couple of partisan war criminals, De Palchi arrives by ferry between bouts of vomiting. It would be easy, here, amid the indifferent flood of History, to engage in a some lofty literary rhetoric on the cheap; in light of the image of this boat transporting accused and accusers, friends and enemies, the conquered and the conquerors, all chained up together.

In the Procida prison De Palchi makes the acquaintance of Ennio Contini, poet and critic, born in Oristano (Cagliari) in 1914, but who had almost always lived in Liguria. Almost every trace of this individual has been lost today. Nevertheless, between the 1930s and 1950s (Contini's last book, which presents his collected poems, *Schegge d'anima* was published by Carpena in 1962 and features a preface by Adriano Grande), he had his role in literary circles and achieved a modest notoriety, as his books of poetry attest. One of them, titled *L'Alleluja* (1952), pairs him as co-author to none other than Ezra Pound. No less significant was his work as a critic: highlights among his essays include those on Emile Schaub-Koch, Armand Godoy, and Renzo Laurano. On Contini there is even a fairly good critical bibliography, in which find the signatures of Enrico Falqui, Adriano Grande, Bartolo Pento and Bonaventura Pecchi.

Ennio Contini is the first to appreciate (he, too, being held political prisoner at Procida) the potential of De Palchi's poetics, as well as the first to encourage and seriously guide him in the direction of poetry. De Palchi himself years later will recognize his debt to his early mentor in the acknowledgments dedicated to him, as

172

well as to Glauco Cambon, Antonio Viscusi, and Sonia Raiziss in his aforementioned first volume of poetry. ("Ringrazio Ennio Contini per avermi messo la penna in mano e 'obbligato' a scrivere," 167; "I thank Ennio Contini for having put a pen in my hand and 'obliged' me to write.")

The years he spends in the Procida penitentiary were, on the one hand, hard and vexing, but extremely rich with reading, stimulation, and literary fantasies, on the other. De Palchi devours a mountain of books that range vertiginously (but also with diligent chronological intent) from the Bible, Dante (especially the *Rime petrose*) and Cavalcanti, to the moderns and his contemporaries, passing through a few Renaissance authors, to arrive (precisely) at Leopardi, Carducci, Pascoli, D'Annunzio, Campana, Govoni, Sbarbaro, Quasimodo, Ungaretti, Montale, his beloved Cardarelli (on whose poetry, while still in prison, he will write a short essay that he sent to Cardarelli himself, who as the editor of the *Fiera letteraria* had it published in the magazine, which caused a sensation and sparked a certain debate), right up to his own virtually contemporary mentors and big brothers: Sinisgalli, Sereni, Caproni, Erba, Zanzotto, Cattafi.

From Italian literature he passes then to the French. It mattered little if he had only an approximate understanding of the language, being particularly taken with François Villon (De Palchi will draw many a later epigraph from this particular poet), Charles Baudelaire, Gérard de Nerval, and, above all, Arthur Rimbaud.

And so from his glum Campanian cell, many a poem will be born, drafted in pencil in various mangled notebooks, attesting not only to the diversity of his sources of inspirations, but also to the variety of expressive modes congenial to them he managed to master. At times he dabbles in a Biblical dimension, rich with visions and oracular ascensions, at times he attains a certain grotesque theatricality, and, most of all, he draws from the savage metaphor of prison life. "La prigione"—one of his more attentive exegetes recently wrote —"con i suoi spazi chiusi e la mancanza di libertà, diventa metafora calzante per l'intera esistenza" (Vettori 1996; "Prison with its closed spaces and lack of freedom, becomes the appropriate metaphor for life as a whole"). This is an annotation that—despite the obvious ideological differences—calls to mind Guglielmo Petroni's first book, *Il mondo è una prigione*, published in 1945 (right around the time of De Palchi's initial experience in prison). Petroni's is a terribly confessional book that not only ruthlessly describes the torture he endured in a fascist prison, but also attests in the first person to the desire to resist at all costs, through his commitment to a fierce moral solitude, "arma vincente sulle condanne a morte, sulle macerie della guerra, sulla ferocia dei sopravissuti" (Luti 1995) ("the weapon triumphant against death sentences, against the rubble of war, against the savagery of the survivors").

The primary nucleus of this chaotic effort is the group of texts that appear in *La buia danza di scorpione*, miraculously preserved by his mother (every so often Alfredo would give her some of his work, during her visits to Procida and later to Civitavecchia). These are the poems that make up the first nucleus or one of the first nuclei of his work (unfortunately almost all the others were either lost or destroyed by De Palchi himself, in a sort of rite of liberation from prison when he was released in the spring of 1951).

The poems of *La buia danza di scorpione* were originally supposed to appear in the volume published by Mondadori in 1967, *Sessioni con l'analista*, but, with Vittorio Sereni's support, De Palchi removed them in order to propose their publication in a subsequent volume that, however, never materialized, at least not until many years later, in 1993, in a bilingual American edition. The motive behind this exclusion—which will become clearer shortly—lies both in the different stylistic expressivity of the two collections, largely in contrast to the impression one gets from a reading of the poems contained in the Mondadori volume (with the exception of the long narrative poem *Un ricordo del '45*), and in an attempt to avoid making the book too long, which had already been more than sufficiently fleshed out.

2. THE SCORPION-POET AND "LA VILE GIOSTRA DEL MONDO"

From all the information presented above, emerges, by now fairly well delineated, both De Palchi's variegated apprenticeship and his formative and expressive plurilinguism. It is, therefore, time to delve into *La buia danza di scorpione* in order to engage in a close reading.

Let's begin with the title, which alludes to the obscurity of the cell in which the author (figured as a scorpion forced to dwell in darkness—this explains his use of the simple preposition "*di*" rather than the compound "*del*")—proceeded to write his poetry and lucubrations of protest, rage, violence, and isolation, against the obtuseness and the abusive atrocities of a social (and military) system that had unjustly condemned him. Right from the start with the verses quoted from Villon in the epigraph ("Ce monde n'est qu'abusion"), De Palchi makes perfectly clear the sulfurous spirit in which his verses have been steeped. By invoking the first poet *maudit* in European literature, more than one biographical analogy and elective affinity are stirred in his mind: Villon, the independent spirit who, like De Palchi, had a conflicted relationship with his native city; Villon, the outlaw autodidact; Villon, the brazen poet in whose verses happiness, sarcasm, melancholy, and derision intermingle; finally, Villon, the frequent prisoner, who was eventually sentenced to be hanged for having dealt a mortal wound to a priest. (Who can forget the memorable incision of the *pendu* of Pierrie Levet's semipirated edition of the *Testaments*?) His sentence was later commuted, *in extremis*, to exile from his city on January 5, 1463, which is precisely the date after which we no longer know anything about François.

The texts that compose *La buia danza di scorpione* are distributed over four sections that bear the following titles: *Il principio, Un'ossessione di mosche, Carnevale d'esilio, Il muro lustro d'aria*. The book, published—as I mentioned—with considerable delay with respect to the period of its original composition, is, practically unknown in Italy even today, with the exception of the poem *Con piedi cercatori* (which was released with other pieces that did not belong to *La buia danza di scorpione* in a collection of ten poems titled *Gentile animale braccato*, in the *Almanacco dello specchio*, Mondadori, 1983, with an introduction by Luciano Erba) along with six other poems ("Mi dicono di origini," "Al palo del telegrafo orecchio il ronzio," "In mano ho il seme nero di girasole," "Inarreso

l'urto del mare escava macerie," "S'abbatte il pugno," "Una scatola")
that the poet included in a little collection in 1988 titled *Mutazioni*, a
short book consisting of heterogeneous texts taken from *La buia
danza di scorpione* as well as other collections published subsequently.

The book was well received in the United States, as attested to
by many reviews as well as several previews of these texts, in English
translations, that appeared in respectable American magazines, as
for example, *The American Poetry Review*, *Granite*, *International
Poetry Review*, *New Letters*, *Paintbrush*, *Poetry Now*, and *Vortex*.

La buia danza di scorpione is the book that most painfully reflects De Palchi's experience in prison. And it is also a book that,
(re)reading it today, half a century after it was initially composed,
reveals a noteworthy innovative force, if one thinks of the sort of
poetry produced in Italy in the years after the war, and without a
doubt anticipatory of that particular anti-hermetic realism, expres-
sionistic-experimental-informal in nature, which will find only in the
late 1950s its first, complete expressivity. I have in mind, emblematically, poets like Giorgio Cesarano, Elio Pagliarani, and a couple
of others (I refer here specifically to exemplary books like the former's *L'erba bianca* (1959) and the latter's *Cronache e altre poesie*
(1954) and *Inventario privato* (1959); authors with whom De Palchi
was obviously not acquainted).

All of this seems to me still more stupefying when understood in
relation to the absolute lack of any kind of literary ferment and cultural *milieu*, which were completely denied to De Palchi, imprisoned in Procida at the time, and that he indefatigably constructed
for himself entirely on his own as an autodidact, without taking for
granted the assistance of Ennio Contini, his companion-in-misfor-
tune.

Right from the opening of the book his very particular and extremely personal "poetic sting" emerges, as Sonia Raiziss intelligently points out in her introduction to the collection. It is worth ex-
cerpting certain passages of it, especially where the American trans-
lator-scholar demonstrates, in her exacting and peremptory way, the

substantial non-dichotomy between De Palchi's life experience and the poetry springing forth from it.

> With Alfredo de Palchi the poet is the man. What he has known, what he has lived, is what he writes. He's one of the most instinctive, shall I say 'natural,' poets I know. [...] The poet is the sufferer, and the experience is the metaphor closest to itself. (xl)

And again, further along Raiziss already seems to have her finger on the pulse of De Palchian exegesis.

> Style makes the man, according to the adage. But in de Palchi's case the formula is reversed. He is altogether himself. [...] The syntax is dictated by his five senses. It is not elaborated for the sake of senti-ment or sensation; there is only enough for the sense. *The Scorpion's Dark Dance* is primal and not pretty. It emerged from the wrenching of body and soul that de Palchi endured for several years in political incarceration. For both man and poet they were unforgettable and un-forgivable years. And the sting is still sharp. (xii-xiii)

And it is in effect that unavoidable unity of life/poetry that emerges in even the earliest pieces in *La buia danza di scorpione*, allegorized starting from *Ovum*: the quintessential metaphor for the concept of "origin," that, in the intricate net of time, in the eyes of the author, has a "spoiled" genesis, dragging with it not a good man but one "congruo d'afflizioni," "congruous in afflictions." Shortly thereafter De Palchi will hint at the necessity of a "seme da trapiantare" ("a seed to transplant"), as the "unico dei sistemi sconosciuti" (10: "only unknown system"); and, yet the poet will return to the tropological image of the *Ovum* over the course of the book, like the symbolic representation of himself as "Nuovo Adamo" ("New Adam") ("Uovo che si lavora nella luce ovale / nuovo adamo / invigorisco nell'altrui simulazione / e quindi anch'io implacabile finzione / anch'io sono [...]" (58); "Egg laboring in oval light / the new adam / I grow stronger through the feigning of others / and therefore impla-cable too a sham / but here I am [...]" [59]). Already entirely in para-hermetic language (though keeping his distance from the formal solutions of the masters of Tuscan hermeticism, who at times run the risk of abstraction), a language polished, edgy, rugged, that constitutes what is most immediately distinctive of De Palchi's style. In this sense, for example, it seems extremely interesting to me to emphasize his use of attributes—which we will see in greater detail as my close reading proceeds—expressionistically "distorted" from their specific semantic value, which lends to the versification of a singular deforming *sprezzatura*. In this regard, I believe Sonia's English translation is very useful, as it is attentive in reproducing De Palchi's pungent *discurrere* along the lines of a greater, plausible pragmatism (perspicuity), without sacrificing the para-hermetic or symbolic halo I mentioned earlier.

Moreover, all that expressive charm, resulting even from an extremely personal adjectival identification (and relative use), returns in a more expansive anarchic/libertarian aspiration (in the tradition of Thoreau, to cite a point of reference) that the experience of prison must have profoundly instilled in the poet's *Stimmung*.

And in fact, to the plot of the time, of the respectable and hypocritical time he inhabited, De Palchi ("figlio limpido") juxtaposes his "io dissennato" ("reckless self"), free and beyond the law; ready, in the restless prehensile capacity of reality, to perceive its confused hum: "... orecchio il ronzio / il sortire incandescente da quando / le origini estreme / provocano la terra / percepisco / accensioni e dovunque mi sparga / chiasso d'inizio odo" (8; "My ear at the telegraph pole I catch the hum / the incandescent emergence since the time / when earliest origins / provoke the earth / I perceive / sparks igniting and wherever I'm scattered / I hear the uproar of beginnings" [9]). But in this molecular and absorbing buzzing of the world the scorpion-poet is always alert, ready to attack and retreat, and even when interrupting the buzzing activity he could be a dove announcing the arrival of the spring to the prisoners. The scorpion-poet, who knows that his spring has not yet come, continues to reside in the shadows, hunched over his paper-thoughts, following the dance of his own "vertiginoso cuore impestato di zanzare" (20; "vertiginous heart plagued by mosquitoes" [21]). Even when confronted by any liberating presence that can distract him: a dove, a fly, a but-

178

terfly, or a moth of any kind. The strong symbolism of this animalization should be noted: the moth and the dove are endowed with wings that permit them to fly; the scorpion, on the other hand, is closed up within himself, "fuori di senno" ("out of his mind"), in his own dark solipsistic dance. Without forcing the comparison, the subversive dimension of the Maldorian bestiary is echoed here— even in the evocation of a *mal d'aurore* self-prohibited to those who, locked up in a cell, hide from themselves and others—of Isidore Ducasse, otherwise known as the Count of Lautrèamont, a writer who was much loved by the Surrealists, whom De Palchi would have read and admired a few years later in Paris, in the famous edition illustrated by Magritte. As was the case for Lautréamont, for De Palchi it is not the thing in itself that "possesses" him, as much as the violent repercussions that act upon his mind. Its *psycho-symbolic expansion* acts in such a way that it metonymically overturns the terms of the vision > perception > fruition > poetic rendering. It is a process that De Palchi will continue to essentialize more and more. We see it, for example, in many poems in *Costellatione anonima*, where the encounter/clash with the city of New York reveals itself in many, meager yet disturbing modalities.

To this "formicolio della natura" ("swarm of nature"), this vile "giostra del mondo" ("merry-go-round"), the poet will never give in; like Villon, he will instead address it with his contempt, his fist, his spittle:

> Al calpestìo di crocifissi e crocifissi
> sputo secoli di vecchie pietre
> strade canicolari
> il pungente sterco di cavalli immusoniti
> in siepi di siccità
>
>> (al gomito dell'Adige allora crescevo
>> di indovinazioni rumori d'altre città)
>
> e sputo sui compagni che mi tradirono
> e in me chi forse mi ricorda (48)

179

(At the trampling of crosses upon crosses
I spit out centuries of ancient stones
dogday roads
and the piquant dung of horses sulking
in the hedges of drought

    (at the elbow of the Adige I grew up
    on guesses, rumors of other cities)

and I spit on the buddies who betrayed me and inside
me on those who may remember [49])

In order to render his "interior monologue" more efficacious and substantial—even in its extremely rough-hewn allure—he supplies a discrete synesthetic presence that is always unfurled (put to use) on his (through his) own body, the axial center of perception that is both contingent and cosmic at the same time ("la pista mi svela / lo scompiglio e odo / una punta di luce scalfirmi gli occhi" [14]; "the pathway reveals / this commotion to me and I hear / a point of light scratching my eyes").

His interior monologue is furthermore suited to the monotony of prison life, which is stuffy and repetitive, though rich with implications that are oneiric and projective of an *autre* life (and that is intensified by a libido of accumulation, as carnally effusive as it is unsatisfied and which will become an important component in his poetry), juxtaposed to which all those elements that can deface or cruelly pervert it—smoke stacks, factories, smog and even cats thrown from bridges. The poem that begins "Estate" (I cite it by its first line because De Palchi's poems never have titles) seems to me, in this sense, the supreme emblematic synthesis. Let's read it:

Estate
frutto propizio   seno biondo
d'una calata di sensazioni

nel belato d'alberi la luce astringente
urta
tutto scompiglia: il verde-

verde
il cielo-cielo e il rombo... (16)

(Summer
propitious fruit   blond breast
heavy with an onrush of sensations

in the bleating of trees the astringent light
collides
upsets it all: the green-
green
the sky-sky and the rumble... [17])

Boredom, fatigue, frustration, anger, desire, nostalgia—these are the buttresses that bear the banner of De Palchi's spleen and that does not allow itself to be overcome by place; on the contrary, it greedily develops an immense desire to transgress imposed limits and to lead him, a scorpion in ambush, toward the light outside, and thus to master with his gaze even all of the humblest things that make their way through the day-to-day routine, with the "volontà di vedere quello che d'abitudine si dimentica" ("will to see that which of habit one takes for granted") and that, given his forced condition, is denied the right of sensory use. A recurring trope in *La buia danza di scorpione* should be annotated here, or rather the obsessive thematic presence of *sight* (*vedere*) and *light* (*luce*), precisely because in the dark and narrow cell, the latter is "dispensata / quanto l'acqua di cisterna" (72; "doled out / like water from a tank," [73]). An American critic hinted at it fleetingly, writing: "His harsh, unrelenting stance and his beautiful and disquieting imagery belong to one who draws in the dark while longing for the light" (Di Pace-Jordan 1994). Thus, of this *topos*, a small but significant sampling:

Percepisco accensioni... [8]
so che la luce cala dietro / l'inconscio... [10]
... e odo / una punta di luce... [14]
... nel belato d'alberi la luce astringente... [16]
... una fiera di ritagli di luce... [20]

... vado incontro alla luce... [22]
Il lepidottero [...] squama alla luce... [24]
... muro circolare che imprigiona la luce... [56]
... nella luce ovale... [58]
... oltre l'ispida luce... [60]
... la città nella conca schiuma di luci...[70]
... voglio luce / mi si impone ombra... [72]
... spula la luce demente di Nerval... [90]

[I perceive sparks... [9]
knowing that the light sinks behind / the unconscious... [11]
... and I hear / a point of light... [15]
... in the bleating of trees the astringent light... [17]
... a festival of snippets of light... [21]
... I shuffle toward the light... [23]
The moth [...] brakes / at the light and flakes off... [25]
... circular wall that imprisons the bed- / lamp...[57]
... in oval light... [59]
... beyond the bristling light... [61]
... the city in the hollow foams with lights... [71]
... I want light / they enforce darkness... [73]
... fan the mad light of Nerval... [91])

And—it may be expressed here incidentally, but I cannot help but mention it—who knows if, any reference to Marinetti aside, whether there was also in De Palchi an unconscious drive behind his decision to name his daughter, Luce, who was born much later following his second marriage (to Rita Di Pace), an annotation that lies beyond the exegetical task of the critic, but that also provides further evidence of how, yet again, life and poetry in De Palchi's human (and psychic) journey constantly intersect.

Over the course of the book, like a rogue wave gathering girth, the poet's biting sarcasm and metaphorical depth are accentuated especially with regard to the military-penitentiary system. Every insult, every humiliation, every "sputo d'arma" ("spit of the gun") are met by the poet's passive attitude, indomitable, his grimace of refusal, in an expressionistic George Grosz style crescendo: "Ad ogni sputo d'arma scatto / mi riparo dietro l'albero e rido / isterico / alla

bocca che sbava / un'ossessione di mosche" (32; "At every spit of
the gun I jump / I hide back of a tree and laugh / hysterically / seeing that mouth slobber / an obsession of flies," [33]); the poet will
again return a little later to his hysterical laughter: "[...] lo sguardo si
diparte e vendicativa / una risata mi regola il polso" (118; [...] "the
stare turns back and a vengeful / laugh corrects my pulse," [119]).

It is possible that, in the mean time, the poet's unyielding antimilitaristic sarcasm was literarily (and existentially) fomented by De
Palchi's gradual, unremitting reading of contemporary poets, which
he practiced throughout his time in prison, readings from which he
was keen to extract formative fuel for his own forays into poetry.
The following example

Una madre sradicata dal ventre geme
per il figlio:
            occhi sbucciati
infiammato groppo di lingua
al palo del telegrafo penzola con me
afferrato alle gambe (34)

[Womb uprooted a mother moans
for her son:
            shelled eyes
swollen knot of a tongue
from the telephone pole he swings with me
clutched to his legs (35)]

irresistibly recalls certain verses of Quasimodo's "Alle fronde dei
salici" (a poet who, like Ungaretti, exterted a profound influence on
De Palchi); a poem that, as we know, evokes one of the most tragic
moments of the Second World War, when following the armistice
of Cassibile as foreigners in our territory, the Germans sought to
impose by means of brutal violence their ferocious oppression. It
seems likely that certain images from this famous lyric resonate in
De Palchi's work. From the "lamento d'agnello dei fanciulli" ("lamb-
like lamentation of the children") killed in the streets, "all'urlo nero
/ della madre che andava incontro al figlio / crocifisso sul palo del

telegrafo" ("to the black scream / of the mother approaching her son / crucified on the telephone pole"). The verses of Quasimodo's poem were published in the 1947 Mondadori volume *Giorno dopo giorno,* but the specific poem in question had already appeared in '46 in *Con il piede straniero sopra il cuore* in Milan, in the *Quaderni di Costume* edited by Giancarlo Vigorelli.

Certainly, unlike the hermetic and para-hermetic poets, De Palchi has a predilection for a discourse that is not modulated, but rugged and compact, comprised of snarled splinters that, in just a few verses, in their flagrant efficacy and livid immediacy, vertiginously sharpens situations, dramatic images, excruciating memories. Yet another two pressing examples (that by no means lack any of Ungaretti or Quasimodo's pregnant vividness) capable of delineating in spare yet extremely effective images of the horrors of war:

> Dopo l'ultima raffica
> il subentrare della calm a orrenda
> un prete esce pazzo dal fosso
> con uno straccio di cristo
> impalato (36)

> After the last hail of bullets
> comes the horrible calm
> out of the ditch a priest madly emerges
> with a scrap of christ
> impaled (37)

> Non più
> udir il tondo dei crivellati nel grano
> urli di vecchie bocche e di bestie
> negli incendi e bui guazzi
> nell'Adige
> [...] (38)

> To hear
> no more the humps of the bullet-riddled in the wheat
> the shrieks of old mouths, the beasts
> trapped by fire and the dark sloshing
> in the Adige
> [...] (39)

Each scene is always expressed in a crushed, broken, anti-naturalistic, analogical language, laden with bold metaphors and, at times, even peppered with biblical references. The author makes explicit reference to his intense biblical readings over the course of *La buia danza di scorpione* (56), and, profoundly permeated with apocalyptic suggestions—as the poet himself attests—were the texts of another manuscript, also drafted in prison, which he later submitted to Giansiro Ferrata who then carelessly misplaced it (more on this later).

Picasso's dove, an allegory of peace, is helpless in the face of the inhuman mess of ruthless violence, but the poet does not allow himself to be "corrupted," he does not compromise, he does not give in to his own brutishness, or to the trappings of conformism, as James Dickey once keenly observed, "De Palchi is absolutely uncompromising, and his poems are painful and exalting to read" (Dickey 1993). His is a scream of innocence, an innocence that will never allow him to accept "il rifugio dell'arca" (44; "shelter in the ark," 45), and even "nel giorno della disfatta" (50; "on the day of defeat" [51]) he will *seek* and he will *find* the truth.

His description of life in prison, with its violent repercussions, reaches its climax in the section titled "Carnevale d'esilio," where the title immediately gives an idea of the boldly detached attitude of the author who endured this painful though absurd experience as though it were merely a prank orchestrated by "omuncoli da circo" (110; "mindless homunculi" [111]) and, as usual, just a few lashing little verses are all he needs to illustrate the semi-life of a prisoner. Here are a couple striking examples:

[...]
– io, ricco pasto per voi insetti,
oltre l'ispida luce
vi crollo addosso il pugno (60)

[...]
– me, a rich meal for you insects,
beyond the bristling light
I crack my fist down (61)

[...] non ho amicizie
non mischio occasionali smanie
con chi persiste (64)

[...] I don't make friends
I don't mix my occasional longings
with those who insist on them (65)

Il mio tempo tra muri infetti
è un ricordo di spighe rovinato dagli uccisi
ancora in fuga (68)

My time between blighted walls
a memory of cornstalks cracked by the slaughtered
still in flight (69)

Età cruda
fame cruda
una gamella al giorno di ceci col baco
e un pane benzoino (76)

Raw times
raw hunger
a daily mess tin of chickpeas with worms
and a chunk of benzine bread (77)

[...]—il pane
sa di petrolio
lo mastico con bucce di limone
raccolte nelle immondizie (76)

[...]—the bread has
a gasoline taste
I chew it with lemon
rinds scrounged from the dump (77)
Il cubicolo è un forno che trasuda

l'umore di me alle prese con la forza
e l'atto di scontare un vivere
ingombro di spurge (82)

The cell is an oven that sweats out
my spirit grappling with their power
and the act of atoning for a life
choked with trash (83)

In the face of such daily compulsion, before which most people would either surrender or adapt ("qui / l'indifferenza livella tutti" [62]; "here / indifference levels us all" [63]), De Palchi develops and reinforces his own *uniqueness*. With respect to the mass of those who "si tentano uniscono e separano" (62; "try to touch, join but part" [63]) he fortified his own unique ego, in both a real and literary sense, under the ideal tutelage of his guardian angels: Villon and Rimbaud ("dopo una lunga attesa la Rimbaudiana / bellezza mi viene sui ginocchi" [54]; "after a long wait the beauty of Rimbaud / comes to sit on my knees" [55]).

And even if his mind is occasionally infiltrated by certain nostalgic glimmers of his youth so preciously spent, the poet does not allow himself any self-indulgence; to the contrary, memories of adolescence only serve to confirm the blind bestiality of those who cut his adolescence so short. In the face of so many "menti carbonizzate dall'odio" (84; "minds scorched black by hate" [85]) and of a "pace finta" (86; "feigned peace" [87]), he is keen on how to counterpoise his revolt and, at the same time, cultivate his slow, inexorable, conscious maturation.

Of course, this is the most tense and intense section of *La buia di scorpione*, where the crude routine of prison life and the poet's pure ideal continually collide, which, like an unyielding flag, one day furled over the Adige, the river of his youth. And from this collision, destined to remain non-pacified, one thing was certain: his desire to "mozzare il guaire di tutti" (104; "cut short your yelps") and his decisive conviction, following Villon, that the world is only an abuse or the dream of a splendid anarchy.

Dalla palma nel cortile la civetta stride
per il topo che sono—in fetore
di bugliolo m'incrosta la gola
e l'impeto della notte
mi spacca la mente

    (mi scaglio nel breve passato
    mi tolgo le scarpe
    ai fossi strappo le canne per soffiarvi
    una bolla di mondo...
    e sogno splendidi anarchici) (92)

(An owl in the jailyard palm
hoots for the mouse I am—the shit
bucket bites my gullet
and the plunge of night
unhinges my mind

    (I rush at my brief past
    pull these boots off
    yank reeds out of ditches for blowing
    the world like a bubble...
    and I dream of magnificent anarchists) [93])

This is De Palchi's signature "explosive, enduring rage," well served by an expressionistic "surrealistic power," mentioned by one critic upon the publication of *La buia danza di scorpione*, (Signorelli-Pappas 1994), or, as another correctly noted, his brusque, disruptive, iconoclastic force (Allen 1995).

A bitter, irritating book that, upon finishing it, leaves in the soul of the reader an unsettling discomfort, but at the same time demonstrates, on the level of style, the poet's extreme capacity for synthesis, proceeding through fulminating enunciations, a gift that will pertain to all of his later writing as well. In order to illustrate this gripping and schizomorphic mode of intensification, which Giuseppe Ungaretti had undisputedly mastered in *Allegria*, I cite five verses that compose one of the last lyrics in the book, which seems to me to provide an extremely efficacious, emblematic synthesis of the solitary and desperate experience of prison.

Una mosca adolescente bruisce
sulla gamella calda di zuppa
annunziando l'infezione
e gira l'orlo come sulle labbra
di me che sogno di uccidermi (112)

(A young fly bustles
over the bowl of hot soup
announcing contagion
and rides the rim as around my lips
while I'm dreaming of suicide [113])

To confirm, after all, that this experience will forever remain an incurable wound, or *permanent scar*, an experience within which—in vain—they attempted to slaughter those who witnessed it.

The conclusive "no / no / no," therefore, resonates like a furious, cosmic scream (à la Munch) that not only stands for the poet who had the courage to express it, but as a scream of revolt for all those victims of history who had to endure so much cruel injustice and human suffering; and, last but not least, it is also a perennial warning against the persecutors who, with impunity, threw their victims into the mud. Thus, it is a scream, as one critic pointed out, directed at all of humankind, "for all of us, swallowed by pragmatism or apathy, against man's inhumanity to man" (Gioseffi 1996). Finally, it is a scream that, for De Palchi's purposes, was intended and still intends to express a radical rejection of all those institutions that cruelly truncated his youth, smothered or attempted to smother his highest ideals and left an indelible mark, but that also—once again—reinforced in him, in an absolute and definite way, the Rimbauldian ideal of the outlaw, nomadic, rebel poet.

3. American Expatriation, Beyond "Conquered" and
"Conquerors"

> *[...] ma è bello*
> *fuggire con*
> *una valigia di poeti scorpioni*
> *le loro menzogne in buona cera*
> *sotto il sedile [...]*

Intimately linked to *La buia danza di scorpione*, in terms of theme and style, is the long poem titled "Un ricordo del '45" (though it is unique in terms of its form), placed at the beginning of the first volume De Palchi published in Italy, *Sessioni con l'analista* (1967).

How De Palchi, the autodidact ex-detainee who expatriated to the United States in '56, came to be published in the prestigious *Specchio* series, under the editorial direction of Vittorio Sereni at that time, is a story too uncanny not to recount. Once again, life and poetry are indissolubly intertwined.

Let's take a step back then to the spring of 1951, when De Palchi, stunned, debased and famished for life, was released from Civitavecchia, after having spent six years of his young life, falsely accused, in Italian prisons. With him he brought "una valigia di poeti scorpioni" ("a suitcase of scorpion poets") full of books lovingly collected in prison (among them were Sereni's *Diario in Algeria*; his beloved Leopardi's *Canti*, Quasimodo's *Giorno dopo giorno*; and once again; Ungaretti, Valéry, Novaro, Negri, Sbarbaro, Sinisgalli, and Cecchi's *Scrittori inglesi e americani* that had been given to him for his twenty-third birthday by Ennio Contini, not to mention, the inseparable Campana and Cardarelli), a suitcase full—it must be said —of dreams and needs.

As soon as he was free, under the impetus of having attainted total freedom (a freedom mixed with discomfort and desperation), he destroyed the notebooks of poetry he had written in the prison: a cathartic gesture with regard to the many hardships that oozed from those pages, which, although expressing his interior world, must have still represented in his eyes, a tangible link to that dismal six-year period. Years later, when he was to arrive at Mondadori's publication of *Sessioni con l'analista*, he will explain *a posteriori* what drove him to destroy those papers: "Il mio mondo adolescente, già crollato sotto una forza creata dalla vigliaccheria italiana, sotto violenze e bastonature da ogni provenienza, e immaturamente entrato in quello susseguente privo di speranze, mi spinse a distruggere gran parte di quei quaderni" ("My adolescent world, crushed under a force created by Italian cowardice, under violence and cudgeling from every origin, and prematurely pushed into the subsequent world devoid of hope, drove me to destroy most of those notebooks").

After having been released from prison, his destination is Paris, which is where his mother Ines had gone to live in 1946 (a year later she marries Carlo Giop who will adopt young Alfredo). He arrives, thus, toward the end of April, in Vercelli where his aunt lives, in order to complete the process of getting a passport. These were difficult months for De Palchi. He (re)discovers the sluggishness of Italian bureaucracy, rendered even more complex by the imprisonment he endured. But this is also a period in which Alfredo discovers love and a renewed (thus never truly dormant) interest in poetry. In fact, in Vercelli, he comes across a couple of notebooks his mother had saved for him (from which he will eventually excavate the texts that will constitute *La buia danza di scorpione*), the poem *Un ricordo del '45*, and a small collection of other short poems strongly influenced by his reading of the Bible in prison, that we will call, for convenience, "the lost manuscript."

Ester Scevola, a university student in Milan (studying literature and a passionate reader of poetry), is the young woman with whom he will fall in love (this youthful love will be re-evoked in certain passages of the eponymous section of the *Sessioni con l'analista*, written between 1964 and 1966), and who will eventually type up this material. And it is also thanks to Ester that "the lost manuscript" will reach the attention of Giansiro Ferrata, the authoritative critic whom in those years—in the wake De Palchi's enthusiastic reading of his introduction to Cardarelli's *Poesie* (1942, 1948)—Alfredo admired more than any other. It is only to Ferrata—and perhaps exclusively to him—that our poet would have been disposed to submit his work.

Ferrata receives the transcript *brevi manu* from Ester in June of 1951, at Caffè Bagutta (while De Palchi timidly hid nearby); it consisted of roughly fifty short poems, extremely different stylistically from those in *La buia danza di scorpione*, though they were composed in the same period of time.

Ferrata's response was positive. And, in what seems like a romanticized episode from a literary life à la Dino Campana, Ferrata left Bagutta and went looking for the timid and elusive Alfredo, showering him with praise and encouragement. According to the direct testimony of De Palchi himself, Ferrata's exact words were, "Sei il nostro miglior giovane poeta"["You are our greatest young poet"]); indeed, he also expressed his personal interest and contextually announced that he would propose the manuscript to Vittorio Sereni. Working in those years for the Milanese publishing house *La Meridiana*, Sereni was in charge of a poetry series that had released (or would release shortly thereafter) the work of poets like Cardarelli, Leonardo Sinisgalli, Nelo Risi, Giorgio Orelli, Luciano Erba, Bartolo Cattafi (it was only a matter of time before Alfredo would become life-long friends with Erba and Cattafi).

Unfortunately, whether it was due to De Palchi's departure for Paris a few weeks later (Alfredo finally obtains his long-awaited passport in the summer of 1951 and bids a painful farewell to Italy and to Ester) or Ferrata's subsequent move from San Babila to via Buenos Aires, every trace of this typescript has been lost. The following year when De Palchi chances upon an encounter with Ferrata in Milan, together with Sonia Raiziss (to whom Alfredo will soon be married; the wedding will be celebrated in Paris on October 24, 1953), he will inquire about the manuscript. Giansiro will candidly confess that he can no longer find it, nor can he remember what he possibly could have done with it. From this moment on De Palchi will become completely uninterested in this line of work. And it would certainly be interesting to know, *à rebours*, if "the lost manuscript" was effectively lost, or if, to this day, it is still lying hidden amongst Ferrata's papers, or amidst Sereni's files or, even—in case Sereni might have passed it along to the small Milanese publishing house—in the archives of *La Meridiana*, if an archive of this publishing house still exists, since, among other things, a few short years later it stopped producing its own publications.

Therefore, of all the poet's work composed between the '40s and the '60s (until the publication of *Sessioni con l'analista* in 1967), all that remain are the texts of *La buia danza di scorpione* that I discussed in the first part of this chapter, and those—after the distant, narrative poem *Un ricordo del '15*—that will constitute the dense 1967 Mondadori volume.

This volume, therefore, was initially "favored" for publication in the *Specchio* series as a result of these first, fruitful yet indirect contacts with Sereni through Ferrata; contacts De Palchi will later nourish from New York, where he will act as a diligent "ambassador" of Italian poetry, both as translator with Sonia Raiziss (they have the honor of granting many Italian poets their first American translations from Saba, Ungaretti, and Montale, to Cardarelli, Piccolo, Sinisgalli, and Sereni: see, above all, the volume *Modern European Poetry*, 1966) and as a critic-correspondent for *Fiera letteraria*. The assiduous correspondence he exchanged with many of the major Italian poets of the time will also contribute to the maintenance of this lively literary relationship (the De Palchi Fund at Yale University's Beinecke Library attests to this). Some of his correspondents gravitated around the so-called *linea lombarda*, including the same Sereni, Erba, Sinisgalli and Cataffi, whom he met in person between 1960 and 1961 and with whom he will forge an authentic friendship, consisting of—more than kindred sensibilities—a profound reciprocal admiration that will persist unaltered right up to Bartolo's death (1979). An enthusiastic reader of *Un ricordo del '15* with close ties to Sereni, Cataffi will in fact eventually be responsible for rekindling a relationship of friendly esteem between Alfredo and Vittorio. Proof of this is found in the fact that, when *Questo e altro* (March 1962) was born, Vittorio did not hesitate—a concrete gesture of his esteem, on the eve of his publication of *Sessioni con l'analista*—to include the long narrative poem in the first issue of this now legendary journal.

It is precisely this official debut, in one of the most significant journals of those years (a debut fiercely, though futilely, opposed by Fortini for purely ideological reasons), that constitutes a precedent for his subsequent publication in the Mondadori volume. For its historical importance, it is worth reproducing here, almost in its entirety, the introduction written by Vittorio Sereni, who (if you exclude Glauco Cambon's short critical note on De Palchi published a year earlier in "La fiera letteraria," February 5, 1961) can, in all senses, be considered the Italian intellectual who baptized Alfredo. Today, his introduction can serve as a basic primer (despite the previsions for the future Sereni adumbrates) for a reading of *Sessioni con l'analista*, which begins with precisely *Un ricordo del '45*:

Oggi, 25 aprile, un quotidiano ci elenca alcuni sgradevoli dati di fatto: generali e colonnelli francesi noti come torturatori e massacratori di patrioti algerini furono a suo tempo eroi o benemeriti della resistenza all'invasore e oppressore tedesco. La conclusion dell'editoriale è semplice e chiara: non intesero, né prima né poi, il senso e il valore della Resistenza. La violenza, la persecuzione, la tortura sono il solo argomento, la sola 'ragione,' ieri dei nazisti, oggi di quelli dell'OAS. L'avere torturatori e massacratori, per ritorsione o altro, tra le proprie file è stato o è un infortunio ieri per la Resistenza, oggi per l' F.L.N. Non sarà mai un argomento contro di essi. Questa premessa abbastanza ovvia era necessaria, a scanso di ogni possibile equivoco, nel presentare qui il gruppo di poesie di Alfredo de Palchi che va sotto il titolo di *Un ricordo del '45*.
Non si tradisce nessun segreto di laboratorio precisando che l'autore ne fece una prima stesura nel '48; e nessun segreto privato, precisando ulteriormente che egli era allora in carere a seguito di avvenimenti in cui era stato coinvolto, poco più che adolescente. [...] Il de Palchi vive oggi negli Stati Uniti. E qui, con la moglie Sonia Raiziss, attende alle sorti di *Chelsea*, rivista di letteratura. Di lui leggeremo prima o poi, in altre sedi, cose più recenti che probabilmente risentono dei nuovi climi—umani e letterari—in cui l'autore vive da tempo. (Di stampo spiccatamente americano è il tirocinio cosciente cui l'autore si è sottoposto, volentieri portato—oggi—ad attribuire un maggiore 'ardimento' alla poesia statunitense rispetto alla nostra—che rappresenta invece il suo tirocinio inconscio o piuttosto la sua preistoria. [...] Sulla

sua vicenda personale di allora—una storia confusa di bastonature, sevizie e confessioni estorte, nella quale si trovò sballottato tra forze avverse che non riusciva, allora, a identificare e che per lui avevano un unico volto: quello dell'orrore—non insisteremmo se non per escludere che sia questa una testimonianza di parte fascista e per richiamare l'attenzione sul titolo, mai come in questo caso, essenziale alla lettura.

Questo ricordo del '45 procede contromano rispetto a ogni ricordo del '45 che ci sia stato tramandato o che si conservi per esperienza diretta. Non viene dalla parte dei vinti né da quell dei vincitori; gli è precluso il beneficio delle speranze che si accesero allora; e se accenna alla colpa, e al senso di colpa, lo fa entro i termini di un destino sentito come ineluttabile e insondabile, metastorico e anonimo: nello stesso modo con cui la vicenda si svolge senza appigli possibili nella storia—nel senso della storia—o nella passione di una scelta.

Non vede le forze in campo se non come cieche fazioni di fatto indifferenziabili, e se avverte un dualismo lo avverte, tragicamente, tra il soggetto commemorante e la guerra civile come fatto uniforme e mostruoso. Si tolga quel titolo e cadremo nell'impaccio e nella miseria delle classificazioni, incerte se trattare questi versi alla stregua di un fenomeno post-ermetico su sfondo genericamente kafkiano o, magari, d'un esercizio in direzione pseudo-informale.

Per noi è il profilarsi—l'abbiamo letto in tal senso—sempre più netto e stringente d'una struttura drammatica dentro e attraverso l'informe; il ripullulare dell'orrore, della fine della guerra civile e dello sterminio, attraverso le speranze stesse e il loro declino, fino alla guerra fredda. (Sereni 1962, 132-133)

[Today, April 25, a newspaper lists several unfortunate facts: French generals and colonels, notorious torturers and murderers of Algerian patriots, had in turn once been heroes or well-deserving participants in the resistance against the German invader and oppressor. The conclusion of the editorial is clear and simple: they didn't understand, not then, not now, the sense and the value of the Resistance. Violence, persecution, and torture are the only issues, the only 'rationale,' that pertained yesterday to the Nazis, today to those of OAS. Having torturers and murderers, whether out of retaliation or for any other reason, in their ranks was (or is) one of the mishaps of the Resistance, and the same can be said of the F.L.N. today. There will never be an argument against them. This rather obvious preamble was necessary in order to avoid any possible misunderstanding in presenting here Alfredo de Palchi's group of poems titled *Un ricordo del '45*.

There is no betrayal of any compositional secret in noting that the author wrote an early draft in '48; nor is any private secret betrayed in noting furthermore that he was already in prison in the wake of a series of events in which he found himself entangled when he was hardly more than a boy. [...] Today De Palchi lives in the United States. And here, with his wife Sonia Raiziss, he tends to the fluctuating fortunes of *Chelsea*, a literary magazine. Sooner or later we will be reading, in other places, more recent works that will probably be redolent of the new climate—human and literary—in which the author has been living for some time now. (The conscious apprenticeship to which the author has subjected himself of a distinctly American brand. Most recently he has willingly been led to attribute a greater 'daring' to the poetry being produced in the United States than to ours, which played a part in the poet's unconscious apprenticeship or rather his prehistory. [...] Regarding his personal experience in the period in question—a confused story riddled with beatings, torture, and extracted confessions, in which he found himself jostled about by adverse forces that he couldn't, at the time, identify and that for him had a single face: that of terror—we will not insist so as not to avoid turning this into a fascist testimony and to redirect our attention to the poem's title, which, more than in the case of any other poem, is essential to our understanding of it.

This memory of '45 moves in the wrong direction with respect to any other memory of '45 that has ever been passed down by tradition or that has ever been preserved through direct experience. It comes neither from the perspective of the losers nor from that of the winners; he was barred from the benefit of the soaring hopes that were ignited in that period; and if he hints at guilt, to a sense of guilt, he does so in terms of a destiny felt as ineluctable and unfathomable, meta-historical and anonymous: in the same way the events unfold without any possible footholds in the story—in the sense of the story—or in the passion of a choice.

He can't see the forces on the field except as blind, fundamentally unidentifiable factions, and if he perceives a duality he does so tragically, between the commemorating subject and the civil war as a uniform and monstrous fact. Take away its title and we fall into the embarrassment and the misery of classifications that are uncertain if we

want to treat these verses according to the standard of a post-hermetic phenomenon against a generically Kafkian backdrop or, perhaps, of an exercise in a pseudo-abstract direction.
For us it is the emergence of the outline—this is how we read it—coming more clearly into focus, of a dramatic structure working within and through the abstract; the palpable return of the terror, of the end of the civil war and of the destruction, through hope itself and the decline of that hope, until the Cold War.]

And what is effectively most immediately striking about this poem in the way it proceeds zigzagging against the grain through a strong impact, knocking the wind out of the reader, like a blow to the stomach, in just a few quick brushstrokes he conjures a scene in the suburbs and a situation—to repeat Sereni—swarming with horror, in which the young De Palchi comes to find himself. The situation is relived in the mind with a rhythm obsessively cadenced by a frantic, drumming scansion in which the nightmare scene of his vexing interrogation, the ruthlessness of his torturers, and the persistence of their cruelty toward the victim in the skeletal nudity of his cell. The entire poem consists of the dark gait of his slave drivers, portrayed in verses that are themselves driving, keen to follow the rhythmic beat of the horrible re-evocation. This vilified and tortured young man is reflected in *Meche* ("soprannome di un matto del mio paese e divenuto tale per le persecuzioni della gente" ["nickname of a mad man from my hometown driven mad by the persecution of the townsfolk"]), who in the poem in question becomes the symbolic scapegoat for the innocent, who "paga per le crudeltà e i crimini altrui" (De Palchi 1967, 167; "pay for the cruelties and crimes of others"). Not a glimmer of hope is to be found in these verses: the distant city is a "verme che divora e che si divora" ("worm that eats and is eaten") and the dawn-like light at the end of the tunnel seems destined to remain a mere apathetic, detached consolatory presence:

Alba
apatia
biancore che non mi schiara;
il passato resta

197

aggrappato e tra le sue maglie
il sogno s'arresta:
presente paleolitico... (17)

Dawn
apathy
whiteness that brightens nothing for me;
the past remains
grappled and the dream checked
between the meshes:
paleolithic present... (33)

This is the source of the eternal impulse that unites and consumes victims and assassins who oppose one another in a History that does not seem to prefer one category to the other.

The second section of *Sessioni con l'analista* is also tied to *Un ricordo del '45*. In "Cancro e meningite," written in the same period of time, the author conjures details and figures from his childhood. First and foremost is that of his grandfather, devoured by cancer ("gran assente / che mi fu padre e visse anarchico"; "great absence / who was a father to me and lived an anarchist") and unremittingly faithful to his libertarian and anticlerical ideals right up to the end. Once again some of the most strikingly seductive verses in all of De Palchi's work reappear, of such an auto-logical force that they almost spurn (or render "useless") any exegetical anamnesis; verses, among other things laden with a strong, expressionistic realism that, written between '48-'50, clearly anticipate "spoken" movements, in fragmentary scraps, and stylistic modalities (previously mentioned) that we will find in Elio Pagliarani's *Cronache* (1954), Giorgio Cesarano's *Erba Bianca* (1959), and, even later, Giancarlo Majorino's *Lotte secondarie* (1967), which will enter into competition with De Palchi for the Viareggio Prize in 1967.

This is the last section of *Sessioni con l'analista* De Palchi wrote in Italy. His move to France in the late summer of '51, his subsequent marriage to Sonia Raiziss, and his definitive expatriation to the United States three years later will mark a distinct turning point in the life (and in part in the poetry, especially from the thematic point of view) of Alfredo de Palchi.

The third section of the book is in fact titled *L'arrivo*, from the title of the eponymous poem written between Bordeaux and New York in '56. In the French city De Palchi passed a couple of spasmodic weeks waiting—yet again!—for his passport to be cleared for an American visa. Yet another instance in which his poetic and existential adventures walk arm in arm over the cobblestone streets near the pier where the Garonne meets the Atlantic, which the poet hopes to finally cross in search of the new world.

> [...] gli scafi
> riattivano scrosci di catene
> gru rottami vengono
> e partono con i continenti.
> Inutile ch'io urli aiuto alla costa,
> lo scheletro degli elementi già spiana
> la massa della distanza.
> [...]
>   Io stesso un'isola
> mi protendo alle navi che vanno
> ma perdo ogni distanza d'oceano
> conflagrante. (50-51)

> [...] and freighters
> busily alive clattering of chains
> cranes junk arrive
> and leave with their continents.
> Useless for me to scream for help of the coast,
> the skeleton of the elements already levels
> the massive distance.
> [...]
>   I myself an island
> Reaching out to the ships that go
> But I lose every distance of the raging
> Ocean. (61)

De Palchi has no anxiety or trepidation regarding his departure, which is the stuff of so much emigrant literature. His attitude toward the category of expatriate is completely different from that embodied by his fellow countryman a generation earlier. In his expectancy, he experiences the thrill of flight, freedom, evasion, mixed also with an apathetic detachment, as in a sort of aprioristic splenetic distrust of that which the new world could be able or will be able to offer him ("con gelido distacco evito l'oceano / purulento e quest'alba / quale alba"; "with icy detachment I avoid the festering / ocean at this dawn / what dawn" [65]). How different, in this sense, is De Palchi's skeptical and disillusioned attitude with respect to the ingenuous enthusiasm that had characterized, half a century earlier, the disembarkation of our compatriots in the new world! And here thoughts can't help but open like a fan and turn backwards, to the very writers I have treated and discussed in this book: from the primogenitor de Amici's *Sull'oceano*, to the likes of Emanuel Carnevali, Arturo Giovannitti, Constantine Panunzio, Pascal D'Angelo, Felix Stefanile, Giose Rimanelli, and Joseph Tusiani.

No different, however, will De Palchi's impact be with respect to his previous companions in fate, an impact anthropologically (but also linguistically) traumatic, harsh, hostile in a city like New York whose ruthless whirlpool of life sprays "fra spacchi di neon / snervanti, muraglie e rombo / di veicoli"; "between flashes of neon / enervating, walls and rumble / of vehicles"). In short, an agonizing America, in which exploitation and racism seem dominant; the poem/manifesto titled precisely *Razzismo* (56) demands to be read in its entirety, which Glauco Cambon liked so much (Cambon 1968), but also an America composed of limitless, evasive, and evanescent spaces, "rupi che sgolano distanze di luce," "boschi di muschio" and finally desert expanses (see *Arizona* and *Sul Delaware River)*.

The dense section *Womanization* is centered on the variegated world of women, perceived as *foemina* and *mulier*, on which, in turn, Marco Forti has written, for the "marasma esistenziale" ("existential decay") that it presents women confronted with the "frana del passato" ("landslide of the past"), which in America is transformed into the "stordimento di nuove metropolis" (Forti 1967; "bewilderment of new cities"). But the term *womanization* also brings with it (mainly) negative and even derogatory connotations, inherent in the expression "andare a donne," the activity of a calloused ladies man, as the corresponding verb, *to womanize*, specifically suggests.

This is one of the crucial aspects of De Palchi's poetry/life, namely an exasperated, almost obsessive search for the feminine subject, which will later congeal in an entire, bilingual volume of erotic poems (*Le viziose avversioni* / *The Addictive Aversions* of 1999). In a passage in *Sessioni con l'analista* at one point the poet states: "so che nulla vale / quanto la totale irruzione dei sensi" (93; "I know nothing's worth / so much as the total eruption of the senses" [101]).

Is it plausible—today, *a posteriori*—to interpret this intense (at times excessive?) addiction to sex or sex mania (experienced through antagonistic acceptation of attraction and rejection at the same time) as the exasperated and exasperating growth of the libido accumulated (and conserved) by the poet over the course of those long and lonely years spent in prison that also coincidentally correspond precisely to those of young Alfredo's pubertal development? An Eros, often resolved in a projective key, that, far from acquiescing with the passing of years, was not only always present in De Palchi's poetry, but we find it again more active than ever and overflowing right up through his most recent output. Here, I refer to a chapbook of twenty-three poems titled "Essenza carnale," written between the winter of 1999 and the summer of 2000, published along with other unpublished pieces, in a supplement of the magazine *Hebenon* (No. 6, Fall 2000), dedicated to De Palchi, and then printed again in a section of its own in the recent volume *Paradigma* (2001).

Running through *Womanization* is a series of erotic situations (actual or only imagined) and feminine figures that rank among the most important in his life: from the years immediately following his release from prison (crucial places: Vercelli, Venezia, Milano, the protean Paris of the '50s, Barcelona, where De Palchi permanently resided from 1954 to 1955), up to those he spent in New York from '56 to '67, the year *Sessioni con l'analista* was published.

This, in my opinion, was one of the happiest and most liberated creative phrases De Palchi's poetry has ever seen. It is a phase in which the author finds a sort of compensation for the nihilistic, punitive emptiness of his youth, which, like an indelible stain (I have already mentioned it, but it needs to be forcefully repeated here), he will carry with him (inside him) his entire life. And it is also, from a linguistic point of view, the phase of his life most unencumbered by para-experimental pitfalls, while always maintaining that fulminating acumen and that tormented projective capacity, typical of his *poiesis*. Here are a few emblematic examples:

> La neve sfuria e sotto il siero livella
> ogni oggetto sporgenza macchia.
> Non sei qui: è domenica
> il marito a casa.
> Aspettandoti al vetro del motel sulla spiaggia
> sento che l'infantile
> gemito dei gabbiani.
> E uguale a quello della mia gola
> ulcerata dalla sigaretta (75)

> (The snow rages and under its serum
> levels every object protuberance blemish.
> You aren't here: it's Sunday
> your husband's home.
> Waiting for you at the window of the motel on the beach
> I hear the seagull's childlike mewing
> so like my own throat ulcerated
> by cigarettes [81])

> [...] La sigaretta mi stordisce
> alle vetrine di reggipetti
> mutandine, umido nylon che mi addossa
> un sapore di bocca seno cosce.
> Guardo chi viene, non dico, la guardo,
> annuso la sottana
> e ho nostalgia di me

dentro il tuo corpo
sinagoga. (76)

([...] a cigarette makes me dizzy
in the shop windows: bras
shorts, limp nylon that swamps me
with the pungency of mouth breast thighs.
I see someone coming, say nothing, glance,
I sniff a skirt
and I am homesick
for the synagogue
of your body. [83])

seguo quelle che
per 10 dollari
entrano nelle auto:
[...] L'insistenza dello sguardo sapiente di soldi
un ondare di natiche
il bisbiglio che non intendo sono
l'invito. Non ne usufruisco; ho moglie
e altro, mi dico—ma ecco,
ce ne è sempre una che mi mette in panico... (79)

(I follow those who
for 10 dollars
get in your car:
[...] The insistence of the knowing gaze of money
a surging wave of buttock
the murmuring that I can't understand are
inviting. I do not partake; I'm married
and all that, I say to myself—but look,
there's always one who sends me into a panic...)

The section that follows *Womanization* is titled *Reportage*, and it is composed of a single, long and caustic narrative poem about New York, a city described in all of its negative aspects and elected the emblematic whorehouse of a corrupt system in which rampant politicians coexist with cynical lawyers, prostitutes, "sodomiti della pubblicità," "elettroesecuzioni dei colombi che piovono dalle finestre / e cornice / sputi catarrosi / escrementi alle gambe lustre / delle signore" (83-84; "electrocution of pigeons that rain down from the windows / and cornices / catarrhal spit / excrement of / dogs lined up at the glittering legs / of women" [89]). In this "reportage" De Palchi does not hesitate to speak openly, through an extremely efficacious technique of accumulation, of an entire catalogue of nefariousness, that runs from the "barboni con bottiglia all'ascella" to "intossicate lesbiche ninfomani" and "voluminose mulatte" and the incessant buzz of life in the hotels. He paints a rotten and ramshackle picture in which nothing seems to be safe from the analytical eye of the author, who proceeds to impiously ransack it. In this whirling, chaotic fresco, "la folla è bestia dal torbido cervello" ("the crowd is a beast with a turbid mind") and "la legge è ingiustizia rispettata" ("the law is injustice respected"), and not even the flag is safe, "uno straccio / per infagottare chi muore per niente" ("a rag / for wrapping those who die for nothing"), while religion, which should represent the last anchor of salvation, is nothing more than "un tumore perché marcisca la razza" ("a tumor so that the race might rot"), the only divinity dominant over everyone and everything is the god Money, which is to be obtained by any means necessary and in any place, from ferocious and sophisticated Wall Street to Central Park where sadistic thugs "al chiodo infilzano lo scoiattolo intanto" ("pierce squirrels on nails in the meantime") and wouldn't think twice about stabbing an incautious passerby for only a few dollars.

This, the suicidal pantomime, the "mefitico miasma" ("mephitic miasma") of an ant farm of a city, erected as a "solenne cattedrale" ("solemn cathedral"), like New York, in which the poet, with nihilistic distrust, has no choice other than to sell and sell himself, following his fictive path (life):

>   – sul filo
>   di ragno
> mi equilibrio mi fingo
> allocco

e l'azzardo offre ogni caduta vizio
l'esperienza di mille
vite e non rimpiango;
                chi mi batte
                     la mano
fredda sulle spalle
può sbilanciarmi

[...] vendo
e mi vendo anch'io ricco
di sconosciuti in attesa [...]
    – seguito la via
di finzione [...]
in bocca la saliva è sale
la cicca morsicata
rancore
[...]
    il mezzogiorno
    irruente
           (fluisce scorie empietà)
un mefitico miasma che amo—questo
è splendore (91-93)

            (- on the cobweb
            of the spider
    I balance I pretend
    that I'm a fool
and the risk offers every fallen vice
the experience of a thousand
lives and I regret nothing:
            whoever slaps
            a cold
hand on my shoulder
can unbalance me

[...] sell
and sell myself even I wealthy
in strangers who wait [...]
    – I follow the path

of deceit [...]
saliva is salt to the mouth
the cigar stub chewed
                      spite
[...]
    the impetuous
    noon
            (flowing slag and impiety)
is a mephitic miasma I love—this
is splendor (99-101)

A scathing reproach, "Reportage" is one of the most cutting and critical poems ever written by a twentieth-century poet on American civilization. With its uneven, mangled, and sarcastic allure, there does not seem to be a single glimmer of hope or faith. Over everything dominates the polyvalent, firm and intransigent *j'accuse* of the poet ("figlio rigettato"), the alienated eyewitness and asymmetrical spectator.

4. THE DOUBLE EXILE

Perhaps in no other poem like "Reportage" does anyone denounce in such a violent and direct way the predicament of alienation and exile (of alienating exile), which was endured, around the middle of the 1960s, by an Italian expatriate writer in New York. In the poem in question, this laceration is flung onto the page in an intentionally free form and threadbare way; it is fully on display, and, in De Palchi, it certainly had to be accentuated, especially following the incipient breaking off of his relationship with Sonia Riaziss and the state of ferocious indigence he suffered in the aftermath. Years later, in the *Almanacco dello specchio* (No. 11, 1983), Luciano Erba introduced, a selection of De Palchi's poems, collected under the title *Gentile animale braccato*. These poems were written for the most part during the 1970s and hinted, although in nuanced tones, at the state of isolation, and more precisely at our poet's "spiazzamento." Although Erba intended "spiazzamento" to refer to the literary aspect of De Palchi's life, the word can also be applied tout court to his existential and psychological states: "[...] poiché Alfredo de Palchi risiedeva e risiede tuttora a New York e il suo status d'isolato andrebbe meglio, se pur più rozzamente, definito come quello di spiazzato. Poeta a New York!, sì, ma..." (Erba 1983; "[...] since Alfredo de Palchi resided and still resides in New York and his status as an isolated individual would be better, if perhaps more crudely, defined as that of one who has been displaced. Poet in New York!, yes, but...").

This then is how, to his initial experience of exile in his homeland, another only apparently milder experience of exile—this time in the adoptive country—was added to this poet's life. What occurred here, in short, is that typical psychic process of acceptance/denial, absorption/refusal, evident in all those Italian writers who, having expatriated to America, and not having been perfectly integrated into the new cultural establishment (or into the new adoptive language), felt, in a lacerating way, in their own words, like "refugees" and "fugitives" at the same time. I am speaking of authors effectively "displaced," who, in order to attain the status of writers of (and in) the Italian language outside Italy, had to undergo a sort of double exile: the first from their literary patria, which no longer recognized them (or only negligently: this is the condition of isolation Erba spoke of), and the second from the new "patria," which they experienced, in a manner of speaking, only transversally, and that therefore could easily ghettoize them. Different, then, is the case of those Italian emigrant writers in America (some of whom were even born here, or rather those who I called in the first chapter "American-Italians"). These writers belonged to the generation prior to that of De Palchi, who even at the price of misunderstandings, sacrifices, and equivocations not only knew how and wanted to integrate into American society, but even adopted its expressive language: as, for example, di Donato, Carnevali, Giovannitti, and Ciardi.

De Palchi's position is therefore more defiladed, more transgressive, and, above all, more anti-academic than any other contemporary Italian emigrant writer in America at the time. (I have in mind names like Cecchetti, Pasinetti, and Tusiani.) Those who were involved in university institutions, for example, had thus "compromised" with the cultural system and were, as a result, very literally, more exposed to linguistic absorption and contamination.

As with his coeval Rimanelli (who came casually to teaching), so with De Palchi we must also speak of a dilatation of the existential-semantic expressive field expanding through the body of his writing.

And so a *second* exile (his adoptive land) is compounded with his *initial* exile (his homeland), both acting together to produce that familiar feeling (which we found in Rimanelli) of belonging neither here nor there, yet also, paradoxically, at the same time, the sense of *belonging any place,* real or imaginary, whatever it may be.

It is precisely this double unresolved knot—returning to *Sessioni con l'analista*—that ignites the mentally ubiquitous deflagration of the last two sections (*Bag of Flies*, written in 1961, and the collection's eponymous section written between 1964 and 1966): experienced on the page as a sort of continuous verbal-mental coming and going between past-present and present-past. When confronted with a present that feels alien, there is the equivalent of a past, equally alien, but that on its auroral side presents "consoling" moments (precisely because they are remote) in which to take "refuge."

Thus, the entire final section of *Sessioni con l'analista* moves between imaginary projections and mnestic border-crossings (the thrilling memories of his adolescence), onto which moments of his present life *are superimposed*. The American existential experience: contemporaneous, that is, to the act of writing the poems of the last two sessions of *Sessioni con l'analista*, the whole thing, in a synchronic *Erlebnis*, experienced, on the page, as a sort of continuum of exceptional self-analytical force. At this level, life experience and imaginary projections are confused into a single flux, a unique storm-of-consciousness à la Svevo (though the comparison should not be forced). Not by chance the eponymous section is titled *Sessioni con l'analista*, where the analyst is not so much an actual character as an emblematic figure that embodies the other to whom he externalizes the fragments of his complex first-person "I" (the "I" of the writer).

Thus, he moves from a condemnation without appeal of a story hypocritically nourished by the mythomaniacs (of the civil war) and vile transformists (the fascists, those lousy turncoats, who as soon as

the war was over nonchalantly changed "sides"), to the disillusionment of every last one of his youthful ideals, brutally trampled under
foot by those who never had any ideals to begin with, if not those
nourished by occasional rewards and various other temporary political advantages, whose "rapacious hands" were keen to obtain and
extort through deceit and violence. After this, there followed, as in a
vicious circle spiraling out of control, wave after wave of infinite violence. This is history. These are its commandments:

Dimentico la pena lacerante, non l'odio
di cui la ragione mi svergogna
per voi tutti.
        Io neppure so più amare,
solo so bruciarvi con i miei anni
di punizione e questa
domenica del patire parolaio / ancora i vosri rami
d'ulivo sono l'infetta infiammazione, torce di numerosi
getzemani dove popolazioni sono triturate
dagli Eichman e da milioni che si lavano le mani (101-102)

(I forget the searing pain not the reason
of your hate that shames me
for all of you.
        Not even I know how to love
but I know how to burn you with my years
for this punishment and this
Sunday of gas bag suffering / yet your olive
branches are the infected inflammation, torches of numerous
Gethsemanes where populations are pulverized
by Eichmanns and by milliions who was their hands clean [109])

Insinuating its way into the thoughts of the poet is the devastating
realization that perhaps he, too, had—despite himself—undergone a
transformation, imposed on him by life; that even he had become
like those whom he had described with greedy hands. This is how
History, in its *fiumana* (to use a Pirandellian expression), drags everything with it, and both the conquered and the conquerors are
mixed up again in the same amalgam. I am reminded of Vittorio

Sereni's bitter reflections on the horrors of civil war, the Nazi extermination, the hope for rebirth, and the subsequent decline of that hope. From here to the radical, sarcastic disillusion of a utopian construction of the "socialist city" is but a short step.

> Ti noto nella tensione
> d'ognuno che in sé mi svela il tuo volto
> qual è, ma ora anch'io tuo (vostro) pari
> ho viltà, magnifiche
> mani ingorde, occhi
> che evitano di sognare o costruire
>
> *la città socialista*
>
> – questo tutto,
> la mia rivoluzione. (103)
>
> (I notice your tension
> in everyone who in himself reveals your face
> to me as it is, but now even I you your kind
> have contempt with our greedy
> hands, magnificent, and eyes
> that avoid dreaming of or building
>
> *the socialist city*
>
> – all this
> my revolution. (111)

In effect, the substantial eponymous section is composed of continuous zigzagging elucubrations, reflections *à rebours*, sudden flashbacks, feverish attenuations, and swift mental contortions. It seems natural that this neurotic coming and going should be served by an intentionally incoherent and informal structure. Very appropriately Giuliano Manacorda, reviewing *Sessioni con l'analista* in *Rinascita* noted that for De Palchi the adoption of "free verse" is the necessary "form" of a precise poetic "content," that expresses itself with "frasi mozze e pur profondamente e logicamente connesse che affiorano alle labbra del nevrotico, dove 'nevrotico' qui è sinonimo di uomo moderno che distrugge se stesso facendo della propria società lo strumento del proprio suicidio" (Manacorda 1967; "broken though profoundly and logically connected phrases that appear on the lips of the neurotic, where 'neurotic' here is synonymous with the modern man who destroys himself transforming society itself into the instrument of his suicide").

We should therefore reject—lingering a moment on the critical reception of *Sessioni con l'analista*—Silvio Ramat's position, who, though emphasizing the schizomorphic meter of De Palchi's versification ("spaccati della mente che l'indagine psichica rivela al suo stesso possessore per squarci insospettati"; "cleft from the mind that the psychic investigation reveals to its very possessor through unexpected fragments"), inquires as to whether the author might be too enchained to free verse as a result of his "costituzionale incapacità di conseguire una 'forma'" (Ramat 1967; "constitutional inability to follow a 'form'").

In reality, in reading *Sessioni con l'analista* properly, the reader soon realizes that he has stumbled upon an actual series of psychoanalytic sessions, one corresponding to each strophe (which are, in fact, duly numbered), almost as if the strophe itself were a stand-in for the psychoanalyst interrogating the author, who gives free reign to his thoughts that spill out onto the page according to their own unique set of pre-logical associations. The whole thing is possible, following a para-surrealist praxis, thanks to a reality in which things that are distant from each other start intersecting with each other uninterruptedly, creating a cluttered mess, yes, but also a considerable alienating effect. In order to obtain this effect De Palchi vertiginously nuances his discourse, leaving only brief traces of it in fragments, shards, fleeting allusions. In other words, he isolates, intentionally, from the verbal-mental "story" only certain pieces, sometimes even individual words, according to a technique—from the point of view of the visual arts—extremely close to the informal. It is a precise, stylistic process, intelligently explained by Carlo Della Corte, who in turn spoke of a "un linguaggio rotto, somigliante a quello che di certa pittura informale" (Della Corte 1967; "a broken language, vaguely resembling that of a certain brand of abstract painting").

Furthermore, we are in the thick of the period in which Free Verse spread throughout Europe, starting in France where De Palchi lived in the first half of the 1950s; and certainly his strong interest in painting led him to an intimate knowledge of the work of Dubuffet, Mathieu, and Fautrier. During his time in Paris, Alfredo took regular courses in painting at the Académie Juliard in Saint-Germain-des Prés. Subsequently, in New York, driven by the same artistic passion, he spent 15 years (1979-1994) working in the diffusion of art books for the largest Italian publishing houses.

Returning to the question of free verse, the Paris School innovated the form, which, from the 1950s on, served as a focal point for similar trends with analogous expressive ends, eventually spread like wildfire to the rest of the western world. Though belonging summarily to abstractionism, abstract painting, in effect, proclaims a triumph over formalism. On equal footing with the work of abstract artists, *Sessioni con l'analista* does not obey any premeditated will: the logical intervention is reduced to the essential; on the canvas (on the page) one finds only fragments of emotions and feverish reactions concentrated in spontaneous lightning-quick movements of the mind. But in De Palchi, beyond the abstract, there is also another element at work—in order to remain in the domain of the visual arts for a moment—the distant memory of the divisionism that brusquely superimposed itself on the experience of the twentieth century. I am thinking, in particular, of an artist like Sironi (whom he very much admired), who exalts the drama of contemporary man, suffocated by the city in an exasperated rigorous use of forms, by dismal and obsessive colors; and I am also thinking of the brusque symbolism and twisted unreality of certain of his compositions, which always denounce the presence of an existential punishment (or of a sense of guilt), over which silence and incommunicability dominate. Let's read, in light of this, an exemplary array of verses:

[...] la geologia ruga,
è

sulla asimmetria
facciale di . .

   il sole che entra a stecche
dalle persiane, la gomma per fregare
(troppo
tardi)
il già scritto [...]

impossibile
comunicare il gergo
inconcluso (107)

([...] geology wrinkles,
lies upon
the facial
asymmetry of . .

   the sun comes in
slatted through the shutters, the rubber for erasing
(too
late)
the document readied [...]

impossible
to communicate the inconclusive
jargon [115])

And still on the subject of "incommunicability," it is worth noting, *en passant*, that when De Palchi writes *Sessioni con l'analista* (in precisely the two-year period from 1964 to 1966) we are in the midst of the period of the most historic films by Antonioni, who, perhaps more than any other artist, adhered to this notion as an ideological/philosophical presupposition in his cinematographic work. On incommunicability, which De Palchi prefers to call *incommunication*, the author will meditate with some frequency. The following is a brief sampling from the eponymous section of the volume:

> (incomunicazione)
> frammenti,
> secchi singhiozzi, turbinio
> interno (109)

> (non-communication)
> fragments:
> harsh sobbing, inner
> turmoil (117)

> il 'perché' è domanda
> stupida,
> incomunicabile; (110)

> the "why" is a stupid
> question—
> incommunicable (119)

> viaggio
> - incomunicabile -
> per altre isole... (126)

> I travel
> - incommunicable -
> to other islands . . (137)

> Inetto —— graffio
> (incomunicazione) la crosta (146)

> inept —— I scratch
> (incommunicable) the crust (165)

To emphasize the stability of his "incommunication," therefore, the scattered fragments and brief glimpses that express it (or do not express it), like verbal sobbing, an S.O.S. transmitted out into a world that seems padded and unresponsive to any cry ("secchi singhiozzi, turbinio / interno—mi ascolti"). In these lightning bursts, like flashes of the most intense light, objects appear and disappear, as well as animals, people and relicts of past-present light (the image of a rabbit with its infant cry); the recurrent crossing and uncrossing of a secretary's legs under the table; a truck bouncing down a dusty road in the country; machine gun and rifle fire; ambushes; the civilian guerilla warriors with whom De Palchi had collaborated, though awkwardly, in a dramatic crescendo slowly building as the memories accumulate (118-119). And emerging again, just as had been the case in *Un ricordo del '45*, is the tattered evocation of the hardships he endured following the incident mentioned above.

All of this testifies to the depth of the wound, still open and vulnerable, which time (we are roughly twenty years after that dark episode) had not been able, and perhaps ever would be able to heal. The only difference, with respect to *Un ricordo del '45*, is that now De Palchi does not hesitate to indicate the precise places and characters of that tragic "theater" and of his ignoble *jeu du massacre*: Carella, Fraccarolo, Luigi [Ferrarin], Dario, Cella Nerone who held a gun to his head and coerced the notorious "confession." Alfredo will write in an annotation to *Sessioni con l'analista* about the last of his "executioners": "Cella Nerone was the monster in charge of the prison. The name means Nero's cell. When the Nazis retreated in 1945, Nerone switched sides. This did not save him from a war trial. He was condemned to life imprisonment for rape and sadistic crimes. To a priest he confided, not without deceit, how Christ and the Madonna had come to him in a vision. After serving a brief sentence, he was set free" (192).

It is easy to understand, *a posteriori*, De Palchi's subsequent complete ideological disillusionment (with regard to both the right and the left), his Serenian indifference (*disamore*) for his time, not to mention his somber depression that for may years accompanied his nomadic existence, which, if it didn't bring him to the act of suicide, certainly, *de facto*, brought him ever closer to affirming his absolute ideological detachment and his most radical denial of all social and political institutions ("ma non mi commetto il colpo / di grazia, ma / *non lo amo il mio tempo, non lo amo*" [129]; "I won't commit the coup / de grâce on me, but / *I don't love our time, I don't*" [141]. Treading the turf of a verse from one of Sereni's poems, entitled *Nel sonno*, the italics are the poet's own;).

Within and amid these bitter biographic episodes, fragments of erotic imagery recur, psychically compensative. Beyond the ephemeral post-prison passions, there is, for example, the persistent evocation of a secretary: an emblematic figure, in a certain way succinctly representative of a repressed Eros, diffusing a libido as dark as it is constant, capable of unleashing the frequent assaults of sexual desires (and projections).

In the last part of the book, all of this solipsistic tangled mess is punctuated in a labyrinthine way by the frequent and obsessive utterance of *perché* (in its double function as adverb and conjunction), as though to stimulate interrogatives or to propose causatives that, nevertheless, are never answered, given, precisely, the basic *incommunication* that pervades De Palchi's entire non-credo. Nor are satire and sarcasm enough to muffle the swift beat of his continuous interior monologue. There are only moments of apparent relenting, born also meta-textually (one example, above all: the ironic, slightly mangled reference to the consolatory title of Guido Da Verona's novel *La mia vita in un raggio di sole*), which, effectively, is this interior roar, unbridledly and haphazardly unleashed by De Palchi, in order to take control of it.

Having conquered every self-indulgence, having vanquished every pseudo-justification, having abandoned any and all "mimetismi / pervasivi / evasivi" (163; "the pervasive / evasive / mimicry" [189]) and the "ostacoli indecenti" (162; "indecent obstacles," [185]), every nostalgia has been eliminated, even the so-called "roots" become an unrelated concept, these nostalgias residing as an extreme reason for being (or rather of one's own "sentirsi esistere"), uniquely and anarchically in writing, in poetry, in love:

   — nessuna nostalgia
   mi rattiene
       spingo la vita oltre

dove non mi occorrono radici
per sapermi
sentirmi esistere;
                  una valigia di libri
un pacco di carta
macchina per scrivere e una donna
mi conchiudono

il resto non importa
                           basta
che la mia sofferenza sia pari
a quella dell'animale sul tavolo
delle ricerche (164)

(— no homesickness
restrains me
                  I thrust my life beyond
where roots are not required
for me to know
or to feel alive:
                  a satchel of books
a batch of paper
a typewriter and a woman
complete me

the rest doesn't matter
                       it's enough
my suffering equals
an animal's in the research
lab [189])

The world (or non-world), De Palchi pessimistically concludes, "è quello che non è e vale / un osso" ("is what it's not, not worth / a damn" [189]). The twice-exiled poet had no choice but to continue pressing on along his own "carro tetro" ("dismal cargo"):

                che nessuno si scomodi
    ora — lo stesso spingo
    in avanti il mio carro tetro sotto

una lapada
>> - solo, incomunicato,
incomunicabile -

>> (may no one bother
now — I thrust my same
dismal cargo forward
under a light
>> - alone, out of touch,
incommunicable—[191])

5. THE BIG (ROTTEN) APPLE

A book that represents a turning point, decidedly innovative (in terms of its expressivity as well as its thematic structure) for the period in which it was written, *Sessioni con l'analista*, "nella sua unicità, lascia il segno nell'odierno panorama letterario" (Cambon 1968; "in its uniqueness, it leaves its mark on today's literary landscape"), and he concedes nothing to the reader, yet he doesn't hesitate to fully disclose himself.

The urgency of his uninterrupted stream-of-conscious is wedded to the accumulation of reflections-judgments-memories-projections that are slowly displayed, analyzed, questioned. The whole, composed of a continually fractured, derisive discourse, reduced to stuttering in those places where even expressive experimentalism with its frequent departures from the norm (reflected in the bold arrangement of certain verses on the page and the irregular use of punctuation, among other things) is not part of a metalingualism premeditated by the author (which is totally foreign to him from the outset), but is always in the service of his incoherent internal motor, that is, in underlining his pauses, his sudden attenuations, his powerful ascensions, in short, his every move.

And as far as the New York scene is concerned, it is ruthlessly discerned in the most penetrating pages of the second part of *Sessioni con l'analista*. Few expatriate Italian writers in America have succeeded like De Palchi—any facile rhetoric of nostalgia aside—in presenting it to us in such a naked and impious way.

In effect, his subsequent collection will be entirely centered on the Big Apple, *Costellazione anonima*, published many years later (first in 1997, in a North American bilingual edition, and the following year in Italy), though the texts that it contains were written in large part shortly after *Sessioni con l'analista*, or rather between the 1960s and 1970s.

Between *Sessioni con l'analista* and *Costellazione anonima* there is obviously *La buia danza di scorpione* and a slender volume titled *Mutazioni* (1988), which Andrea Zanzotto honored at the Premio San Vito al Tagliamento, justifying his decision in the following speech:

La poesia di De Palchi si inscrive con originalità nel campo dello sperimentalismo di questo dopoguerra, senza cedere mai alle mode o a velleità di eversioni totali, ma provando fin dall'inizio un suo equilibrio fondato su una risentita partecipazione al moto della storia di questi decenni. L'espressione di De Palchi è limpida e nello stesso tempo acre e tagliente. In generale vi domina una concisione che tende a fissare in lampeggianti immagini il senso intero dei componimenti. I ritmi ne risultano fratti e scossi, quasi come un diagramma dei moti interiori, ma contenuti sempre ad un livello che rifiuta l'enfasi e l'ostentazione, anche della stessa tragicità.

In questo si potrebbe riscontrare un'analogia di De Palchi con i poeti della "linea lombarda" e con Cattafi o Accrocca. La violenza che si scatena più o meno sordamente, o sfacciatamente, entro un ambiente di metropoli che ha un sottinteso americano, ma che riflette una situazione generale del nostro tempo, viene riconnessa da De Palchi a un osceno errore della Natura, in cui sembra imperare una maligna selezione, ma non a vantaggio del più forte (o intelligente), come spesso si dice, bensì del più "scaltro," del cinico che nell'inganno ha la sua più pericolosa arma. De Palchi oltre a dimostrare qui la sua attenzione alle scienze umane, come psicanalisi e antropologia, manifesta una sua presa di posizione altamente etica, anche se nel rifiuto di ogni ideologia. E la configurazione stilistica del suo lavoro è pienamente congrua, nella sua decisione e immediatezza, a tale vissuto ed interpretazioni del vissuto.

[De Palchi's poetry asserts itself with originality in the field of post-war experimentation, without ever giving into the trends or to the foolish aspirations of total subversion, but attempting from the beginning to establish a balance based on his resentful participation in the movement of these most recent decades of history. De Palchi's expression is limpid and at the same time piercing and harsh. In general it is dominated by a concision that tends to fix in flashing images the entire sense of his poems. His rhythms come off broken and shattered, almost like a diagram of interior movements, but contained always on a level that refuses emphasis and ostentation, even of its very tragedy.

In this we can find De Palchi's analogy with the poets of the "Lombard line" and with Cattafi or Accrocca. The violence that is unleashed with a more or less dull thud, or shamelessly, in an metropolitan environment that is implied to be American, but that reflects a general situation of our time, is reconnected by De Palchi to an obscene error of Nature, in which a malicious selection seems to rule, but not for the benefit of the fittest (or most intelligent), as one often hears, but for the most "cunning," the cynic who finds his greatest weapon in deceitfulness. Beyond demonstrating here his attention to the humanities, like psychoanalysis and anthropology, De Palchi manifests his highly ethical stance, even if in his rejection of every ideology. And the stylistic configuration of his work is fully congruous, in its decisiveness and immediacy, to his lived experience and interpretations of that experience.]

I have reproduced Zanzotto's explanation in its entirety because it not only effectively synthesizes De Palchi's work as a whole, but also because *Mutazioni* is composed of a selection of texts culled from the output of an abundant twenty-year period (we can also even call it a forty-year period, since the little book in question also included six poems from *La buia danza di scorpione*). In this book there are three pieces that come from *Costellazione anonima* and the one that would immediately follow, titled *Le viziose avversioni*.

Zanzotto's note, therefore, rightly provides an opportune exegetical basis for understanding how De Palchi's work evolves over the course of the 1970s and 1980s.

All the better for proceeding directly to a reading of *Costellazione anonima* and *Le viziose avversioni*, books in which, in a more organic way (inasmuch as they have been thoroughly mixed in with the others), the reader can find poems (hastily anthologized) that had initially appeared in *Mutazioni*.

Costellazione anonima (my textual references refer to the first edition) is also fundamental for our understanding of De Palchi's entire American experience. The main inspirational force behind the book is New York City, the huge, chaotic metropolis in which Alfredo has lived for more than fifty years, and in which he continues to live.

With respect to his previous attempts, this collection also possesses a greater formal equilibrium while maintaining unaltered his uncanny finesse at synthesis, though it is perhaps slightly less transgressive on the linguistic level than his previous books (notice the kinks he ironed out and certain variants, in three cases in particular, drawn from Sessioni con l'analista, namely "In Times Square," "Hanno sparato il negro," and "Gigantiacciai," which had formerly born the titles "Times Square", "Razzismo," and "Il saldatore," respectively).

The bilingual volume presents forty-seven poems translated over the course of the 1970s and 1980s by Sonia Raiziss, with whom Alfredo, even once their marriage ended in 1970, maintained a fruitful cultural relationship. They even co-edited the magazine *Chelsea* for many years (founded in 1958 in New York, the magazine ceased publication in 2007).

Certainly, a profound chronological hiatus separates the publication of *Sessioni con l'analista* and that of *Costellazione anonima*. The gap is partially compensated for by the appearance of the English translation of *Sessioni con l'analista* by I. L. Salomon (1970), the fine translator of Carlo Betocchi and Dino Campana; not to mention the frequent contributions to newspapers and periodicals—especially American—of his creative work (and methodically translated by Sonia Raiziss), written in the twenty-year period from 1970 to 1990: I cite, among many others (beyond those already mentioned in the context of *La buia danza di scorpione*), *The American*

Poetry Review, The Nation, Pittsburgh Quarterly, The Antioch Review, Contemporary Literature in Translation, Gradiva, and *Testo a fronte.*

To this I add the intense work of translation into English of a good deal of Italian poetry on which he collaborated with Sonia, for the magazine *Chelsea* and for other American publishers, beginning in 1960 with Bantam Books (together they edited—as I have already mentioned—the entire Italian section of *The World's Love Poetry*); which led in 1962 to a collaboration with the Modern Library (they translated and edited the *Anthology of Medieval Lyrics*); New Directions in 1965, (*Selected Poems* of Eugenio Montale); and again in 1966 with Bantam Books, for which they curated the entire Italian poetry section in the volume *Modern European Poetry.*

To all of this, let us not forget his translation work and the presentations he wrote for "Chelsea" (introducing numerous Italian poets translated from 1961 on: including Sinisgalli, Risi, Sereni, Della Corte, Erba, and Cardarelli, just to name a few); in *Poetry* (in this historic magazine Montale made his debut in America thanks to the translation of a couple of his poems by De Palchi/Raiziss, for the 1958 issue; and again in *Poetry* (September 1961), his translations of a group of poems by Lucio Piccolo appeared); *The Atlantic Monthly* (December 1958, translations of Saba, Montale, Quasimodo, and Sinisgalli); and I could also list other important periodicals like *The Transatlantic Review* (No. 7, 1961, translations of Saba, Cardarelli, Ungaretti, Sinisgalli, Gatto, Caproni, and Sereni); *Poetry Now* (December 1965, Sereni; June 1979, Davide Maria Turoldo); and many others.

I have limited myself in this brief excursus to citing only a fraction of the variegated and stratified body of translation work De Palchi produced between 1970 (the year of the publication in English of *Sessioni con l'analista,* which was well received in America, as demonstrated by the positive reviews it garnered from Brendan Kennelly, Priscilla Whitmore, and Glauco Cambon, among others; see also the bibliography in the appendix) and 1983, when he staged his comeback on the Italian poetry scene with a group of poems printed in the *Almanacco dello Specchio* of that year, which I mentioned above. His translation work should give you an idea of the intense laboratory *for* poetry (though not *his* poetry per se) that in part justifies his long silence.

And so, as I was saying, the forty-seven (mostly short) incandescent poems that compose *Costellazione anonima* have as their essential theme the American metropolis: from the years of De Palchi's traumatic first impressions to his experience over the course of the following several years (the book, with the exception of the three poems taken from *Sessioni con l'analista*, as I mentioned above, effectively covers the work of roughly a fifteen-year period: 1965-1980).

His quotidian encounter/confrontation with the city is documented in a dramatic way under the double banner of "rejection" and "revolt." Furthermore, the Villonian epigraph, not his first, placed in the opening ("Pour ce qui'il est tout insensé"), is an extremely precise semiological hint at the meaning of the whole. The shamelessness of the world finds in a metropolis like New York its quintessential concentration and manifestation.

Out of this shamelessness—in the very way the poet embraces it, in particular, in the heart of Manhattan—De Palchi derives a mini-epopea of daily life in the city, as candid as it is cruel, and he blurts the whole thing out into the face of the reader with scabrous and piercing verses that concede nothing to the tourist-visionary fascination that punctually strikes the (superficial) visitor of the Big Apple. The quotidian dimension comes through loud and clear, as brash as it is threadbare, of the *homo homini lupus*, to which the only solution seems to consist, primarily, of enslaving oneself to the miserable existence that renders individuals "manichini col motore al culo" ("manikins with a motor in our tails").

[...]
È un mondo breve composto, simbolo atroce
di quello fuori... Schiavi della meschina
esistenza, ammutoliti e restii a dire
buongiorno, siamo
manichini col motore al culo. (28)

[(...)
It's a proper brief world, odious symbol
of that big one outside... we're tools of a wretched
life, tongue-tied and dreading to say
hi there, nothing
but manikins with a motor in our ass. (29)]

On this level the metaphor for the world is truly that of "un ingi-nocchiatoio" ("a kneeling stool"), and the life of the individual who is both the subject and its object at the same time, is reduced to a "pura costellazione anonima" ("pure anonymous constellation"). It is worth reproducing the composition that gives the collection its title.

Polvere dovunque su tutto polvere su ciascuno
su me un cadere continuo di polvere dal soffitto
sul letto tappeti bottiglie dalle pareti
che mi Serrano nella morsa del mio futuro cadavere
già sepolto sotto il cumulo di polvere di questa
polvere che rassodata nello spazio gira su sé stessa
e intorno il sistema termonucleare come me cadavere
che rigiro su me stesso e spostato di quel tanto
dal mio centro intorno a me stesso:
costellazione anonima. (38)

[Everywhere dust on all things on all of us dust
on me a continuous drizzle of dust from the ceiling
covering the bed carpets bottles
from walls which lock me in the vise of my future
cadaver already buried under the cumulus of dust this
dust that curdles in space, spins round itself
round the thermonuclear system a cadaver like me
coiling self-centered and displaced by that much
from my axis, I go round myself:
anonymous constellation. (39)]

Here, the Leopardian sense of the void that surrounds the poet is based on the insistent presence of Death that engulfs everyone and everything.

The "Big (rotten) Apple" puts on a fictitious, elusive and dismal theatrical spectacle. And to express this spectacle, which anyone can watch for free, De Palchi privileges a discourse that, with respect to the complex and completely wanton register of *Sessioni con l'analista*, branches out in a decisively paratactic, enunciative, icastic way. Beneath the surface, of course, the poet's monstrous observational skill remains extremely lucid. The poet punctually undermines even those images that could carry an affective or consolatory charge. One example among many is that of the "neve" ("snow"), an image recurring more than once in *Costellazione anonima* ("pila di neve sulla città informe" |40|; "snow drifts over the shapeless city" |41|; "La neve che alla porta si asfalta di ghiaccio" |42|; "The snow at the door that turns into icy asphalt" |43|; "Questa neve m'indietreggia" |44|; "This snow pushes me back" |45|).

In effect, other aspects (cruder and more disturbing ones) really strike the poet, like the poverty, the violence (on all levels), the hypocrisy, the daily insults, the racism that suddenly explodes in that image of the black man killed in a greengrocer, in one of the tensest and most intense poems in the whole collection, that we have already been able to appreciate in *Sessioni con l'analista*.

Costellazione anonima is one of the cruelest, most penetrating books written by an Italian poet in America. Not since the time of Arturo Giovannitti had we seen, on the part of a transplant poet in America, urban alienation so shamelessly exposed. It is also the book with which De Palchi makes his comeback in his native land after a decade of silence (*Mutazioni*, as I have already stated, appeared in 1988).

After a thorough reading of the volume, one picks up on an overarching skeptical and pessimistic attitude toward the "magnifiche sorti e progressive" of the biggest city in America, most of all with respect to categories like history, that great comb for the bald, which is apparently instructive, but ultimately teaches nothing. Man is a tree torn to pieces ("mi contorco / risentito di essere / uomo" |70|;

"I twist resentful for being / human" [71]), rootless, destined to both weighty and petty daily insults; the city in which he lives intensifies his alienation and the subsequent internal laceration, where "è inutile pretendere, ognuno / è per sé stesso / e sta in sé stesso" ("it is useless to pretend, everyone / is out for himself / and remains in himself"). There is, therefore, scarcely a glimmer of *hope*, which, if anything, the poet exalts his own *will*, which is capable of placing itself in opposition to the chaos of history and paradoxically accepts permanent *anonymity* as his only proper *identity*.

Two American critics, both very attentive readers of *Costellazione anonima* in its English version, came to these conclusions. The first, Kenneth Scambray, noted that, after all, "De Palchi does offer in his poems that at least the will of the individual can survive the chaos of history and betrayal of comrades" (Scambray 1998). The second, John Taylor, after commenting on the tensive and epigrammatic nature of the book, also finds a formidable grain of wisdom in it: "These disturbing poems cumulate into a redoubtable wisdom: accepting one's 'identity' as no more permanent than an 'anonymous constellation' of dust" (Taylor 1998).

6. EROS AND THE "VASITÀ DELL'INFERNO MENTALE"

It is time to address De Palchi's most recent output, without obviously having the pretense of drawing any conclusions, since, in this case we are dealing with a writer still in the flower of his creativity.

De Palchi's most recent work has taken the form of two volumes respectively titled *Addictive Aversions / Le viziose avversioni* and *Paradigma*. The first, completely bilingual right down to its title as it was published in the United States (1999), avails itself of the translations of Michael Palma, Sonia Raiziss, I. L. Salomon, and Alethea Gail Segal as well as an introduction by Alessandro Vettori; the second, entirely in Italian, was released in 2001.

Addictive Aversions contains old and new pieces. The old poems, constituting the majority, were drawn from *Sessioni con l'analista* in its dual Italian and American editions (it should be noted that the American edition was slightly altered with respect to the version published by Mondadori). The new ones were written in the 1970s and 1990s, but never included in the collections that made it into print.

Divided in three sections, respectively titled, *Momenti / Momenti, Movimenti / Movements* and *Mutazioni / Mutations, Addictive Aversions,* he collects his entire body of work in the amorous-sensual vein. Additionally, De Palchi recovers poems from *Mutazioni,* released, as we saw, in an autonomous little book in 1988, which obviously presented the text only in Italian.

Despite the chronological dilation of the anthologized texts, *Addictive Aversions* is a "libro fortemente coeso" (Buffoni 1991; "an extremely cohesive book"]; the fact that the book is structurally and thematically compact is evidence, among other things, of the author's desire to systematize and, in a way to confirm, a posteriori, the relevance of the erotic theme in his work. (Indeed, at a certain point, the author felt the need to collect in a single work all of the erotic poetry he wrote over the course of roughly half a century; the oldest text, *Colonne di vento permeano* dates to 1951.)

It should nevertheless be immediately understood that the locution "erotic poetry" is not limited to the variously colored sensual-sexual-amorous world (which is nevertheless poignant and predominant); it extends also to the world of expressive language. It is the author himself who articulates this extension in an explanatory note, in the *Mutazioni* section, which is worth reproducing here:

La sensualità e/o sessualità è qui espressa nel linguaggio e in immagini non esplicitamente o graficamente attinenti all'amore o al sesso. Questo poemetto [composto di 13 pezzi per lo più brevi] fu composto nel 1987, nella mia testa, mentre camminavo per le strade di Manhattan, in preda a un'agitazione emotiva. Erano le 2-3 del mattino. Debiti personali mi spingevano a pensare, ossessivamente, a una sola cosa sicura: il sesso. La parola finale, 'Justine,' si riferisce alla protagonista dell'omonimo romanzo del marchese di Sade. (134)

[The sensuality and/or sexuality is here expressed in language and images not explicitly, or graphically, related to love or sex. This 1987 poem [composed of thirteen mostly short pieces] was written in my head while I was walking the streets of Manhattan in emotional turmoil at 2-3 o'clock in the morning. Personal debts made me think, with obsession, of only one secure subject: sex. The final word, '*Justine*,' is a reference to the protagonist of the Marquis de Sade's novel.]

The title, *Addictive Aversions / Le viziose avversioni* seems immediately to highlight the oxymoronic dimension that makes up the book in question: sex as an ineluctable "vice," a sort of drug, seductive and repulsive at the same time, which the writer cannot live without. He is (and has always been) so obsessed with sex that he is fatally addicted to it. It is a preliminary aspect that Daniela Gioselli, an Italian-American poet and scholar, notes in her reading of *Addictive Aversions*: "De Palchi is both enthralled by sexuality and its pleasure and repulsed by the addictive grip in which it holds him. He is angered by his lack of control, his driving need, represented by his own animal nature" (Gioselli 1999).

Sexuality—Sigmund Freud taught us—is also a thirst for knowledge, and De Palchi gave himself to it as early as his errant youthful years. The book has its own dense, inspired concentration, which unfolds, as is the case in all of De Palchi's work, through his vertiginous deft hand at synthesis, flowing often in figurative abstractions of great symbolic efficacy and of a pronounced psycho-physical seduction; indicative, in short, of a liberating desire deprived of any "costrizione morale e costumi sociali" (Vettori, xiv; "moral resrtiction and social customs"). The following is an emblematic excerpt, taken from the earliest poem in the collection:

Ti presentisco alla pioggia –
l'uscio alle spalle mi è chiuso
e l'urto solleva mulini di foglie
lamenta lampade
alla nerezza, provoca afrore
di catrame e pozzanghere guizzanti.
Un crepitìo di ramaglie si prolunga
nel vortice e allo scheletro
arcuato del viale; e tu sorgi
dal buio, con pulsare

violento alle mie tempie
e nella veste intuisco lo slancio
il guanto al collo. (30)

I scent you in the rain—
the door slams shut at my shoulder
and the crash lifts the leaves in a whirl
the lamp laments
in the darkness, raises a stench
of tar and flickering puddles.
A crackle of broken branches goes on and on
in the whirlwind and along the arched
skeleton of the avenue; and you
emerge from the dark, with a violent
pounding at my temples
and in your dress I sense the urgency
the glove at my neck. (31)

The tensive force that excitedly runs through the poems in *Addictive Aversions* speaks to us, after all, of an actual "storia di un'ossessione sessuale" ("story of a sexual obsession") that certainly for a long time—an inexhaustible period, as more recent texts in *Essenza carnale* demonstrate—must have dominated the author. He knew how to exorcise it once and for all through poetry, by means of rendering linguistically, with equally obsessive concentration, the impulse that had possessed him.

And Eros appears, in fact, in its entire expressive range, not only in its most obvious manifestation, but in the variegated psychological geography that accompanies it: from jealousy to deceit, to prohibited (and prohibitive) playfulness, spasmodic expectations, nostalgia, anger, frenzied longing, and to sadomasochistic delights, of which we have many examples in the Latin classics, from Catullus, Propertius, Tibullus, Ovid (authors our poet devoured and admired), right up through the moderns, such as Lawrence, Miller, Nabokov, and Durell. Even certain keen readers of *Addictive Aversions* have mentioned these authors: I am thinking of Carlo della Corte, who spoke, regarding *Addictive Aversions*, of "sessualità rapinosa, complessa, molestata, disordinata, disagiata" (Della Corte 1999; "rapacious, complex, tormented, chaotic, agitated sexuality"); and I think also of Giose Rimanelli who, beyond his mention of Latin poetry, spoke of verses "intrisi di lacrime sorde e di stravolta, allucinante sessualità, temperate da uno stile accorto, severo, senza sbavature" (Rimanelli 1999; "imbued with mute tears and a twisted, intoxicated sexuality, tempered by a shrewd, severe style, without the dribble").

Therefore, the poetry of *Addictive Aversions* is truly "physical," well endowed with a language, as usual, spare, essential, where at times we truly seem to hear heavy breathing, exhausted panting, the hammer of a heartbeat in the temples, the fingernails on flesh, the feverish search for the body of the other, screams hardly held back, a precise and savage gaze, while the body is completely engulfed in a passionate flame.

Such a thirst for vital tension cannot help but correspond, in inverse proportionality, as an overturned correlative, to the death drive. The obligatory constellation of Eros/Tantalos finds throughout this volume (and even more so in *Essenza carnale*, though in a projective sense) its own unresolved, anguished representation. Behind the milky windows of a motel, of a sultry, dimly lit room, there lies a world of unspoken anguish, the planetary melancholy of a tormenting solitude, the desperation of a man fending for himself. Death is the antidote to Eros. Sex emerges, as one critic wrote, as a "simbolo di forza vitale e appiglio contro la solitudine e il silenzio" (Ricchi 2000; "as a symbol of vital force and bulwark against solitude and silence"); but it also represents, in an irreducible way, up to vital exhaustion, a sort of *cupio dissolvi* in which everything annihilates itself, as in a happy though tragic tornado.

An almost totally unique book in the panorama of Italian literature-in-verse in America—and even virtually peerless in contemporary Italian literature, *tout court*: the only book that comes to mind while reading *Addictive Aversions* is *L'odore del sangue* by Goffredo Parise, a contemporary of De Palchi, who wrote a novel in which sex and death are inextricably intertwined in an obsessive and reciprocally contagious way. Here, as in many morbidly erotic pages of *Addictive Aversions*, the author truly let himself go, with an extreme and vital shamelessness; I am even tempted to say vitally extreme.

ℂ

This very shamelessness, though expressed in a versification measured to the millimeter in order to achieve the greatest concentration, we also find in the twenty-three pieces that compose *Essenza carnale*, the second section of *Paradigma*, which constitutes the true novelty of this last volume, since the first section is composed of texts mostly from *Sessioni con l'analista*, either in its Italian incarnation of 1967, or of its American counterpart in 1970. Various other texts are equally reprints of pieces that had already appeared elsewhere, like *Fungo amletica*, a poem in thirty-two short segments that appeared in 1997, in a bilingual presentation in *International Quarterly* and two others from the anthology *Dal Po al Potomac: esperienze di poetica e poesia italiana in America* (1998).

Essenza carnale is a coagulation in its own right, stylistically extremely compact, composed of twenty-three poems of dark, exasperated eroticism, anticipated in a monographic issue of the magazine *Hebenon* (No. 6, October 2000), with various critical essays and a comment by De Palchi himself (my citations from *Essenza carnale* all refer to pagination of the volume *Paradigma*).

With the exception of the first two pieces in *Essenza carnale*, dating respectively back to November 1998 and November 1999, the other twenty-one were written in a rather contracted period of time spanning from January to August 2000. Eight months of complete and utter immersion into the world of Eros, in which the darkest meanders are subtly explored, the most intimate and delicate, and at the same time, the most transgressive and bold recesses.

A full autumnal immersion—to be understood symbolically but also realistically in an extistential sense (De Palchi was born in 1926), as one gathers from the first poem—featuring, however, the vibrant, warm, sensual colors of New England foliage, with which the author experiences an instinctive, symbolic osmosis ("Giallo / rosso cinabro / arancione / il verde malato dell'autunno che trasgre-

231

disce / sfogliandosi insieme a te che scegli quali colori / ora che tra-
passi le date e le febbri" (73); "Yellow / vermillion red / bright or-
ange / the diseased green of the autumn that transcends / unleaving
itself with you choosing which colors / now that you pass through
dates and fevers"), precisely in the dialectic of the "spogliazione"
and of the "rinascita," or rather of a renewed, irreducible *enérgeia*,
within the very "corpus scribendi/vivendi."

Furthermore, the erotic and erotogenic intensity is present even
in the precise sexual modalities and its obsessively repetitive, per-
verting concreteness (but every perversion is considered thus only if
it reproposes itself, in its execution, *ad infinitum* and *ad libitum*),
corresponds to an unfolding (a *mise en scène*) of a projective sort
that does not make it any less efficacious in its gripping, anaphoric
valence/violence:

> Si vola leggeri con ali
> di risa e sciochezze colmando l'universale
> e qui dentro mi scopro quale pensi
> di vedermi, con la testa che spazia oltre il corpo.
> La distanza frantuma la mente che t'insegue
> e ti nutre in me con assoluta debolezza: ancora
> il tuo viso si culla accarezzato nelle mani e si specchia
> nei frantumi di luce dell'Adige e del Mincio
> dove insieme con il grembo a volte
> sofferente tenebroso cùpido lugubre lunatico
> si trasforma in letizia solare
>   – o lunare, emblema
> sempreverde di rugiada dell'alba giovane nel puslare
> dell'universo di stella ovale ascoltato nella mano;
> dal fondame mensile denso di spezie e di rossori
> insieme con la tua voce tremula di tortora ferita
> rinasco meravigliato. (75)

where the para-hynagogic and pan-sexual orchestration are directed
by, precisely, either a return to a panic and pagan, festive and pre-
logical innocence (for example, the insistent aquatic symbolism of

the river of his adolescence, the Adige), or the simple nagging mental obsession, flowing into imaginary and oneiric projections.

Shortly thereafter, nevertheless, and as if in a burning progression, the erotic figurations reach a paroxysmal concentration in his unsatisfied *désir*, which he openly acknowledges in certain verses, shamelessly peppered with remarkably arousing "illustrations," touching on the most provocative carnal lasciviousness (the figures massively dominating this "profane" representation are cunnilingus and irrumation—otherwise known as oral coitus), not to mention a dense tactile-visual-visionary conglomeration of breasts, with a female character who remains in the shadows, but who is, nevertheless, an active and engaged interlocutor.

The entire arc of *Essenza carnale* comes to a rest in this spasmodic search or visual "reconstruction" of this eidetic feminine character, who is both real and ideal at the same time (in the sense that she could be a specific woman, like any number of others who equally inhabit the poet's memory); the eternal feminine, in short, now invoked, now lusted after, now scolded, in a desire for self-annihilation coinciding precisely with the moment in which his phantasmatic possession is realized, whose distance from the writing-imagining subject can kill or become more intense until it reaches fever pitch.

In this specular concentration of the erotic game/yoke, lust at times reaches peaks as extreme as they are unsettling: sexuality comes to identify itself as a *return* (or even better, as a *reentry*)—through coitus—to an ancestral amniotic dimension, a sort of re-birth, the woman is *foemina* but also *mater terraquea*; a dimension internal to which man and woman identify themselves: the one is the other and inside the other; the other is the one and contains him. Two appropriate though perturbing examples:

Guardami, dimmi, è così per te, trafissa nell'astruso
esplodere di parole vocali insensate,
udite con tenerezza mentre ciascuno percepisce
penetrando l'immagine che l'una ha dell'altro,
e generate nel tuo terreno seminabile a onde assiderato

con fioriture sotto una coltre di polvere;
io sono chi tu cerchi [...] (80)

[...]

uguale al serpe ti assorbo intera
e tu da madre terracquea
chimai alla nascita il mio ritorno nell'aurora
del grembo, la dimora
di ascendente devozione per lo spirito in frammenti. (90)

[As a serpent I absorb you whole
and you like a terraqueous mother
call to birth my return in the dawn
of the womb, the abode
of ascending devotion for a spirit in fragments.
(Translations from *Essenza carnale*, when available, by Barbara Carle,
IPR IV (2009): 245]

The dense, spasmodic, erotic tension loosens its grip only at
times. And it is in moments like these that he rediscovers any happy
shred of authentic, surrealist *imagerie* ("le grida di addio / che
mandi da dietro i vetri serrati / le senti e le ascolti / chiusa nella
vestaglia in fiamme / di pelle ancora notturna"; "the farewell cries /
you send from behind sealed windows / you hear them and listen to
them / you closed in the flaming robe of skin still nocturnal"). And
still it is to the influence of surrealism, which was the historic avant-
garde movement he studied most profitably, along with futurism and
Dadaism (De Palchi actually made the acquaintance of Tristan
Tzara in 1961), that we can trace *Le sacre du printemps*, the first
piece featured in *Paradigma*, written on the same wavelength as Igor
Stravinsky's famous opera.

The poetry that blossoms out into *Essenza carnale* is intensely
and fundamentally liberating. Such a profane representation was
born of the erotic poetry of Verlaine and Apollinaire (or, in part, to
bring our point of reference a little closer to home, that of D'Annunzio or Ungaretti—but these comparisons should not be forced),

though theirs was not expressed—I would almost dare say exhibited—in quite the same audacious and joyous, long-suffering and shameless way. De Palchi manages to make of it, with his usual analytical and pointed dictation, a sort of party in which the obsessive dance of Eros is mixed with its projectively consumed "sacrifice," and, therefore, in one of its perfect executions (and execrations), like an atemporal construction, that is physical and metaphysical, tangible and transcendental, in the "vastità dell'inferno mentale."

7. (PROVISIONAL) CONCLUSIONS

It is time to conclude my excursus on this "transversal" poet, who certainly among those expatriates in the United States over the course of the migratory wave that followed the Second World War managed to maintain, in subsequent decades, an identity of his own and a stylistic coherence. And more than any other poet in America, De Palchi is also the one who remained faithful to his own personal linguistic constitution. Unlike what happened to some of his transoceanic traveling companions—and perhaps more than just a few—he neither conceived nor wrote a single poem or critical text in English. (Alfredo also established himself as a critic, but all things considered, it seems negligible with respect to his poetic work.)

This is obviously not a sort of self-closure or defense to the bitter end of his own expressive language, since that constitution, from a literary point of view, never was rigid or treated as an end in itself in the first place; rather, with time, it grew richer, whether through De Palchi's intense work with the magazine *Chelsea* (the many contacts and exchanges with American poets and intellectuals that it entailed: it is enough to cite here the names of some of the poets and intellectuals, like William Carlos Williams, David Ignatow, James Dickey, and more recently Charles Wright, Rosanna Warren, Jonathan Galassi, W. S. Piero, with whom he has cultivated and continues to cultivate to this day (with those who are still living) fruitful friendships); or through his noteworthy translation work; or finally—last but not least of all—through his innate, inexhaustible human and cultural curiosity (profoundly anti-academic) that was always unique to him.

And so, it should not seem strange or rash to state today that his poetry seems to be among the most significant and original (at its origin it went "against the grain," as Sereni had intuited more than forty years ago) not only in the panorama of the second half of the Italian twentieth century (and beyond, having followed De Palchi's output over these last eleven years), but even on the America poetry scene *tout court,* one of the most learned American critics, Burton Raffel, editor of the *Literary Review,* wrote that "De Palchi's terse, sparse lines are a kind of lesson in musicality, and a text that many contemporary American poets would do well to study" (Raffel, vol. 43, no. 2, 2000).

In my mind, not since the time of Emanuel Carnevali (from whom De Palchi inherited his contemptuous and equally candid impudence) has such recognition been attributed to one of our expatriate poets. A recognition, I add, so much more relevant if one thinks that the linguistic reception of De Palchi's poetry occurred in the United States only in a metaphorical way, and not in a direct way like that of Carnevali, who, though hunger and poverty were ever-present, had the "fortune" of working in one of the most stimulating and innovative intellectual milieus of the twentieth century in North America (I am referring above all to the brief but intense period he spent in Chicago at the magazine *Poetry,* as we saw in the first chapter).

Alfredo de Palchi was, therefore, a poet who, at the cost of enormous existential difficulties, and after having endured atrocious ideological misunderstandings (vexations) in his homeland, managed, in 2003 (forty-seven years after his expatriation), to give himself his own constitution and his own dignity (precisely the "lyrical affirmation of his own lonely dignity," the Irish critic Brendan Kennelly wrote over forty years ago, reviewing *Sessioni con l'analista* in the *Sunday Independent,* June 28, 1971), to which a certain literary quality is also attributed.

I think that because of all of this (and for other reason as well, if one considers also the impressive work he has produced as an "ambassador" of Italian poetry in America), it is essential to give De Palchi his just due. This rings especially true in light of so much feeble, intellectualistic, confessional, and/or unforgivably partisan poetry produced today by so many Italian poets (at this point, it little matters whether dealing with America or Italy). Indeed, in spite of it all, De Palchi has always maintained his convictions and irreverent, internal coherence, while knowing how to keep his distance. He has also known when and how, in those impious moments, to make light of any quaint literary convent as well as of all the useless hullabaloo associated with it; in this, always in his own unique, countercurrent though coherent way, following his own rogue star; also fully aware, in short, that true poetry is, à *la* Rimbaud, elsewhere.

BIBLIOGRAPHY

In this expanded English version of my original Italian study, I have included in this bibliography all of the works that are cited herein. In addition, I have divided the many works referenced throughout this study between "primary" and second-ary" sources. Furthermore, since chapters two through five are dedicated to a specific author, I have decided to separate out those secondary works so that the reader shall have a better idea of the criticism that has been dedicated to each of these four writers throughout the years. Finally, I wish to thank both Joan Taber and Bordighera Press for the final preparation of this bibliography.

PRIMARY SOURCES

Barolini, Helen. *Umbertina*. New York: Seaview, 1979.

Berto, Giuseppe. *Il male oscuro*. Milano:Rizzoli, 1964.

Buranelli, Prosper. *You Gotta Be Rough*. New York: Doubleday, 1930.

Calitri, Charles. *Rickey*. New York: Charles Scribner's Sons, 1952.

Caillois, Roger. *Les jeux etre les homes*. Paris, Gallimard, 1967.

Carnevali, Emanuel. *Il primo Dio*. Milano: Adelphi, 1978.

Carrol, Lewis. *Alice's Adventures in Wonderland*. Old Saybrook: Konecky & Konecky, 2000.

Cautela, Giuseppe. *Moon Harvest*. New York: Dial Press, 1925.

Ciambelli, Bernardino. *I misteri di Mulberry Street*. New York: Frugone e Balletto, 1893.

_____. *I misteri di Bleeker Street*. New York: Frugone e Balletto, 1899.

_____. *La trovatella di Mulberry Street*. New York: Societá libreria italiana, 1919.

Ciardi, John. *Homeward to America*. New York: Henry Holt & Company, 1940.

D'Agostino, Guido. *Olives on the Apple Tree*. New York: Doubleday, 1940.

_____. *Hills Beyond Manhattan*. New York: Doubleday, 1942.

_____. *My Enemy the World*. New York: Dial Press, 1947.

D'Angelo, Pascal. *Son of Italy*. New York: MacMillan, 1924.

_____. *Le poesie di Pascal D'Angelo*. Francesco Mulas, ed. Sassari: Università degli Studi di Sassari, 1989.

_____. *Canti di Luce*. Luigi Fontanella, ed. Sant'Eustachio di Mercato S. Severino, SA: Edizioni Il Grappolo, 2001.

De Amicis, Edmondo. *Sull'oceano*. Milan: Treves, 1889.

De Capite, Michael. *Maria*. New York: John Day Co., 1943.

_____. *No Bright Banner*. New York: John Day Co., 1944.

_____. *The Bennett Place*. New York: John Day Co., 1948.

De Palchi, Alfredo. *Sessioni con l'analista*. Milano: Mondadori, 1967.

_____. *Sessions with My Analyst*. Translation by I. L. Salomon. New York: October House, 1970.

_____. *Gentile animale braccato*. Introduction by Luciano Erba, Almanacco dello Specchìo 1. Milan: Mondadori, 1983.

_____. *Mutazioni*. Udine: Campanotto, 1988. Winner of the Premio Città di San Vito al Tagliamento.

_____. *The Scorpion's Dark Dance – La buia danza di scorpione*. Introduction and translation by Sonia Raiziss, Riverside (California): Xenos Books, 1993.

_____. *Anonymous Constellation – Costellazione anonima*. Introduction by Alessandro Vettori, translation by Sonia Raiziss. Riverside (California): Xenos Books, 1997.

_____. *Costellazione anonima*. Introduction by Alessandro Vettori. Marina di Minturno: Caramanica, 1998.

_____. *Addictive Aversions – Le viziose aversion*. Introduction by Alessandro Vettori, translation by Sonia Raiziss et al, Riverside (California): Xenos Books, 1999.

_____. *Paradigma*. Marina di Minturno: Caramanica, 2000.

_____. *Paradigma. Tutte le poesie: 1947-2005*. Preface by Roberto Bertoldo, introduction by Alessandro Vettori. Milan: Associazione Culturale Mimesis, 2006.

Di Biasio, Rodolfo. *I Quattro camminanti*. Florence: Sansoni, 1991.

Di Donato, Pietro. *Christ in Concrete*. Indianapolis: Bobbs-Merrill Co., 1939.

_____. *This Woman*. New York: Ballentine books, 1959.

_____. *Three Circles of Light*. New York: Julian Messner, 1960.

_____. *Naked Author*. New York: Phaedra, 1970.

Fante, John. *The Road to Los Angeles*. Santa Rosa, Ca.: Black Sparrow Press, 1999.

_____. *Dago Red*. New York: Viking Press, 1940.

_____. *Wait Until Spring, Bandini*. Santa Barbara, Ca.: Black Sparrow Press, 1983.

Faulkner, William. *The Sound and the Fury*. New York: Random House, 1929.

Forgione, Louis. *Reamer Lou*. New York: Dutton, 1924.

_____. *The Men of Silence*. New York: Dutton, 1928.

_____. *The River Between*. New York: Dutton, 1928.

Francavilla, Carlo. *Le terre della sete*. Manduria: Lacaita, 1977.

Fuentes, Carlos. *Aura*. Trans. Carmine Di. Michele. Milan: Feltrinelli, 1964.

Fumento, Rocco. *Devil by the Tail*. New York: McGraw Hill, 1954.

_____. *Tree of Dark Reflection*. New York: McGraw Hill, 1954.

Galletti, Alfredo. *L'eloquenza*. Milano: Vallardi, 1938.

Gioseffi, D. "Universe." *Small Press Review* (June-July 1997).

_____. "Erotic Poems." *Small Press Review* (May-June 1999).

_____. Poetry in *The Cortland Review* 8 (1999).

Giovannitti, Arturo. *Arrows in the Gale*. New York: Hillacre Bookhouse, 1914.

_____. *Collected Poems*. Chicago: E. Clemente, 1962; reissued by Arno Press, NY, 1975.

Kerouac, Jack. *On the Road*. Trans. by Magda de Cristofaro. Milan: Mondadori, 1959.

Lapolla, Garibaldi Mario. *The Fire in the Flesh*. New York: Vanguard Press, 1931.

_____. *Miss Rollins In Love*. New York: Vanguard Press, 1932.

_____. *The Grand Gennaro*. New York: Vanguard Press, 1935.

Mangione, Jerre. *Mount Allegro*. Boston: Harper and Row, 1942.

_____. *Reunion in Sicily*. Boston: Houghton Mifflin, 1950.

Novalis (Friederich Leopold Von Hardenberg). *Enrico di Ofterdingen*. Translated by Tommaso Landolfi. *Germamica*. Ed. Leone Traverso. Milano: Bompiani, 1942.

Pagano, Jo. *The Paesanos*. Boston: Little Brown, 1940.

_____. *Golden Wedding*. New York: Random House, 1943.

_____. *The Condemned*. New York: Prentice Hall, 1947.

Palazzeschi, Aldo. "*La Piraminde*." *Opere Giovanili*. Milano: Mondadori, 1958.

Panetta, George. *We Ride a White Donkey*. New York: Harcourt, Brace & Co., 1944.

_____. *Jimmy Potts Gets a Haircut*. New York: Doubleday, 1947.

Panunzio, Constantine. *The Soul of an Immigrant*. New York: MacMillan, 1924.

Pouget, Émile. *Sabotage*. Chicago: Charles H. Kerr & Company, 1913.

Rimanelli, Giose. *Tiro al piccione*. Milan: Mondadori, 1953. New edition edited with an excellent introduction by Sebastiano Martelli. Torino: Einaudi, 1991.

_____. *Peccato originale*. Milan: Mondadori, 1954.

_____. *Biglietto di terza*. Milan: Mondadori, 1958. New edition with afterword by Giuseppe Prezzolini, Weland (Ontario): Soleil, 1998.

_____. *Una posizione sociale*. Florence: Vallecchi, 1959; republished as *La stanza grande*, with introduction by Sebastiano Martelli. Cava de' Tirreni: Avagliano, 1996.

_____. *Il mestiere del furbo*. Milan: Sugar, 1959 (published with the pseudonym A. G. Solari).

_____. *Carmina blabla*. Padova: Rebellato, 1967.

_____. *Monaci d'amore medievali*. Preface by Ugo Moretti. Roma: Trevi, 1967.

_____. *Graffiti*. Edited by Titina Sardelli. Isernia: Marinelli, 1977.

_____. *Molise Molise*. Preface by Giuseppe Faralli. Isernia: Mannelli, 1979.

_____. *Arcano*. Preface by Luigi Reìna, *La poesia di Giose Rimanelli*. Salerno: Edisud, 1989.

_____. *Benedetta in Guysterland*. Introduction by Fred Gardaphé. Toronto: Guernica, 1993.

_____. *Alien Cantica. An American Journey 1964-1993)*. Translated and edited by Luigi Bonaffini. Preface by Alberto Granese, afterword by Anthony Burgess. New York: Peter Lang, 1995.

_____. *Da G. a G.: 101 Sonnetti,* in collaboration with Luigi Fontanella. Edited by L. Bonaffini. New York: Peter Lang, 1996.

_____. *Moliseide and Other Poem*. Translated and edited by L. Bonaffini. Preface by G. Rimanelli. Brooklyn: Legas, 1998.

_____. *Familia. Memoria dell'Emigrazione*. Introduction by Luigi Fontanella. Isernia: Cosmo Iannone, 2000.

_____. *Detroit Blues*. Welland (Ontario): Soleil, 1996.

_____. *Accademia*. Toronto: Guernica, 1997.

_____. *L'arcangelo* e *il ragazzo,* recital by Giose Rimanelli and Claudia Pescatori. Directed by Pierluigi Giorgio. Auditorium M. Pagano, Campobasso, December 21, 1998.

_____. *The Three-legged One: A Glossed Novel*. New York: Bordighera Press, 2009.

Rossi, Mark Anthony "Metaphoric Journey." *Collages & Bricolages* 10 (1996).

_____. "Answers in Acts of Intimacy." *Collages & Bricolage* 13 (2000).

Stefanile, Felix. *A Fig Tree in America*. New Rochelle, NY: The Elizabeth Press, 1970.

Tucci, Niccoló. *Gli Atlantici*. Milano: Garzanti, 1968.

Tusiani, Joseph. *Amedeo di Savoia. Poemetto in isciolti*. Preface by P. Ciro Soccio. Sant'Agata di Puglia: Casa del Sacro Cuore, 1943.

_____. *Peccato e luce. Preface by* Cesare Foligno. New York: The Venetian Press, 1949.

_____. *M'ascolti tu mia terra? Ode al Gargano*. Foggia: Stab. Tip. Cappetta, 1955.

_____. *Melos Cordis*. New York: The Venetian Press, 1955.

_____. *Lo speco celeste*. Siracusa, Ciranna, 1956.

_____. *Odi sacre*. Preface by Alfredo Galletti. Siracusa: Ciranna, 1957.

_____. *Rind and Ali. Fifty Poems*. New York: The Monastine Press, 1962. Also available in Italian in *Mallo e gheriglio e La quinta stagione*. Translated and edited by M. Pastore Passaro. Roma, Bulzoni, 1987.

_____. *The Fifth Season. Poems*. New York, Obolensky, 1964. Also available in Italian in *Mallo e gheriglio e La quinta stagione*. Translated and edited by M. Pastore Passaro. Roma, Bulzoni, 1987.

_____. *Gente Mia and Other Poem*. Stone Park, Illinois: Italian Cultural Center, 1978. Also available in Italian in *Gente mia e altre poesie*. Preface by Ennio Bonea. Translated and edited by M. Pastore Passaro. San Marco in Lamis: Gruppo Cittadella Est, 1982.

_____. *Tireca tàreca, Poesie in vernacolo garganico*. Edited by A. Motta, T. Nardella and C. Siani, San Marco in Lamis: Franco Troiano, 1978.

_____. "The Making of an Italian American Poet" in *Italian Americans in The Professions*, a c. di Remigio U. Pane. Staten Island, N.Y.: The American Italian Historical Association, 1983.

_____. *Rosa rosarum. Carmina latin.*, Oxford (Ohio): American Classical League, 1984.

_____. *In exilio rerum*. Edited by Dirk Sacré. Avignone: Aubanel, 1985.

_____. *Confinia lucis et umbrae*. Edited by D. Sacré, Lovanio, Peeters, 1989.

_____. "Cain, The Better Giver. A Lyrical Monologue," *Italian Quarterly* XXVIII, 108 (Spring 1987).

_____. *La parola difficile*. Fasano: Schena, 1988.

_____. "A Luxury of Light," *Italian Quarterly* XXX, 117 (Summer 1989).

_____. *La parola nuova*, presentazione di Angelo Di Summa. Fasano: Schena, 1991.

_____. *La parola antica*. Introduction by A. Di Summa. Fasano: Schena, 1992.

_____. *Il ritorno. Liriche italiane*. Preface by Pietro Magno. Fasano: Schena, 1992.

_____. *Carmina latina*. Introduction and translation by Emilio Bandiera. Fasano: Schena, 1994.

_____. *Carmina latina Ii*. Introduction and translation by E. Bandiera. Galatina: Congedo, 1998.

_____. *Leopardi's Canti*. English edition, Introduction by P. Magno. Preface by Franco Foschi, Fasano, Schena, 1998.

_____. *Dante's Lyric Poems*. Introduction and notes G. Di Scipio. New York: Legas, 1999.

_____. *Lu deddù*. Edited by Anna Siani, note by Antonio Motta. San Marco in Lamis: Quaderni del Sud, 1999.

_____. *Ethnicity. Selected Poems,* with two essays by Paolo A. Giordano. West Lafayette (Indiana): Bordighera Press, 2000.

_____. *Radicitus. Poesie latine.* Introduction and translation by E. Bandiera. San Severino (SA): Il Grappolo, 2000.

_____. *Maste Peppe cantarine.* Edited by Anna Siani. San Marco in Lamis: Quaderni del Sud, 2000.

_____. *Lu ponte de sola.* Edited by A. Siani, note by A. Motta. San Marco in Lamis: Quaderni del Sud, 2001.

_____. *L'ore de Gesù Bambine.* Edited by A. Motta. San Marco In Lamis: Quaderni del Sud, 2002.

_____. *La prima cumpagnia.* Edited by A. Siani. San Marco in Lamis: Quaderni del Sud, 2002.

Van Doren, Carl. *Three Worlds.* New York: Harper, 1936.

_____. *The Roving Critic.* New York: Knopf, 1923.

Villa, Silvio. *The Unbidden Guest.* New York: MacMillan, 1923.

Vivante, Arturo. *The French Girls of Killini.* Boston: Little Brown, 1958.

_____. *A Goodly Babe.* Boston: Little Brown, 1959.

_____. *Dr. Giovanni.* Boston: Little Brown, 1959.

SECONDARY SOURCES

GENERAL

Alba, Richard. *Italian Americans: Into the Twilight of Ethnicity.* Englewood Cliffs: Prentice Hall, 1985.

Alfonsi, Ferdinando, ed. *Poeti Italo-americani.* Catanzaro, Italy: Carello, 1985

_____. *Dictionary of Italian-American Poets.* New York: Peter Lang, 1989.

Ashbery, John. *Reported Sightings.* Ed. David Bergman. New York: Knopf, 1989.

Barolini, Helen. *The Dream Book: An Anthology of Writing by Italian American Women.* New York: Schocken, 1985.

_____, *Chiaroscuro. Essays of Identity.* West Lafayette, Indiana: Bordighera, 1997.

Barone, Dennis. *America / Trattabili.* New York: Bordighera Press, 2011.

Basile Green, Rose. *The Italian-American Novel: A Document of the Interaction of Two Cultures.* Madison: Fairleigh Dickinson University Press, 1974.

Benét, William Rose. *The Readers Encyclopaedia.* New York: Thomas Y. Crowell, 1948.

Boelhower, William. *Immigrant Autobiography in the United States.* Verona: Essedue, 1982.

Bona, Mary Jo. *Claiming a Tradition: Italian American Women Writers.* Southern Illinois University Press, 1987.

_____. *By the Breath of Their Mouths: Narratives of Resistance in Italian America.* Albany, NY: SUNY P, 1998.

Boyle, Kay, ed. *The Autobiography of Emanuel Carnevali.* New York: Horizon Press, 1987.

Butor, Michel. *La modificazione.* Milan: Mondadori, 1959.

Caetura, Linda, ed. *Growing Up Italian.* New York: William Morrow & Co., 1986.

Carravetta, Peter and Paolo Valesio, eds. *Paesaggio.* Treviso: Pagus, 1993.

Coleman, Terry. *Passage to America.* Harmondsworth: Penguin Books, 1974.

Della Terza, Dante. *Da Vienna a Baltimore. La diaspora degli intellettuali europei negli Stati Uniti d'America.* Roma: Editori Riuniti, 1987/2000.

Di Biagi, Flaminio. "Emanuel Carnevali: un 'American Poet'" in *La letteratura dell'emigrazione.* Jean-Jacques Marchand, ed. Turin: Edizioni della Fondazione Giovanni Agnelli, 1991.

Fink, Guido. "Le bugie colorate di Carnevali." *Paragone* 280 (1973): 85-88.

Fontanella, Luigi. "Poeti italiani espatriati negli Stati Uniti." *La letteratura dell'emigrazione.* Ed. Jean-Jaques Marchand. Turin: Fondazione Giovanni Agnelli, 1991 459-66.

_____. "Poeti emigrati ed emigrant poeti negli Stati Uniti." *Il sogno italo-americano.* Sebastiano Martelli, ed. Naples: Cuen, 1998.

Franzina, Emilio. *L'immaginario degli emigranti.* Treviso: Pagus, 1992.

_____. *Dall'Arcadia in America.* Turin: Edizioni della Fondazione Agnelli, 1996.

Freud, Sigmund. *L'interpretazione dei sogni.* Turin: Boringhieri, 1973.

Gambino, Richard. *Blood of My Blood.* Toronto: Guernica, 2000.

Gardaphé, Fred. "From Oral Tradition to Written Word." *The Margin. Writings in Italian American Americana.* Ed. Anthony Tamburri, et al. W. Lafayette, IN: Purdue University Press, 1991.

_____. *Italian Signs, American Streets: The Evolution of Italian American Narrative.* Durham, N.C.: Duke University Press, 1996.

_____. *Dagoes Read: Tradition and the Italian/American Writer.* Toronto: Guernica, 1996.

_____. ".Academic Archetypes." *Fra Noi.* Chicago 5 (February 1998).

_____. *From Wiseguys To Wise Men: The Gangster And Italian American Masculinities.* New York: Routledge, 2006.

_____. *The Art of Reading Italian Americana: Italian American Culture in Review.* New York: Bordighera Press, 2011.

Gioia, Dana. "What is Italian-American Poetry?" *Voices in Italian Americana* 4.2 (1992).

Haller, Hermann. *Una lingua perduta e ritovata.* Florence: La Nuova Italia, 1993.

Hart, James D. *Oxford Companion to American Literature.* London/New York: Oxford University Press, 1941, 1948.

Hine, Daryl and Joseph Parisi. *American Poetry Anthology.* New York: Houghton & Mifflin, 1978.

Ignatow, David. On the back cover of *The Scorpion's Dark Dance.*

Kennelly, B. "Poets of Hope and Suffering." *Sunday Independent,* Dublin, 28 June 1971.

Kunitz, Stanley and Howard Haycraft, eds. *Twentieth Century Authors.* New York: H. E. Wilson, 1942.

Lalli, Renato. *Arturo Giovannitti.* Campobasso: Editoriale Rufus, 1981.

Lawton, Ben. "What Is 'Italian American' Cinema?" *Voices in Italian Americana* 6.1 (Spring 1995).

Mangione, Jerre and Ben Morreale. *La Storia. Five Centuries of the Italian American Experience.* New York: Harper Collins, 1992.

Marazzi, Martino. "Le fondamenta sommerse della narrative italoamericana." *Belfagor* 3 (31 May 2000).

_____. *Misteri di Little Italy. Storie e testi della letteratura italo-americana.* Milano: Franco Angeli, 2001.

Marchand, Jean Jaques, ed. *La letteratura dell'emigrazione.* Torino: Fondazione Giovanni Agnelli, 1991.

_____. "Dalla letteratura dell'emigrazione agli scrittori di lingua italiana nel mondo," *Profili letterari* II.3 (November 1992).

Martelli, Sebastiano. *Letteratura contaminate. Storie parole immagini tra Ottocento e Novecento.* Salerno: Laveglia, 1994.

_____. *Il crepuscolo dell'identità.* Salerno: Laveglia, 1988.

Masters, Edgar Lee. *Spoon River Anthology.* Fernanda Pivano, ed. Turin: Einaudi, 1981.

Monroe, Harriet and Alice Corbin Henderson. *The New Poetry: An Anthology of Twentieth-Century Verse in English.* New York: Knopf, 1936.

Peragallo, Olga. *Italian American Authors and Their Contributions to American Literature.* New York: S.F. Vanni, 1949.

Pane, Remigio U. *Italian-Americans in the Professions.* Staten Island, NY: AIHA, 1979.

Prezzolini, Giuseppe. *America in pantofole.* Florence: Vallecchi, 1956.

_____. *I trapiantati.* Milan: Longanesi, 1963.

Rimanelli, Marco and Sheryl L. Postman, eds. *The 1891 New Orleans Lynching and U.S. – Italian Relations. A Look Back.* New York: Peter Lang, 1992.

Scambray, Kenneth. *The North American Italian Renaissance.* Toronto: Guernica, 2000.

Sollors, Werner. *Beyond Ethnicity: Consent and Descent in American Literature and Culture* (New York: Oxford, 1986).

Tamburri, Anthony Julian, *To Hyphenate or not to Hyphenate: the Italian/American Writer: Or, An Other American?* Montreal: Guernica Editions, 1991.

_____. "In (Re)cognition of the Italian/American Writer: Definitions and Categories." *Differentia,* Spring/Autumn (1991).

_____. "Italian/American Poetry." *Encyclopaedia of Italian American Culture.* Eds. Frank Cavaioli and Salvatore La Gumina, New York: Garland, 1997.

_____. *A Semiotic of Ethnicity: In (Re)cognition of the Italian/American Writer.* Albany, NY: SUNY P, 1998.

_____. *Una semiotica dell'etnicità. Nuove segnalature per la scrittura italiano/americana.* Franco Cesati Editore, 2010.

Tedeschini Lalli, Biancamaria. "La metapoesia di Arturo Giovannitti" in *L'America degli Italiani.* Rome: Bulzoni, 1986.

Tzara, Tristan. "Manifesto sull'amore debole e l'amore amaro" in *Manifesti del dadaismo.* Turin: Einaudi, 1964.

Valesio, Paolo. "Lo scrittore fra i due mondi," *Italian Literature in North America*. Eds. John Picchione and Laura Pietropaolo, Ottowa: Canadian Society for Italian Studies, 1990.

_____. "Italian Poets in America." *Gradiva* 10-11 (1993): Introduction

_____. "*I fuochi della tribú.*" *Paesaggio.*

_____. "I fuochi incrociati delle tribú" in *The Craft and the Fury.* J. Francese, ed. *Italiana X.* West Lafayette, IN: Bordighera, 2000.

Van Doren, Carl. *Three Worlds.* New York: Harper, 1936.

_____. *The Roving Critic.* New York: Knopf, 1923.

Verdicchio, Pasquale. *Bound by Distance.* Madison, NJ: Farleigh Dickinson University Press, 1997.

Viscusi, R. "'De vulgari eloquentia': An Approach to the Language of Italian American Fiction," *Yale Italian Studies* 1.3 (1981).

_____. "Circles of the Cyclops: Schemes of Recognition" in *Italian American Discourse in Italian Americans.* L. Tomasi, ed. Staten Island, NY: Center for Migration Studies, 1986.

_____. "A Literature Considering Itself. The Allegory of Italian America." *From the Margin: Writings in Italian Americana.* Eds. Anthony Tamburri, Paolo Giordano, and Fred Gardaphé. West Lafayette: Perdue University Press (1991): 265-81.

ON PASCAL D'ANGELO

Anelli, Luigi. "Il piú bel libro dell'anno, scritto da un lavoratore abruzzese immigrato," *Il Vastese d'oltre Oceano* 28 (December 1924).

Barone, Dennis. "Immigrant Enigma: Pascal D'Angelo, Son of Italy," *Voices in Italian Americana* 11.2 (2000).

Benét, William Rose. Rev. of *A Son of Italy,* by Pascal D'Angelo. *Saturday Review of Literature* (27 December 1924).

_____. "Round about Parnassus," *Saturday Review of Literature* 26 (March 1932).

Candeloro, Gabriele. "Echi d'oltre Oceano," *Il Vastese d'oltre Oceano* (15 February 1925).

Chierici, Maurizio. "Emigranti. Le voci della nostalgia." *Corriere dell Sera,* 9 December 2000.

Colombo, Furio. Rev. of *Son of Italy,* by Pascal D'Angelo. *La Repubblica,* 5 August 1999.

D'Agnese, Generoso. "Il poeta della vanga," *America Oggi,* 27 December 1998.

Esposito, Pasquale. "Emigranti. Lo spaccapietre scrittore." *Il Mattino,* 17 August 1999.

Fontanella, Luigi. Introduction. *Canti di Luce.*

_____. Introduction. *Son of Italy.*

Mulas, Francesco. "La poetica di Pascal D'Angelo." *Le poesie di Pascal D'Angelo.*

Mann, L. Rev. of *A Son of Italy*, by Pascal D'Angelo. *Boston Transcript* (6 December 1924).

Murphy, Jim. *Pick and Shovel Poet. The Journeys of Pascal D'Angelo.* New York, Clarion Books, 2000.

Panza, Rino. *Il mondo di Pascal D'Angelo, poeta del piccone e della pala.* Sulmona: Fondazione Ignazio Silone-Voci della Provincia, 2002.

Prezzolini, Giuseppe. "Stati Uniti: autobiografia e romanzo," *Gazzetta del popolo,* 19 December 1934.

Richter, R. "A Pick and Shovel Poet." *New York Evening Post,* 13 December 1924.

Van Doren, Carl. Introduction. *Son of Italy*

ON ALFREDO DE PALCHI

Alicco, Sebastiano. "Contro il Nulla. La poesia di Alfredo de Palchi" in *Una vita scommessa in poesia. Omaggio ad Alfredo de Palchi / A Life Gambled in Poetry. Homage to Alfredo de Palchi.* Edited by Luigi Fontanella. Stony Brook, NY: Gradiva Publications, 2011.

Allen, William. Rev. of *The Scorpion's Dark Dance*, by Alfredo de Palchi. *Another Chicago Review* 29 (Spring 1995).

Battilana, Marilla. *La Nuova Tribuna Letteraria* 65 (2002).

Bertoldo, Roberto. Rev. of *Costellazione anonima*, by Alfredo de Palchi. *Hebenon* 3 (1999)

_____. Rev. of *Paradigma*, by Alfredo de Palchi. *Hebenon* 9-10 (April-October 2002).

"Leggere Alfredo De Palchi," *Hebenon, rivista internazionale di letteratura,* special issue, "Scritti sulla poesia di Alfredo De Palchi," 6 (2000).

_____. "Intervista ad Alfredo de Palchi" in *Alfredo de Palchi. La Potenza della poesia.* Alessandria: Edizioni dell'Orso, 2008.

Bisutti, Donatella. "Alfredo de Palchi" in *Una vita scommessa in poesia. Omaggio ad Alfredo de Palchi.*

Bonafini, Luigi. "Preliminary Comments on De Palchi's Diction" in *Una vita scommessa in poesia. Omaggio ad Alfredo de Palchi.*

Buffoni, Franco. Rev. of *Addictive Aversions*, by Alfredo de Palchi. *Testo a fronte* 21 (1999).

Caddeo, Rinaldo. "Alfredo de Palchi *Paradigma*: una vorticosa, apocalittica testualità" in *Alfredo de Palchi. La Potenza della poesia.*

Cambon, Glauco. "Alfredo de Palchi," *La fiera letteraria* (5 February 1961).

_____. Rev. of *Sessioni con l'analista*, by Alfredo de Palchi. *Books Abroad.* January 1968.

_____. Rev. of *Sessions with My Analyst*, by Alfredo de Palchi *Books Abroad.* Winter 1972.

Capello, Dario. "Del pulsare. Note su 'Essenza carnale" di Alfredo de Palchi" in *Alfredo de Palchi. La Potenza della poesia.*

Carle, Barbara. "An Introduction to De Palchi's Recent Poems." *Gradiva* 19 (Spring 2001).

_____. "'Dal Fuoco all'Acqua': sulla poesia di Alfredo De Palchi," *Hebenon, rivista internazionale di letteratura.*

_____. "The American Editions of Alfredo de Palchi's Poetry: *The Scorpion's Dark Dance, Sessions with My Analyst, Anonymous Constellation, Addictive Aversions,*" *Gradiva* 30 (2006).

_____. "The lexicon of *Costellazione anonima*: a paradigmatic poem" in *Alfredo de Palchi. La Potenza della poesia.*

_____. "Alfredo de Palchi's Anarchic Paradigm: *Non li scrive sul quaderno*, A New Translation and Commentary" in *Una vita scommessa in poesia. Omaggio ad Alfredo de Palchi.*

Condini, Ned. "Carnalità mistica nel *Paradigmi* di de Palchi" in *Alfredo de Palchi. La Potenza della poesia.*

De Angelis, Milo. "Il sorriso di Alfredo" in *Una vita scommessa in poesia. Omaggio ad Alfredo de Palchi.*

Della Corte, Carlo. "*Sessioni con l'analista* di Alfredo De Palchi," *Oggi*, 9 September 1967.

_____. "Quelle viziose avversioni. Dietro l'eros ossessivo c'è una musa elegante," *Nuova Venezia*, 5 August 1999.

_____. Rev. of *Addictive Aversions*, by Alfredo de Palchi. *Gradiva* 18 (2000).

Dickey, James. On the back cover of *The Scorpion's Dark Dance*.

Di Pace-Jordan, Rosetta. Review of *Mutazioni*, by Alfredo de Palchi, *World Literature Today* (Autumn 1989).

_____. Review of *The Scorpion's Dark Dance*, by Alfredo de Palchi, *World Literature Today* (Summer 1994).

Erba, Luciano. "Alfredo de Palchi." *Almanacco dello Specchio* 11 (1983).

Fantato, Gabriela. "Versi incisi nella pietra. Note di lettura sulla poesia di Alfredo de Palchi" in *Alfredo de Palchi. La Potenza della poesia.*

_____. "Una parola erotica: la poesia di Alfredo de Palchi" in *Una vita scommessa in poesia. Omaggio ad Alfredo de Palchi.*

Ferramosca, Annamaria. "Tutte le poesie di Alfredo de Palchi" in *Alfredo de Palchi. La Potenza della poesia.*

_____. "Il tremore terrestre. Eros e donna nella poesia di Alfredo de Palchi" in

Una vita scommessa in poesia. Omaggio ad Alfredo de Palchi.

Ferrarelli, Rina. "Metonymies and metaphors in the poetry of Alfredo de Palchi" in *Alfredo de Palchi. La Potenza della poesia.*

Ferreri, Rosario. Rev. of *Anonymous Constellation,* by Alfredo de Palchi. *World Literature Today* (Autumn 1997).

Ferri, Gio. "La rabbia e l'amore: Alfredo de Palchi, sessant'anni di poesia" in *Una vita scommessa in poesia. Omaggio ad Alfredo de Palchi.*

Flecchia, Piero. Il corpo come orizzonte nella scittura. Una nota sulla poesia di Alfredo de Palchi" in *Alfredo de Palchi. La Potenza della poesia.*

Fontanella, Luigi. "New York la crudele." *America Oggi,* 1 June 1997.

_____. "Un italiano a Manhattan." *Gazzetta di Parma,* 25 June 1997.

_____. "Introduzione. Perché De Palchi," *Hebenon, rivista internazionale di letteratura.*

_____. "Per le *Memeorie Scheletriche* di Alfredo de Palchi" in *Alfredo de Palchi. La Potenza della poesia.*

_____. "Fra saggio e racconto: la scommessa di Alfredo de Palchi" in *Una vita scommessa in poesia. Omaggio ad Alfredo de Palchi.*

Forti, Marco. "*Sessioni con l'analista.*" *La Nazione,* 15 August 1967.

Gioseffi, Daniela. "Dark Outrage." *American Book Review* XVII.3 (February-March 1996).

_____. "Reading Alfredo de Palchi's Poetry: *The Scorpion's Dark Dance,*" *Voices in Italian Americana* 1 (1996).

_____. Rev. of *Anonymous Constellation,* by Alfredo de Palchi. *Voices in Italian Americana* 2 (1997).

_____. "*Anonymous Constellation,*" American Italian Historical Association Bulletin, April 1997.

_____. Rev. of *Addictive Aversions,* by Alfredo de Plachi. *Yale Italian Poetry* (Fall 1998).

_____. "*Addictive Aversions,*" The Independent Publisher (September-October 1999).

_____. "Intervista a Alfredo de Palchi," *Cortland Review* 15 (February 2000).

"Vita e poesia di Alfredo De Palchi di Ferrea individualità e duro oltraggio.' la poesia di Alfredo De Palchi," *Hebenon, rivista internazionale di letteratura.*

_____. "A Retrospective Essay: The Poetry of Alfredo de Palchi" in *Una vita scommessa in poesia. Omaggio ad Alfredo de Palchi.*

Kvitko, Karl. "Alfredo de Palchi Says No" in *Una vita scommessa in poesia. Omaggio ad Alfredo de Palchi.*

Laiolo, Andrea. "Un incipit depalchiano e la quartina di Villon" in *Alfredo de Palchi. La Potenza della poesia.*

Linguaglossa, Giorgio. "'Lateralità' di de Palchi" in *Alfredo de Palchi. La Potenza della poesia.*

Macchia, Annalisa. "Su una poesia di Alfredo de Palchi" in *Una vita scommessa in poesia. Omaggio ad Alfredo de Palchi.*

Malanga, Gerard. "Alfredo de Palchi, Racconti" in *Una vita scommessa in poesia. Omaggio ad Alfredo de Palchi.*

Manacorda, Giuliano. Rev. of *Sessioni con l'analista,* by Alfredo de Palchi. *Rinascita* 22 (1967).

Manzi, Luigi. "La poesia di Alfredo de Palchi il corpo e corpo con la parola poetica" in *Una vita scommessa in poesia. Omaggio ad Alfredo de Palchi.*

Marchegiani, Irene. "Poesia e coraggio" in *Una vita scommessa in poesia. Omaggio ad Alfredo de Palchi.*

Montalto, Sandro. "Alfredo de Palchi: un perpetuo scoppio di vita" in *Alfredo de Palchi. La Potenza della poesia.*

_____. "Biglietto per Alfredo de Palchi" in *Una vita scommessa in poesia. Omaggio ad Alfredo de Palchi.*

Moroni, Mario. "Note su Foemina Tellus di Alfredo de Palchi" in *Una vita scommessa in poesia. Omaggio ad Alfredo de Palchi.*

Nanni, Luciano. "La bellezza sopra le macerie" in *Alfredo de Palchi. La Potenza della poesia.*

Paganardi, Alessandra. "La fenice poetica di Alfredo de Palchi," in *Alfredo de Palchi. La Potenza della poesia.*

Pallalardo La Rosa, Franco. "Nella 'buia danza' dell'esistenza. Appunti sulla poesia di Alfredo de Palchi" in *Alfredo de Palchi. La Potenza della poesia.*

Palma, Michael. "'To Live Tomorrow': Three Poems by Ennio Contini" in *Una vita scommessa in poesia. Omaggio ad Alfredo de Palchi.*

Panella, Giuseppe. "Nel caos. La scrittura poetica di Alfredo De Palchi," *Gradiva* 30 (2006).

_____. "Ritratto (in piedi). La lezione poetica di Alfredo de Palchi" in *Alfredo de Palchi. La Potenza della poesia.*

_____. "Alfredo de Palchi: Writing Poetry as a Form of Life" in *Una vita scommessa in poesia. Omaggio ad Alfredo de Palchi.*

Perilli, Plinio. "'Urlo al mondo la truffa': Omaggio ad Alfredo de Palchi" in *Una vita scommessa in poesia. Omaggio ad Alfredo de Palchi.*

Raffel, Burton. "Six Poets of 1999," *The Literary Review* XLIII.2 (Winter 2000).

Ramat, Silvio. "Due poeti contro la storia," *La fiera letteraria,* 27 July 1967.

_____. "Il fuggitivo che insegue se stesso," *Hebenon, rivista internazionale di letteratura.*

Ricchi, Renzo. Rev. of *Addictive Aversions,* by Alfredo de Palchi. *La nuova Antologia,* April-June 2000.

Rossella, Maurizia. "Alfredo de Palchi" in *Alfredo de Palchi. La Potenza della poesia.*

Rimanelli, Giose. "Alfredo de Palchi nelle trasformazioni della memoria d'amore," *Gradiva* 30 (2006).

Scambray, Kenneth. Rev. of *Anonymous Constellation*, by Alfredo de Palchi. *L'Italo-americano*, 31 December 1998.

———. "*Addictive Aversions*," *L'Italo-americano*, 31 January 2002.

Sereni, Vittorio. "Alfredo de Palchi," *Questo e altro* 1 (1962).

Signorelli-Pappas, Rev. of *The Scorpion's Dark Dance*, by Alfredo de Palchi. R. *Small Press Review* (Spring 1994).

Surliuga, Victoria. "Dire e non dire: il controllo della parola in *Sessioni con l'analista*" in *Una vita scommessa in poesia. Omaggio ad Alfredo de Palchi.*

Tamburri, Anthony Julian. "A Semiotics of Ambiguity: Indeterminacy in Alfredo de Palchi's *Anonymous Constellation*" in *Una vita scommessa in poesia. Omaggio ad Alfredo de Palchi.*

Taylor, John. "Between the horizon and the leap: the poetry of Alfredo de Palchi" in *Alfredo de Palchi. La Potenza della poesia.*

———. "Guardami, dimmi, è così per te" in *Una vita scommessa in poesia. Omaggio ad Alfredo de Palchi.*

Valesio, Paolo. "Alfredo de Palchi e la libertà d'espressione" in *Una vita scommessa in poesia. Omaggio ad Alfredo de Palchi.*

Veco Riccardo, Angelo Lippo, Domenico Cara. "Tre letture" in *Alfredo de Palchi. La Potenza della poesia.*

Vettori, Alessandro. "*La buia danza di scorpione*: Uno specimen della poesia contemporanea," *Nuove lettere* 5-8 (1996).

———. "Il carcere come metafora nell'evoluzione poetica di Alfredo De Palchi," *Hebenon, rivista internazionale di letteratura.*

Whitmore, Priscilla. Rev. of *Sessioni con l'analista*, by Alfredo de Palchi. *Library Journal*, 15 September 1971.

Zagaroli, Antonella. "Alfredo de Palchi. Alcuni paradigmi dell'opera poetica" in *Una vita scommessa in poesia. Omaggio ad Alfredo de Palchi.*

Zanzotto, A. "Motivazione Premio di Poesia." Città di S. Vito al Tagliamento, 30 July 1988.

ON GIOSE RIMANELLI

Attanasio, Salvator. "A Surgical Survey of a Center of Learning" in *Rimanelliana. Studi su Giose Rimanelli / Studies on Giose Rimanelli.* Edited by Sebastiano Martelli. Stony Brook, NY: Forum Italicum, 2000.

Axelrod, Mark. Rev. of *Accademia*, by Giose Rimanelli. *World Literature Today* (Summer 1998).

Axelrod, Mark. "From *Alien cantica* to *Dirige Me Domine*: The Biblical Dimension in Rimanelli's Latest Works" in *Rimanelliana. Studi su Giose Rimanelli*.

Betti, Franco. "Nota critica su *La stanza grande* e *Detroit Blues*" in *Rimanelliana. Studi su Giose Rimanelli*.

Bonaffini, Luigi. "Rimanelli e la poesia dialettale in America" in *Rimanelliana. Studi su Giose Rimanelli*.

Bosch, Rafael. "The Surprising Study of *Anaconda*" in *Rimanelliana. Studi su Giose Rimanelli*.

Burgess, Anthony. Afterword. *Alien Cantica*.

Capek-Habekpvic, Romana. "Texts within the Texts: Hermeneutics of the 'Fluid' Novel *Benedetta in Guysterland* for the Jabberwocky Reader," *Voices in Italian Americana* 6.2 (1995); republished in *Rimanelliana*.

Cecchetti, Giovanni. "A Quest for Love" in *Rimanelliana. Studi su Giose Rimanelli*.

_____. "Autobiografia mitografica in Giose Rimanelli" in *Rimanelliana. Studi su Giose Rimanelli*.

Fontanella, Luigi. "La poesia di Giose Rimanelli: un 'Maudit' tra gioco e autodistruzione," *Su/per Rimanelli. Studi e testimonianze*, special issue of *Misure Critiche* (October 1987-June 1988).

_____. Introduction. *Familia*.

_____. "*Detroit Blues*: riscostruzione (parziale) e lettura" in *Rimanelliana. Studi su Giose Rimanelli*.

Gardaphe, Fred. "Giose 'The Trickster' Rimanelli's Great Italian/American Novel" in *Rimanelliana. Studi su Giose Rimanelli*.

_____. Introduction. *Benedetta in Guysterland*

Giordano, Paolo. "Giose Rimanelli: A Bibliogrpahy" in *Rimanelliana. Studi su Giose Rimanelli*.

Granese, Alberto. "Le anamorfosi di Rimanelli. Testo pre-testo e contest del romanzo Graffiti." *Su/per Rimanelli. Studi e testimonianze*.

_____. Preface. *Alien Cantica*.

_____. "Tra i manoscritti di Rimanelli: nella *Macchina paranoica* l'origine di *Detroit Blues*" in *Rimanelliana. Studi su Giose Rimanelli*.

Maffia, Dante. "Il Molise come 'voce' del profondo" in *Rimanelliana. Studi su Giose Rimanelli*.

Martelli, Sebastiano. Introduction. *Tiro al piccione*

_____. "Un 'irregolare' nella letteratura degli anni Cinquanta" in *Rimanelliana. Studi su Giose Rimanelli*.

Matteo, Sante. "Trovatello o Rinamello sul ponte? A quale riva arriva e a quale sponda risponda Rimanelli?" in *Rimanelliana. Studi su Giose Rimanelli*.

Moretti, U. Preface. *Monaci d'amore medievali*.

———. "Disertore amato," *Su/per Rimanelli. Studi e testimonianze*.

Pietralunga, Mark. "Giose Rimanelli: An Honorary Piedmontese" in *Rimanelliana. Studi su Giose Rimanelli*.

Postman, Sheryl Lynn. "A Bridge to America: *Biglietto di Terza e Tragica America*" in *Rimanelliana. Studi su Giose Rimanelli*.

———. *Crossing the Acheron: A Study of Nine Novels by Giose Rimanelli*. Brooklyn: Legas, 2000.

Prezzolini, Giuseppe. "*Elogio di un 'trapiantato' molisano, bardo della libertà negli Stati Uniti,*" *Il Tempo*, 10 May 1964.

Ragni, Eugenio. "*Il mestiere del furbo. Un 'suicidio' annunciato*" in *Rimanelliana. Studi su Giose Rimanelli*.

Reina, Luigi. "*La poesia di Giose Rimanelli*"; preface to *Arcano*.

Sciascia, Leonardo. Rev. of *Il mestiere del furbo*, by Giose Rimanelli. *L'Ora* 26 (February 1960).

Tamburri, Anthony Julian. "Rimanelli's *Benedetta in Guysterland*: A 'Liquid' Novel of Questionable Textual Boundaries," *World Literature Today* 68.3 (Summer 1994); republished in *Rimanelliana*.

Valorba, Franco. "An Absolutely New Novel" in *Rimanelliana. Studi su Giose Rimanelli*.

Vitti-Alexander, Maria Rosaria. "L'America di mio padre" in *Rimanelliana. Studi su Giose Rimanelli*.

ON JOSEPH TUSIANI

Bandiera, Emilio. "Lessico, prosodia e metrica nella poesia latina di Joseph Tusiani" in *Joseph Tusiani: Poet Translator Humanist. An International Homage*. Edited by Paolo A. Giordano. West Lafayette, IN: Bordihera Press, 1994.

———. "Il tema dell'emigrazione nella poesia Latina di Joseph Tusiani" in "*Two Languages, Two Lands*": *L'opera letteraria di Joseph Tusiani*, Cosma Siani, ed. (San Marco in Lamas: Quaderni del Sud, 2000)

Bonaffini, Luigi. "La poesia dialettale di Joseph Tusiani" in *Joseph Tusiani: Poet Translator Humanist*.

Bonea, Ennio. Preface. *Gente mia e altre poesie* by Joseph Tusiani.

Borrelli, Franco. Rev. of *La parola difficile* by Joseph Tusiani. *America Oggi* (8 January 1989).

———. "Un colloquio con Joseph Tusiani." *America Oggi* (1 November 1992).

———. Rev. of "*Lu dedhì*" by Joseph Tusiani. *America Oggi* (29 August 1999).

_____. Rev. of "*La prima cumpagnia*" by Joseph Tusiani. *America Oggi* (8 September 2002).

Cecchetti Giovanni. "Joseph Tusiani e l'emigrazione coatta" in *Joseph Tusiani: Poet Translator Humanist.*

Cipolla, Gaetano. "Tusiani as Translator" in *Joseph Tusiani: Poet Translator Humanist.*

Fanciullo, Maria Carmela. "Il romanzo di Joseph Tusiani: dal *Dante in licenza* ad *Envoy from Heaven*" in *"Two Languages, Two Lands": L'opera letteraria di Joseph Tusiani*, Cosma Siani, ed. (San Marco in Lamas: Quaderni del Sud, 2000)

Fontanella, Luigi. "Da Tusiani e Tusiani: Appunti sulla poesia in italiano e in inglese" in *Joseph Tusiani: Poet Translator Humanist.*

_____. Rev. of *Il ritorno. America Oggi* (11 October 1992).

_____. *Intervista Joseph Tusiani*, 1990 (unpublished manuscript).

_____. Rev. of Leopardi's *Canti, Carmina latina* II, *Lu deddú. Gradiva* 18 (2000).

Galletti, Alfredo. Preface. *Odi Sacre* by Joseph Tusiani.

Giordano, Paolo A., ed. *Joseph Tusiani: Poet Translator Humanist. An International Homage.* West Lafayette, IN: Bordihera Press, 1994.

Giordano, Paolo A. "Tusiani Explores Lives of Italian Immigrants," *Fra Noi,* Chicago (November 1987).

_____. "Joseph Tusiani and the Saga of Immigration" in *Joseph Tusiani: Poet Translator Humanist.*

_____. "Emigrants, Expatriates, and Exiles." *Beyond the Margin. Reading in Italian Americana.* Eds. Paolo Giordano and Anthony Tamburri, Rutherford-Madison-Teaneck: Farleigh Dickinson University Press, 1998.

_____. "From Southern Italian Immigrant to Reluctant American: Joseph Tusiani's Gente Mia and Other Poems" in *Ethnicity: Selected Poems.* Edited by Paolo Giordano. West Lafayette, IN: Bordighera Press, 2000.

_____. "The Writer between Two Worlds: Joseph Tusiani's *Autobiografia di un italo-americano*" in *Ethnicity: Selected Poems.* Edited by Paolo Giordano. West Lafayette, IN: Bordighera Press, 2000.

Kirby, John T. "The Neo-Latin Verse of Joseph Tusiani" in *Joseph Tusiani: Poet Translator Humanist.*

Lèbano, Edoardo. "Tusaini, Translator of Pulci's *Morgante*" in *Joseph Tusiani: Poet Translator Humanist.*

Magno, Pietro. Preface. *Il ritorno*

_____. "L'ultima poesia italiana e garganica di Joseph Tusiani" in *Joseph Tusiani: Poet Translator Humanist.*

Marazzi, Martino. "Da un 'angolo di vantaggio'. Intorno alla parola autobiografica di Joseph Tusiani," *Il Giannone* 5.9-10 (2007).

Pastore Passaro, Maria. Maria. "Il 'non detto' biblico nella poesia di Tusiani" in *Il filone cattolico nella letteratura italiana del secondo dopoguerra*. Ed. Florinda M. Iannace. Rome: Bulzoni, 1989.

_____. "La parola difficile. Autobiografia di un italo-americano" in *La letteratura dell'emigrazione*.

_____. "L'autobiogrofia di Joseph Tusiani" in *To See The Past More Clearly: The Enrichment of the Italian Heritage, 1890-1990*. Hasrral E. Landry, ed. Austin, TX: Nortex Press, 1994.

_____. "Gente mia, Part Two: An Indispensable Reading" in *Joseph Tusiani: Poet Translator Humanist*.

Petracco Sovran, Lucia. *Joseph Tusiani poeta e traduttore*. Perugia: Sigla Tre, 1984.

_____. "Joseph Tusiani's Lyrical Monologues of the Holy Week" in *Joseph Tusiani: Poet Translator Humanist*.

Rimanelli, Giose. "A Mesmeric Sculpture: Tusiani the Humanist" in *Joseph Tusiani: Poet Translator Humanist*.

Sacré, Dirk. "Joseph Tusiani's Lating Poetry: Aspects of Its Originality" in *Joseph Tusiani: Poet Translator Humanist*.

Siani, Cosma. "Tusiani's Italian Years: A Study of Background Influences" in *Joseph Tusiani: Poet Translator Humanist*.

_____. *L'io diviso. Joseph Tusiani fra emigrazione e letteratura*. Rome: Edizioni Cofine, 1999.

INDEX OF NAMES

Mazza, Armando 28
Miller, Henry 117, 124, 229
Minor, Roberto 38, 46
Mirbeau, Octave 46
Molinari, Giovanni 26
Monicelli, Mario 104
Montaldo, Giuliano 98
Montale, Eugenio 173, 193, 222
Moore, Harriet 3, 18, 20
Moretti, Ugo 97, 118
Mulas, Franco 52
Munch, Edward 189
Muscetta, Carlo 97, 123
Musso, Giuseppe 26
Mussolini, Benito 11

Nabokov, Vladimir 117, 123, 142, 144, 157, 158, 229
Neagol, Peter 4
Negri, Ada 169, 190
Novalis (Friederick Leopold von Hardenberg) 165
Novaro, Angiolo Silvio 169, 190

Orelli, Giorgio 192
Ovid, N. P. 229

Pagano, Joe 17
Pagliarani, Elio 176, 198
Palazzeschi, Aldo 146, 149
Palma, Michael 226
Panetta, George 17
Panunzio, Constantine 16, 50, 200
Papini, Giovanni 5, 24, 27, 32
Paris, Jean 145
Parise, Goffredo 230
Parisi, Joseph 18
Pascoli, Giovanni 173
Pasinetti, Pier Maria 207
Passaro, Maria 79
Pavese, Cesare 98, 100, 102, 123, 142
Pento, Bartolo 172

Pescatori, Claudia 164
Pessoa, Fernando 93
Peterkiewicz, Jerzy 123
Petracco-Sovran Lucia
Petrarch, Francis 8, 102
Petroni, Guglielmo 174
Picasso, Pablo 98, 185
Piccolo, Lucio 193, 222
Pirandello, Luigi 8
Ponti, Carlo 98
Postman, Sheryl Lynn 102, 161
Pouget, Emile 20
Pound, Ezra 97, 143, 144, 172
Prezzolini, Giuseppe 3, 16, 17, 19, 29, 52, 77, 82, 169
Prisco, Michele 113
Propertius, S. 229
Proust, Marcel 76, 83
Puzo, Mario 7, 8

Quasimodo, Salvatore 173, 183, 184, 190, 222

Raffel, Burton 236
Ragni, Eugenio 100
Rago, Michele 2
Raiziss, Sonia 162, 173, 176, 177, 192, 193, 194, 221, 226
Ramat, Silvio 167, 211
Rappolo, Leon 161
Reina, Luigi 115, 125
Ricchi, Renzo 230
Rimanelli, Giose 2, 5, 6, 7, 84, 95-166, 167, 171, 200, 208, 230
Rimanelli, Marco 161
Rimbaud, Arthur 167, 173, 187, 237
Risi, Nelo 192, 222
Robichaux, John 161
Rossi-Drago, Eleonora 98
Rotolo, Lucrezia 145
Roulston, Jane 43, 47
Rousseau, Jean-Jacques 102

ABOUT THE AUTHOR

LUIGI FONTANELLA studied at the University of Rome, "La Sapienza" (Laurea in Lettere), and at Harvard University (Ph.D. in Romance Languages and Literatures). Fulbright Fellow (Princeton University, 1976-78), he has taught at Columbia, Princeton, and Wellesley College. Presently, he is Professor of Italian and Director of the Italian Program at Stony Brook University.

Poet, critic, translator, playwright, and novelist, Fontanella has published fifteen books of poetry, nine of literary criticism, and three books of narrative. His most recent volumes are: *Pasolini rilegge Pasolini* (Milan: Archinto-Rizzoli, 2005, translated into several languages), *Land of Time* (New York: Chelsea Editions, 2006), *L'azzurra memoria* (Milan and Bergamo: Moretti & Vitali, 2007, Città di Marineo Prize, Laurentum Prize), *Oblivion* (Milan: Archinto-Rizzoli, 2008), the novel *Controfigura* (Venice: Marsilio, 2009), *Soprappensieri di Giuseppe Berto* (Turin: Aragno, 2010), *L'angelo della neve. Poesie di viaggio* (Milan: Mondadori, 2010).

He is the Editor of the journal *Gradiva* and president of the Italian Poetry in America (IPA). In 2005, Carlo Azeglio Ciampi, President of Italy, nominated Fontanella *Cavaliere all'Ordine del Merito della Repubblica Italiana*.

SAGGISTICA

Taking its name from the Italian—which means essays, essay writing, or non fiction—*Saggisitca* is a referred book series dedicated to the study of all topics, individuals, and cultural productions that fall under what we might consider that larger umbrella of all things Italian and Italian/American.

Vito Zagarrio
  The "Un-Happy Ending": Re-viewing The Cinema of Frank Capra. 2011. ISBN 978-1-59954-005-4. Volume 1.

Paolo A. Giordano, editor
  The Hyphenate Writer and The Legacy of Exile. 2010. ISBN 978-1-59954-007-8. Volume 2.

Dennis Barone
  America / Trattabili. 2011. ISBN 978-1-59954-018-4. Volume 3.

Fred L. Gardaphè
  The Art of Reading Italian Americana. 2011. ISBN 978-1-59954-019-1. Volume 4.

Anthony Julian Tamburri
  Re-viewing Italian Americana: Generalities and Specificities on Cinema. 2011. ISBN 978-1-59954-020-7. Volume 5.

Sheryl Lynn Postman
  An Italian Writer's Journey through American Realities: Giose Rimanelli's English Novels. "The most tormented decade of America: the 60s" ISBN 978-1-59954-034-4. Volume 6.

The following volumes are forthcoming:

David Barone and Peter Covino, editors
  Essays on Italian American Literature and Culture. ISBN 978-1-59954-035-1. Volume 8.

Peter Carravetta
  After Identity: Critical Challenges in Italian American Poetics and Culture. ISBN 978-1-59954-036-8. Volume 9.

CPSIA information can be obtained
at www.ICGtesting.com
Printed in the USA
FFOW02n2325131216
30148FF